D0560419

Couple Found Slain

Couple Found Slain

After a Family Murder

Mikita Brottman

Henry Holt and Company
New York

Henry Holt and Company
Publishers since 1866
120 Broadway
New York, NY 10271
www.henryholt.com

Henry Holt ® and 🏢 ® are registered trademarks of Macmillan Publishing Group, LLC.

Library of Congress Cataloging-in-Publication Data

Names: Brottman, Mikita, 1966– author.
Title: Couple found slain : after a family murder / Mikita Brottman.
Description: First edition. | New York : Henry Holt and Company, 2021. |
Includes bibliographical references.
Identifiers: LCCN 2020034388 (print) | LCCN 2020034389 (ebook) | ISBN
9781250757449 (hardcover) | ISBN 9781250757456 (ebook)
Subjects: LCSH: Bechtold, Brian, 1968–| Mentally ill
offenders—Maryland—Case studies. | Murderers—Maryland—Case studies. |
Parricide—Maryland—Case studies. | Psychiatric hospital
patients—Maryland—Case studies.
Classification: LCC HV9468.B33 B76 2021 (print) | LCC HV9468.B33 (ebook) |
DDC 364.152/3092 [B]—dc23
LC record available at https://lccn.loc.gov/2020034388
LC ebook record available at https://lccn.loc.gov/2020034389

Our books may be purchased in bulk for promotional, educational, or business
use. Please contact your local bookseller or the Macmillan Corporate and
Premium Sales Department at (800) 221-7945, extension 5442, or by e-mail at
MacmillanSpecialMarkets@macmillan.com.

First Edition 2021

Designed by Meryl Sussman Levavi

Printed in the United States of America

1   3   5   7   9   10   8   6   4   2

Contents

Couple Found Slain

Introduction

Through our many conversations, through his own written recollections, and by providing me with his psychiatric and police records, Brian Bechtold has helped me write this book. I've also relied on other primary documents: court audio and transcripts, police logs, diagrams, photographs, incident reports, and in-person interviews. This is a work of nonfiction; however, some of the dialogue has been re-created based on information from various sources and some of the names and identifying details have been changed.

Most true crime stories focus on the buildup to the crime, the incident itself, and the quest for justice. They're propelled by the need to solve a mystery or find resolution. They end, inevitably, with the arrest and confinement of the perpetrator. The prosaic life, lit up for a moment by the thrill of the crime, returns to obscurity. The curtain comes down. But the end of one story is the beginning of another.

Most murders are committed by young men under thirty. These men disappear from public view, but they're still here. Their lives go on: in maximum-security prisons, in forensic hospitals, and even on death row. They change and grow. They develop new interests, form new friendships, work at different jobs. People no longer recognize their names. Eventually, they become middle-aged or elderly, long-timers going about their daily routines: washing floors, cleaning bathrooms, serving food. Sometimes they even return to live quietly among us. One famous example: Nathan Leopold (of the Leopold and Loeb case) was released from prison at age fifty-four, married a widowed florist, and moved to Puerto Rico, where he wrote a well-received book on the island's bird life.

True crime deals with the victim's before and after, the community's suffering, the hunt, the cops, the capture, the trial, the verdict. This book is about another part of the story, the part that begins when the verdict is announced, the sentence handed down. "Couple Found Slain" is a compelling headline. The scene it conjures up is lurid and frightening. It shuts out further thought. It's like a burst of gunfire, explosive and short-lived.

The rest of the story, dense and messy, lies beneath.

1

Still Life

Port St. Joe, Florida
Friday, February 21, 1992, 1:30 p.m.

Officer Timothy Hightower was finishing up some paperwork at the front desk of police headquarters. It had been a quiet week. The district, whose population was small and mostly rural, had seen its usual share of petty thefts and burglaries, but nothing more serious. Tourists were scarce in February. Scallop season was over. Other than the mosquitoes, the biggest problem was hurricanes, which could move in unpredictably from the Gulf of Mexico to make landfall on Cape San Blas. But it wasn't the season for storms.

The front door opened. Hightower looked up and saw a young man walking toward the desk. He was thin, pale, and jittery.

"What can I help you with, sir?" the officer asked, suddenly feeling uneasy.

The young man held his gaze. "Something bad happened," he said.

Jim Drewry, a homicide detective in the Montgomery County Police Department, was driving home from work when he picked up a dispatch call on the radio asking for officers to respond to a residence in Hillandale, a suburb of Washington, DC, just north of Silver Spring, to check on the welfare of the occupants.

Because Drewry wasn't far from the address given by the dispatcher, he decided to drop by and see if he could help out. He arrived at around 3:30 p.m.

The house on Green Forest Drive was a split-level brick home set back about two hundred feet from the road on a slight incline. There were signs of neglect: two empty trash cans sat out in front of the house, the mailbox was full, and a package sat unclaimed on the front porch. The responding officers told Drewry that the house was locked. They'd rung the bell and hammered on the front door, but no one had replied. If the residents were out, Drewry reasoned, they couldn't have been gone long, because they'd left the television on; he could hear it playing somewhere inside the house. Yet, according to its postmark, the package on the front porch had arrived almost a week ago, and there was a note on the door from someone named Theresa expressing her concern about the residents and asking the police to get in touch.

Drewry went around the back of the house, crossed a small patio, and approached a sliding glass door. Pressing his face against the glass, he could make out what appeared to be a woman sitting in a chair in the living room. Her body was covered by a multicolored quilt; only her head was visible. It was obvious to Drewry that she was dead. He also saw the feet and lower legs of a man lying facedown on the kitchen floor. The detective pulled out his radio and called headquarters. They had a double homicide on their hands.

The sliding doors at the back were locked, and so were the windows. Not wanting to break the glass, Drewry decided to call the Fire and Rescue team and get them to force the doors open. He also placed a call to John Tauber, the Maryland deputy medical examiner. By the time Fire and Rescue had arrived, the crime scene technicians were on the scene, along with four more detectives from the Homicide/ Sex division of the Montgomery County Police Department. They entered the house at around 4:40 p.m.

The odor was almost unbearable. The rear door led into an openplan dining room, which was separated from the kitchen area by a stone-and-wood counter. The chandelier in the dining room was on; so were the overhead lights in the kitchen. A man's body lay on the kitchen floor. He appeared to have been killed while preparing a meal. On the kitchen table was a bowl containing the remains of what looked like breakfast cereal, and on a plate beside the stove were some bits of fish; fish bones lay on a sheet of aluminum foil. The body was fully clothed, the skin bloated and bluish green. From the state of decomposition, Drewry estimated that the man had been dead for at least ten days. There was a shotgun wound to the back of his right shoulder and some blood splatter on the front of the dishwasher, to the left of his head. On the floor near the body, the red linoleum was black with dried blood, which made Drewry suspect the man may have been moved or rolled over. Both pockets of his pants were empty.

Inside, the place was a mess. The trash hadn't been taken out for weeks, and the water had been cut off. Dirty dishes and utensils were stacked on the counter and the kitchen table, along with cans of food; a box of Rice Krispies; a spray can of insect repellent; a box of tea bags; bottles of cooking oil, Gatorade, condiments, and medicine; a bag of oranges; an open container of milk; empty takeaway cartons; and a half-eaten baguette.

The woman's body lay on a recliner beside the living room fireplace, in front of the still-playing television. This body, too, was dark and bloated by decomposition. The skin was coming loose, and the flesh swarmed with maggots. A tube sticking out from under the quilt was connected to an oxygen cylinder on the floor. When police uncovered the woman's body, they found two shotgun wounds, one to her right breast and the other to the front of her throat. (A gold crucifix around her neck had been damaged by the bullet.) Shotgun pellet holes were also found in the back of the recliner. Police found a spent twelve-gauge shotgun shell on the couch and another on the living room floor by the entryway to the kitchen.

At 5:10 p.m., the medical examiner arrived. Detective Drewry told the responding officers to secure the house, then called the police photographer, Joseph Niebauer, to take shots of the scene. He also placed a call to the State's Attorney's Office, informing them of the crime, and another to Bell Funeral Home, asking the mortician to transport the bodies to the Office of the Chief Medical Examiner in Baltimore in preparation for autopsy.

Like the rest of the house, the living room looked as if it hadn't been cleaned for months. The surfaces were dusty, and the floor was ankle-deep in trash: newspapers, telephone directories, candy wrappers, empty boxes of Oreos and breakfast cereal, videocassettes, towels, drinking glasses, dirty utensils, medicine and pill bottles, an electric blanket, a heating pad, wadded-up tissues, various items of clothing, a teddy bear, a walker, pillows, blankets, paper towels, two cans of talcum powder, the leg of a plastic doll, a hairbrush, a Bible, an emesis basin, and an oxygen tank. There was also a *TV Guide* open to a page on which the phrase "Go to Hell" had been smeared, apparently in blood.

Walking down the hall to the front of the house, Detective Drewry came to a foyer from which a short flight of stairs led down to a basement den. This was just as messy as the living room, only here, all the trash had been pushed to the sides of the room, uncovering a large circle of empty carpet. In the middle of the circle was a black stain, as if something had been spilled or burned there. A blanket had been hung over the window. Near the left wall of the den was a stained couch, an armchair with its stuffing coming out, a table, and a dusty stereo system with two large speakers. The piles of trash contained a pair of jeans, candy wrappers, blankets, plastic bags, more empty Oreo boxes, towels, tissues, magazines, athletic clothing, two tennis rackets, a pair of shorts, peanuts, coins, potato chips, packaging, cassette tapes, an ironing board, a briefcase, and twenty-three empty Coke and Pepsi cans, many of them crushed or flattened. On a side table was the cutoff portion of a shotgun barrel and an empty Styrofoam box that had once contained a shotgun. One of the police officers found the primer end of a twelve-gauge shotgun shell on the bookcase.

Upstairs, in the four bedrooms, things were a little more orderly. The first room Drewry entered appeared to have been unused: the bed was neatly made and the walls bare, apart from a large wooden crucifix. On the dresser lay a pile of blankets, a letter opener, and a Panama hat. The second bedroom he investigated overlooked the backyard and contained a king-size four-poster bed. This bed, too, was neatly made. A bedside tray contained a jumble of pill bottles, medicines, droppers, and tissues. The room was cluttered with cardboard boxes, an inflatable mattress, laundry hampers, and piles of clothes. The two other bedrooms were even more cluttered. The first contained piles of papers, an unmade queen-size bed, and mounds of sheets, pillows, and dirty laundry.

The fourth bedroom was small and narrow. There were four indentations in the door that looked as though they had been made by someone punching the wood with a fist. On the floor around the unmade bed were magazines and piles of dirty laundry. A large television set faced the bed. On top of the television set was a bare lamp with no shade, nine empty Pepsi cans, two half-empty two-liter soda bottles, a glass serving bowl full of quarters, a dish of dried-up used tea bags, an empty bottle of soy sauce, a hairbrush, a stereo, two electric heaters, a nasal spray, and a pile of wadded-up tissues. On top of a chest of drawers were fourteen martial arts trophies. A shelf on the opposite wall held another twelve. To the right of the headboard, on the floor, police found a spent twelve-gauge shotgun shell.

Whatever had happened to this family, Drewry realized, had taken place some time ago; the detritus had been accumulating for years. At the same time, the house still contained recognizable signs of ordinary domestic life: framed baby pictures on the living room wall, dried flower arrangements, Catholic prayer cards attached with magnets to the doors of the fridge. The garage contained a lawn mower, garden tools, and bags of mulch. The valance and tiered curtains in the living room window looked homemade. On a side table in the foyer, clay pots held peace lilies, maidenhair ferns, and fiddle-leaf figs that were growing healthily, oblivious to the surrounding decay.

The call for officers to check on the occupants of the house on Green Forest Drive had come from Detective Joseph Mudano at Montgomery County Police Department headquarters. About an hour before the bodies were discovered, Mudano had received a telephone call from an officer who identified himself as Timothy Hightower of the Port St. Joe Police Department in Florida. Hightower told Mudano that a young man had just come into the station and confessed to shooting his parents in Maryland some time ago—perhaps two weeks or ten days; the young man wasn't exactly sure.

Hightower told Mudano that the man had given his name as

Brian Anthony Bechtold; his parents were George and Dorothy. Mudano had checked the files. There'd been no murders reported in Hillandale during the last two weeks, and no one had reported a retired couple missing. Still, Mudano had put in the call to dispatch, just to be sure.

Now Mudano gave Detective Drewry information about the decedents for the medical examiner's report. The male victim was George Bechtold, sixty-five, a white male six feet tall and weighing 215 pounds. The female was Dorothy Bechtold, sixty-two, a white female five feet six inches tall and weighing 160 pounds. The suspect in custody in Port St. Joe was their son, Brian Anthony Bechtold, twenty-two, a white male five feet nine inches tall and weighing 150 pounds.

At 7:20 that evening, Drewry obtained a warrant for the arrest of Brian Bechtold on two counts of murder and called Hightower in Port St. Joe with the warrant number. Hightower said he'd secured the car Bechtold had been driving. The suspect had a dog with him, Hightower added, which had been sent to the city pound.

By 8:30 p.m., Detective Drewry had tracked down two of the deceased couple's daughters and called them to break the news. Cathy Bechtold, thirty-six, lived with her family in Pasadena, Maryland, about half an hour from Hillandale, and Carole Prentiss, thirty-four, lived in Emmitsburg, about an hour away. Once the immediate shock was over, the sisters provided Drewry with some basic information about the suspect. Cathy told the detective that her younger brother was "a loner who did not talk much to anyone," had spent time in a psychiatric hospital, and had "never been right in the head." She said she was unsure if he'd ever been diagnosed with any particular condition, but she believed that whatever had been done in terms of mental health treatment was "too little, too late."

Drewry also tracked down the author of the note left on the Bechtolds' front door. Theresa Rizak, fifty-five, lived in Hyattsville, a nearby suburb, and identified herself as Dorothy's closest friend. Mrs. Rizak told the police that eleven days earlier, on Monday, February 10, George Bechtold had dropped by to give her an update on Dorothy's health. During the visit, he'd mentioned that the couple was planning a trip to Florida, where they owned a vacation home, but Mrs. Rizak didn't get the impression they were leaving immediately. Over the next few days, she called the Bechtold residence, but got no response. On February 13 or 14, she stopped by the house and left a note on the front door.

"She was always upset over Brian," said Mrs. Rizak of her friend Dorothy Bechtold. She didn't know the specifics, she admitted, but she knew he had a history of mental problems. "We had prayer groups for him," she said. She added that, according to Dorothy, Brian had recently purchased a gun.

Although the Bechtolds had lived on Green Forest Drive for almost twenty years, apparently they kept to themselves. None of the street's residents knew them well. They described Dorothy Bechtold as an invalid who used an oxygen tank and had a nurse come by to visit her every week. George Bechtold was more elusive. There was a rumor that he was some kind of government scientist. Some thought he was a retired engineer; others said he worked at the U.S. Navy's nearby Naval Surface Warfare Center.

The neighbors didn't have much to say about Brian Bechtold, either. They described him as a shy, clean-cut young man who, until recently, had spent most of his time alone with his two Rottweilers. A few months ago, one of the dogs had died. Brian had been seen burying its body in his backyard. A high school student who lived across the street said Brian used to play basketball with the other boys on the block, but he'd stopped a few years ago, becoming quiet and withdrawn. Another neighbor recalled that Brian had gone away to college, but only for a semester, and since then, he'd worked delivering pizza. Everyone agreed that while he had never caused any problems in the neighborhood, he seemed troubled, sullen, and withdrawn.

The autopsy showed that George Bechtold was shot from behind while sitting at the dinner table eating a bowl of breakfast cereal. Dorothy Bechtold, who was suffering from advanced heart disease, had been shot once from the front and once from the back.

2

"Honor Thy Father and Mother"

Mental illness ran in the family, though they called it by different names. Brian had an uncle who suffered from delusions, a cousin who "went nuts." His paternal grandfather walked out on his family to start a new one with a woman who lived down the street, leaving his wife with five sons and a case of venereal disease. This led to a "nervous breakdown," and she was sent to a sanatorium. The five sons were farmed out to relatives. The second of these sons was Brian's father, George.

Born into a working-class Catholic family in Depression-era Pittsburgh, George Bechtold had a mean streak and a quick temper. Hard to handle, he was shuffled around from one relative to another until his mother was well enough to leave the sanatorium and care for her sons again.

Despite his bad temper, George Bechtold was considered the smartest and most promising of the five brothers. He joined the navy when war broke out and, later, went to college under the G.I. Bill, attending Duke University, in Durham, North Carolina. He graduated with a bachelor of science degree in 1946, and then a master of science in electrical engineering in 1948. Smart, focused, and mechanically minded, George had an aptitude for solitary study. After graduation, he was employed in the research and development laboratory at the Westinghouse Electric Corporation and started work on the project that would later become his doctoral thesis, which involved ultrasonic waves and electromagnetic pulse analysis.

It was at Westinghouse that George Bechtold, twenty-four, met Dorothy Eichel, a twenty-three-year-old secretary who operated a Computype machine, a kind of early electric typewriter designed to process business data. Dorothy was stunning, with dark hair and pale skin. She came from a comfortable middle-class background, and George, who was smart and well built but socially awkward, admired her poise, refinement, and grace. In this, he wasn't alone—Dorothy was popular, with plenty of suitors to choose from, and George realized that if he wanted to pin her down, he had to make a move. But when he proposed in 1951, Dorothy told him she couldn't marry him—at least, not without confessing a painful secret.

Dorothy was an only child who was raised by her mother and grandmother. She'd always wanted to have brothers and sisters and couldn't wait to get married and have a large family of her own. She didn't even finish high school, but quit at age sixteen to take a secretarial job with the aim of meeting and marrying a handsome businessman. Whoever her future husband might be, Dorothy hoped he didn't plan to keep her in Pittsburgh—she hated the city's cold weather, gloomy skies, and the soot from the coal plants that coated her clothes and dirtied her skin.

Charming but naïve, Dorothy fell for the first good-looking guy who came along. Bud Eichel was handsome, but he wasn't in business—he was a smooth-talking technical illustrator looking for a steady girl. The deal was clinched when, during the war, Bud was deployed as an airplane gunner and stationed in sunny Miami. Dorothy was thrilled. As soon as she could, she took the bus from Pittsburgh to Florida, chaperoned by her mother and grandmother, and waited for Bud to get leave from the army so they could be married. In the meantime, she found work as a pinup model and got sunburned so badly her complexion was almost ruined.

Not long after marrying Bud, Dorothy discovered she'd made a terrible mistake. First, it turned out Bud couldn't afford to stay in Miami; once the war was over, the couple returned to gloomy Pittsburgh, where they lived in a converted apartment in Dorothy's grandmother's house. Second, they argued constantly. Third, Bud had no ambition at all, and a nasty temper. He got his pilot's license after the war, and all he seemed to care about was flying planes. He wasn't serious about settling into a career, saving money, or working to buy the couple a home and start a family. The marriage lasted less than two months.

As a Catholic, Dorothy couldn't remarry after a divorce—at least, not in the Catholic Church. George had no qualms about this, but he knew his family would be less forgiving, and he never told his mother about his wife's divorce. George and Dorothy were married quietly in a civil ceremony in 1951 and moved right away into their own apartment. But the fact of her previous marriage always weighed heavily on Dorothy, and while she continued going to church every Sunday, she never took Communion or went to confession, not even after her first marriage was annulled sixteen years later, when annulments were easier to obtain. Neither she nor George ever spoke of this first marriage to any of their five children, who learned about it only after their mother's death.

In Pittsburgh, the couple settled into the traditional roles of husband and wife. George went to work every day and attended graduate school at the University of Pittsburgh most evenings. He expected Dorothy to stay home and do the housework. The apartment wasn't especially large, but George had high standards, and Dorothy, who'd led a sheltered life, was overwhelmed by the work. She'd never had to clean before, never had to do the laundry, shop for groceries, or prepare meals. To make matters worse, in 1952, less than a year after her marriage, she became pregnant with her first child. The baby was a girl, and the couple named her Marcia.

When George had completed his master of science degree in electrical engineering, he got a job at Link Aviation, working on flight simulators and automatic checkout equipment, and the young family moved to New York City. Unlike Dorothy's first husband, Bud Eichel, George Bechtold was intelligent, ambitious, and disciplined. He worked full-time while studying for his PhD, but despite his professional success, he was emotionally distant and drank more than was good for him. He also had a bad temper, and although he worked hard in the lab, he didn't believe in helping out around the house. This was unfortunate, because very soon, Dorothy once again began to feel overwhelmed.

After two years in New York, George got a job at the RCA Research Laboratories in New Jersey, where he worked on the development of tracking radar and magnetic video recording systems. George, Dorothy, and two-year-old Marcia moved to Princeton, along with the couple's baby son, George Bechtold Jr., who was born in 1954. Money was tight, as George was traveling to the University of Pittsburgh two or three evenings a week to work on his PhD at night school, and it got even tighter when Dorothy got pregnant again. (Like many Catholic couples in the 1950s—even those who were halfhearted about churchgoing—the Bechtolds observed the prohibition against contraception.) A second daughter, Catherine, was born in 1956, and a third, Carole, in 1958.

While Dorothy seemed to enjoy her children when they were infants, her affection appeared to fade as they grew older. Cathy Bechtold remembers her mother saying that she liked babies best because "they stayed where you put them." Dorothy seemed to lose her bearings when, rather than extensions of herself, her children became individuals in their own right. George, for his part, was too impatient to deal with babies. Carole's wailing grated on his nerves, and one day, in a moment of cruelty brought on by her crying, he told Dorothy he'd never wanted more than two kids. If they hadn't been Catholic, he told her, he'd have made her get rid of the second two. Dorothy was appalled. She was also taken aback by the fact that, even with four young children to look after, she still had to go out to work. She'd always assumed her place in the workforce would be temporary—she'd planned to stay home once she got pregnant and devote herself to taking care of the family—but every month, they struggled to meet the mortgage.

To shore up the couple's finances, Dorothy modeled clothes in a department store, did a little hairdressing, and learned to upholster furniture. Working part-time outside the home made it even more difficult for her to do the household chores, prepare the family's meals, and take care of four children. It was still the age of cloth diapers, and while the Bechtolds had a washing machine, there was no dryer, and laundry had to be hung outside to dry. Dorothy was often driven to tears by the endless household responsibilities and the demands of the children and of a difficult, angry husband. "She grew up in a very sheltered situation. She wasn't prepared," her daughter Cathy recalled. "She was from a very strange family. Her parents hadn't taught her how to do anything." Despite his wife's struggles, George still refused to lift a finger. Every Sunday morning, he'd sit on the couch and complain about how long it took Dorothy to get herself and the four children ready for church, never once offering to help her fasten their coats or tie their shoelaces.

For some couples, having children can disguise or displace their incompatibility; for the Bechtolds, it did just the opposite, bringing out their differences. Dorothy had a lively personality; she was chatty and social. As a mother, she could often be delightful, singing and dancing for the children, decorating their bedrooms in colors and patterns designed to stir their imaginations. George, however, was always surly and standoffish. He disliked shows of sentiment and was contemptuous of affection. Even his hugs were mean-spirited, as if he were trying to squeeze the life out of you. People who knew the couple couldn't imagine what kept them together. The only thing they seemed to share was a love of swing dancing to Big Band music. When they were dancing together, they looked happy.

As her husband grew colder and more remote, Dorothy turned to her friends for companionship. She grew close to some of the other neighborhood mothers and, while George was at work, would invite them over for coffee, telling them to bring their children along. The moms would chat and socialize while the kids played together. A couple of these women were in a local bridge club, and they invited Dorothy to join. She also became part of a neighborhood bowling league, and proved to have a knack for the game, winning local titles and trophies.

Her friends and hobbies provided Dorothy with relief from housework and child care, which she found stifling and oppressive. She got out of the house as often as she could, and by the time Marcia was seven, Dorothy was regularly leaving her in charge of the younger children. Five-year-old George Jr. was badly behaved, always in trouble, and six-month-old Carole cried all the time. Marcia was terrified of the enormous responsibility. Left at home with her siblings on one cold winter's night, she became so anxious at the baby's nonstop wailing that she took her sisters and brother out into the snow to knock on a neighbor's door and ask for help.

Dorothy clearly knew it was important to maintain a sense of structure in the household; she just wasn't able to keep it up, often growing impatient with everyday chores. Still, because she loved everything to do with design and décor, she would orchestrate elaborate ceremonies for the holidays. She designed four different sets of drapes for the windows and slipcovers for the furniture, one set for each season of the year. Every Christmas, she'd buy a live tree and keep it on the porch until Christmas Eve, when each child would be presented with a new set of pajamas to sleep in that night. Dorothy would then stay up late to decorate the tree with lights and gifts, setting up a toy train that puffed its way in circles around the room and bringing out valuable wind-up toys that the children were allowed to play with only once a year.

These holiday treats were memorable because, most of the time, the family lived frugally. George repeatedly promised Dorothy that when he finished his PhD, he'd get a high-paying job and make up for all the time he'd missed as a husband and father. He was right about the high-paying job, which he was offered even before he'd finished writing his thesis. For a while, it seemed as if all the family's sacrifices were about to pay off.

In 1965, avionics was booming; George Bechtold was given a contract to work for the federal government on military technology at Martin Marietta in Orlando, Florida, where he'd be researching applied quantum electronics. With four children aged between seven and thirteen, the Bechtolds moved to Orlando, where they rented a place to live while looking for a home to buy in the right neighborhood. When George finally finished his PhD, as a treat, he flew the whole family from Orlando to Philadelphia to attend his graduation ceremony and see the Liberty Bell. It was their first time on a plane. It seemed as though, in more than one way, the Bechtolds were finally moving up in the world.

In Orlando, the family moved into a ritzy, newly built home surrounded by tall trees covered in Spanish moss. The children had the run of the neighborhood, an idyllic suburb full of lakes, woods, stables, and orange groves. The new house had a swimming pool in an enclosed glass atrium and polished terrazzo floors for which Dorothy, who no longer had to work outside the home, designed brightly colored child-friendly chairs out of glued-together tires with foam-and-vinyl cushions on top.

By this time, the children had developed distinct and separate personalities. Marcia, now fourteen, had inherited her father's intelligence and her mother's artistic flair, but she exhibited none of Dorothy's exuberance or playfulness. Parental neglect had forced her to become serious beyond her years. As her eldest daughter was growing up, Dorothy had made her into a surrogate partner, and it was Marcia to whom Dorothy would go crying at night after heated arguments with George. Dorothy began relating to Marcia as if she were her spouse, and Marcia not only began to act as her confidante but also served as her protector against her abusive husband. Mother and daughter became tangled up together in a kind of emotional incest.

The quarrels between George and Dorothy were often about George's physical punishment of their twelve-year-old son, George Jr., whose bad behavior drove his father wild with rage. Cathy, ten, was a typical middle child, forced to compete for the time, love, and attention of her parents and siblings. She was also turning into the beauty of the family, with high cheekbones and thick, waist-length dark hair. Her sister Carole, eight, was small and shy. Cathy recalls that as Dorothy's favorite, Carole was rarely punished for neglecting her chores, while the other children would be reprimanded severely, even beaten. Their mother seemed to get an almost sadistic pleasure from pitting the children against one another and playing favorites.

Beatings became more common as time passed, and Dorothy became increasingly inconsistent with the rules. She clearly knew it was important to lay down permissions and injunctions, but she'd uphold them on some days and not on others. When the children went out to play after school, sometimes they had to be back by a certain time and sometimes it didn't appear to matter. If they were late, sometimes they were beaten; at other times, no one seemed to care. Only one thing was clear: the older the children became, the more aggressively they were punished. Dorothy appeared to think physical punishment was vital to successful parenting. "She seemed to believe she ought to be beating us all the time," Cathy recalls.

Still, if Dorothy was hard and cruel, she was also—when she wasn't rubbed raw by the burden of caring for four young children—loving and affectionate. George, though, had only two moods: cold and colder. Unsurprisingly, after finishing his PhD, he didn't change his ways and spend more time helping out at home. He didn't become a loving husband and father. On the contrary, he became increasingly aggressive and abusive. He enforced strict beatings for any infringement of the rules. He'd poke and taunt his children and couldn't even manage to feign interest in them—he memorized facts about them to recite when strangers or colleagues asked. The children were afraid of him and avoided him whenever possible, doing their best to keep a low profile so they wouldn't attract his attention.

In short, the family was falling apart.

Then Brian came along.

3

Accident of Birth

It was 1968. Dorothy, at forty-two, had assumed her childbearing years were over. Although the Bechtolds were Catholics, when Dorothy learned she was pregnant again, she wanted to have an abortion. She could hardly deal with the four children they already had; she thought another child might push her over the edge. Plus, at her age, a pregnancy was considered high-risk. (For this reason, if no other, an abortion would have been easy for her to obtain.) But even though George had told Dorothy he wished she'd aborted Cathy and Carole, he insisted she carry her new baby to term. His apparent interest in the child didn't stop him from punching Dorothy in the stomach while she was pregnant, an act of cruelty witnessed by the young Marcia. It was an inauspicious beginning, but Brian Anthony Bechtold arrived in the world intact. He was seventeen years younger than his oldest sister and fifteen years younger than his brother.

However unfavorable the circumstances of his birth, it was widely agreed that Brian was a beautiful baby. His bright blue eyes, golden curls, and happy disposition led the nurses on the maternity ward to christen him "Prince Charming." The excitement caused by the new baby lasted a few months at most, at which point his parents lost interest in him. But Marcia and Cathy continued to find him delightful. They treated him like a favorite doll, taking him for walks in his stroller and pulling him around the pool in an inner tube.

By the time Brian was born, George Bechtold had grown secure in his position with the federal government. The more his power and salary increased, the less interest he showed in his newborn son. His older son, however, due to his constant misbehavior, got more than his share of George's attention. At fifteen, George Jr. was tall and strong, and he felt big enough to meet his father blow for blow. The two of them would get into fistfights that terrified the other children—once, memorably, in the front of the house, in broad daylight. Even worse, George's violence seemed to make Dorothy feel that the use of force was an acceptable way to exert authority. She, too, physically abused and humiliated the children more and more often, once giving Cathy a black eye by hitting her in the face with a belt buckle. Dorothy was beginning to lose sight of the needs of her children beyond the basics of food, shelter, and clothing—she was too bound up with her own affairs and those of her husband. As problems in the family increased, the Bechtolds became more and more isolated in the community.

The children were sent to a Catholic school where, as at home, it wasn't unusual for them to be humiliated. Cathy had a learning disability and was shamed by the nuns for her failure to memorize facts. This didn't help her; indeed, it made things worse, and when she moved to a large public junior high school, she was unable to keep up with the homework. There were so many students that she felt lost in the crowd, unable to get the attention she craved. One day at the end of the school year, Cathy deliberately missed the school bus and then swallowed an entire bottle of pills that she'd found in her mother's bathroom cabinet. Dorothy, unaware of what her daughter had done, reprimanded her for missing the bus, drove her to school, and left her sitting outside the principal's office, waiting to be reprimanded again.

As soon as her mother left, the pills began to take effect. Observers said Cathy suddenly became violent and unruly, yelling, cursing, and banging her head against the wall over and over again. She was taken to the hospital to have her stomach pumped, then admitted to a children's psychiatric ward. She has no memory of being offered any counseling, either during her time in the hospital or afterward, when she got home. At school, she was simply passed on to the next grade, no questions asked. This was the first of Cathy's many suicide attempts, one of which left her in a coma from which it seemed, for a while, that she might not recover.

In keeping with her unpredictable nature, Dorothy, when she arrived to bring Cathy home from the hospital, was in her most winning mood. Knowing her daughter loved pretty clothes and accessories, she had brought her a beautiful bright yellow dress and a pair of new white sandals to change into. Instead of going straight home, the two went to an upscale French restaurant surrounded by high brick walls and lit by oil-burning torches. Dining with her mother in high style, Cathy was thrilled.

Her suicide attempt went unmentioned.

Dorothy could be thoughtlessly cruel. She told Cathy about a pediatrician who'd wanted to adopt her. Dorothy said she often wished she'd let him. Later, when Brian was older, Dorothy told him more than once that while pregnant with him, she'd wanted to get an abortion.

George's contract at Martin Marietta lasted for five years; after leaving, he took an adjunct job teaching engineering at Georgia Tech in Atlanta and moved into the student dorms while the family's house was put on the market. When it sold, in 1970, George found a house in Atlanta, and the rest of the family joined him there. Brian was two when they moved. His only memories of Orlando are headaches so shocking he'd faint from the pain.

The family was already in a state of high tension before the move, and in Atlanta, the tension came to a crisis. George was drinking heavily. He'd constantly get into fistfights with George Jr., now seventeen, who was getting into trouble with the law. On one occasion, he got involved in a plot to hold up a convenience store. When he got home from the police station, George gave him a dreadful beating—an incident that traumatized Cathy and Carole, both of whom witnessed it. After this, whenever family fights broke out, Cathy would take Brian and hide him in her room, away from the noise and violence.

George Jr. was turning into a replica of his father. As Cathy recalls, he began using his size and strength to bully his sisters and threaten his mother, whom he cajoled into giving him money and cooking him special meals. If she resisted or complained, he would respond with profanities and, sometimes, violence. He'd bring his jock buddies over to the house when his father was at work, and they'd sit around drinking, smoking pot, and teasing his sisters. He seemed to have little moral compass or sense of responsibility. Only his prowess at sports stopped him from dropping out of school. Tall and tough like his dad, he was a natural athlete and star of his high school football team. His commitment to sports helped him focus his drive and energy, although his parents had no interest in his successes—a fact that didn't stunt the growth of his already inflated ego.

Shortly after the incident with the police, George Jr. was sent away to a Catholic camp for juvenile delinquents. This was the beginning of a pattern for the Bechtolds of turning to therapeutic interventions (camps, day programs, psychiatric clinics) after disturbing incidents with their children.

Cathy's role in the family was to display all the feeling and sympathy her parents seemed to lack. While her siblings grew stoical about their beatings, she grew more sensitive, weeping on their behalf. Unconsciously, she took on the burden of the family's emotional well-being, silently absorbing their anger and pain.

While Cathy retreated inwardly into suicidal depression, the Bechtolds' youngest daughter, Carole, now in her early teens, rebelled outwardly. From the age of thirteen, she started to sneak out of the house at night to hang out in downtown Atlanta. George responded by beating her, which made her even more eager to run away. Finally, George and Dorothy committed her to a psychiatric hospital for children in southern Georgia, where she remained for a year before being joined by Cathy, after another suicide attempt. The sisters spent another year at the hospital together.

When Dorothy's mother died, the Bechtolds moved to Pittsburgh to take care of the estate, leaving the two older siblings behind in Atlanta. George Jr. was engaged to his high school sweetheart and was planning to become an accountant. Marcia was enrolled in nursing school.

In Pittsburgh, things were a little better, but after the sunshine of Orlando and Atlanta, Cathy and Carole both hated the damp, gray weather and gritty industrial town. Their new house was in a very rough, working-class neighborhood, and the girls felt alienated and out of place. While Brian stayed at home with his mother, his sisters were enrolled in school and found it difficult to get used to the toughness and teasing of their fellow students. They were both miserable.

While Cathy made it through the school year, Carole, more rebellious than her sister, kept running away. When she was fifteen, she escaped, hitchhiking to New York, where she lived on the streets for a while before getting caught up in a cult called the Forever Family. Its leader was Stewart Traill, a charismatic vacuum cleaner salesman. According to Carole, cult members lived in a big warehouse, ate oatmeal served from vats, performed exorcisms, and worked, at minimum wage, for Traill's carpet cleaning business. It was an unusual life, but it gave Carole a family and a job. Brian was especially fascinated by the cult's exorcisms. When he was six or seven, Carole sent him a recording of one, and he listened to it over and over again. He was gripped by the thought that a person could be possessed by the devil.

In 1973, George Bechtold was offered a position at the then-named Naval Surface Weapons Center in White Oak, Maryland, and the family moved to a new home in nearby Hillandale. It was a relief to be settled at last. The previous year had been particularly disruptive. Cathy, now sixteen, had spent tenth grade in four different high schools; Brian, who was not yet five, had already lived in three different states.

The Bechtolds' new home was a split-level, ranch-style house built in 1957 and set about two hundred feet back from the road, on a slight incline. It had two and a half bathrooms, a finished basement, and a shady yard out back. There was a small patio outside the front door, which opened onto a split-level foyer. On the first floor were the living room, kitchen, and dining room, which had sliding glass doors leading out to a paved area beside the backyard. The second floor contained four bedrooms; the basement served as a den.

Hillandale is part of Montgomery County, an area noted for its high median household income, safe and desirable neighborhoods, and first-rate public schools. Its close proximity to Washington, DC, makes the county an appropriate location for large government offices, military bases, and research headquarters like the weapons center where George would be working as a research engineer.

In Hillandale, Dorothy tried to settle into the neighborhood. She enrolled Cathy in a Catholic school and tried to befriend other local mothers, but whenever anyone came over to the house, George's rudeness would drive them away. When the phone rang, which was rarely, it was always for Dorothy—unless it was business. The family never had guests over, and after a while, Dorothy stopped cleaning the house. The only place the couple ever went was to church, which they'd started attending again in middle age. St. Camillus, in nearby

Silver Spring, was an active Catholic church with a lively parish community. George attended Mass once a week, but Dorothy got more involved, joining a Bible study group and going to prayer meetings. Together, the couple still enjoyed listening to Big Band music, but they didn't dance much anymore. Dorothy wasn't in the best of health.

George, however, was in great shape, exercising fanatically. He'd jog in the morning, then go to the gym, where he'd hook two eighty-pound dumbbells to a two-hundred-pound bench press and do power lifts in sets of ten. But his new interest in health didn't stop him from drinking. By now, he was unquestionably an alcoholic and, according to Brian and Cathy, tyrannical in eccentric ways. For example, while he'd always been frugal, he now became positively tightfisted, and despite making a decent salary, he kept everyone on a strict budget. He'd buy old cars and fix them up himself. He threw nothing away, making his family eat stale bread and meat that had gone bad. "There was something wrong with my father," Cathy recalls. "I don't know what it was, but something was definitely wrong with him. He had no friends. He wasn't the type to have friends. He didn't even seem to like any of his children."

The summer of the year they moved to Hillandale, Dorothy was still working hard to make friends, and she was often distracted, leaving Cathy to take care of Brian. One day, the two children took a walk to the neighborhood pool. There, Cathy lay in the sun while Brian splashed around in the shallow end. Another boy, a little older than Brian, had brought a metal watering can to play with and was throwing it up in the air. While Brian was paddling in the water, the can came down right on his head. Hearing his cries, Cathy ran over and found her brother covered in blood. She picked him up and, with assistance from the lifeguard, cleaned off the blood in the changing room. There was a deep cut on her brother's head.

The mother of the boy who'd thrown the watering can put Brian and Cathy in her car and drove them home. When the children arrived, however, their father was at work, and Dorothy, talking on the phone, was uninterested—in fact, she seemed annoyed at having her conversation interrupted. Without even coming out of the house to see Brian's injury, she told Cathy to let the other child's mother take them to the hospital. Terrified and embarrassed, Cathy had to ask a complete stranger to give them a ride—in bathing suits and flip-flops, with Cathy's hair dripping wet.

At the hospital, the doctors told Cathy they couldn't treat her brother unless a parent or legal guardian gave permission. Cathy gave the hospital staff her home phone number, but it was busy; Dorothy was still on the line. Finally, one of the doctors got the operator to interrupt the call to ask Dorothy for permission to stitch up her son's head. Cathy was shocked and scared by the incident. Even at the time, she wondered what impact it might have on Brian.

Unsurprisingly, Cathy Bechtold was eager to get away from home. She finished high school early, taking classes over the summer so she wouldn't have to attend her senior year. After graduating, she went to Atlanta and lived with her sister Marcia for six months. Even though she was still very young, she wanted to learn to take care of herself and to earn a living. She took a waitressing job and made enough money to buy a car and pay for insurance. When she returned home, she'd matured significantly and began dating an older boy she'd known in high school. She stopped coming home at night, and her parents told her she was no longer welcome, so she moved in with her boyfriend's family full-time. George and Dorothy didn't seem unhappy to let her go.

If Cathy acted out the family's unfelt emotions, Brian's role was to manifest the tension and anger that everyone else ignored. He was too young to understand how dysfunctional the situation had become, but old enough to know he was unwanted. His parents would talk about him in the third person, even though he was right there in the room. They seemed to be ashamed of him. By the time Brian was in junior high, Dorothy was depressed, tired, and often unwell. She began asking her husband to look after Brian—which meant dropping him off somewhere while George went to a bar to drink. Later, she learned that George had given Brian a knife and told him he should use it if he thought anybody was going to cause him any trouble.

Now Brian was alone, without his sisters to protect him from parental neglect. The less George and Dorothy acknowledged him, the more attention he seemed to need. His migraines grew worse as he got older; sometimes they were bad enough to make him hallucinate. When he was in junior high, a doctor prescribed Dexedrine, which made him jumpy and aggressive. Dorothy thought he should find an outlet for his anger. George thought his son should be encouraged to fight, so Dorothy enrolled him in a martial arts studio in Rockville, a half-hour drive from home.

For a time, like Carole with the Forever Family cult, Brian had found a home. At the martial arts studio, he fell under the calm, benign influence of Korean grandmaster and guru Ki Whang Kim. Known to his acolytes as Master Kim, he based his tough fitness regime on the lessons he'd learned in Korea, where as a schoolboy from a wealthy family he was terrorized by less fortunate classmates. Along with martial arts, Master Kim taught honesty, patience, and humility. Brian was a diligent pupil. He'd never liked playing team sports at school, but karate made sense. Everything was up to him. He could train at his own pace, without pressure, on his own terms. For the first time, he knew what it felt like to be motivated, and he made his way swiftly through the ranks. Soon, he began asking Dorothy to drive him to the studio every day after class.

Brian's most frequent sparring partner was a Korean boy named Kyu (pronounced "Q"), who was a second-degree black belt and Master Kim's godson. "Brian was very good at martial arts," Kyu told me. Master Kim, who'd trained in China and Japan, supplemented his students' training in karate and taekwondo with lessons in meditation, which came easily to Brian. He'd always been the silent type. Meditation strengthened his character, and by the time he was sixteen, he, too, had a black belt.

Brian and Kyu became close, and Brian would go along with Kyu to eat after practice with Master Kim. "We spent almost every day of the week with him," Kyu told me. Because they were now old enough to work part-time, Brian and Kyu got jobs at the same pizzeria, delivering pies. For a while, Brian felt that his life was back on track. He had a new pastime, a new friend, a new job, and a new mentor. Soon, the karate studio became the center of his life. "Everything we did was related to martial arts," said Kyu, "whether it was practicing for a tournament or just sparring together." Brian hoped to teach karate one day, like Master Kim.

Kyu, like Brian, didn't get along with his parents and wasn't comfortable at home, but he liked visiting Brian's house, just as Brian liked visiting Kyu's, so they alternated staying over each weekend. Neither of them regarded the other's family as dysfunctional; in fact, each idealized the other's home life, and both sets of parents were friendlier in front of an outsider and put on a show of civility. Kyu never noticed anything unusual or extraordinary about the Bechtold family except the fact that their house was untidy. "I was on very good terms with his parents. I thought they were great," said Kyu. "It was always fun to go over there. I'd spend the holidays there. At Thanksgiving, his sister Cathy would come. At Christmas, there'd be Marcia, and Carole and her boyfriend, Henry. When I was around, it was usually a happy time."

4

Thicker Than Water

If things at the Bechtold residence seemed stable to an outsider, it was a precarious illusion. More and more, Brian appeared to take on and act out the tension between George and Dorothy. At school, his grades were getting worse. Even though his karate lessons were supposed to be character-building, he sometimes lost his temper and used his moves against his classmates, which got him into trouble. He was suspended more than once for fighting. One day, he was called out of class to see the school psychologist, which puzzled him, as he hadn't done anything wrong. The psychologist questioned him about his state of mind. She wanted to know if he'd ever thought about suicide. Brian thought the questions must have something to do with his sister Cathy, who was often suicidal. Unguarded, he told the truth. Of course, he'd thought about suicide. Who hadn't?

It was the wrong thing to say. Given Cathy's history of self-harm, and Brian's increasing isolation from his family, the psychologist decided that he, too, was a suicide risk, and informed George and Dorothy. After a conversation with well-meaning friends from church, Brian's parents decided it was time for an intervention—and they had him locked up. More specifically, they signed papers to have him hospitalized at the Psychiatric Institute of Montgomery County, where he was kept on a maximum-security ward for children. Here, at age sixteen, he was diagnosed with a mental illness for the first time in his life ("atypical depression") and put on lithium, which made him talkative, and Haldol, which made him sleepy. His intelligence was tested and shown to be average, his brain and body proved to be functioning normally, and the Rorschach test personality description ("sexual identity confusion and a strong feeling of hostility and aggressiveness towards other people") might have described any unhappy adolescent.

Brian was on the psych ward for only thirteen days, but it was a huge disruption. The kids there had done terrible things. One of them had killed his stepfather with a shotgun. Another had molested little girls. The medication was no help. Brian was relieved when Dorothy changed her mind about the whole thing and came to take him back home ("against medical advice," according to Brian's records).

It was a relief for him to stop taking the meds, but other than that, things weren't much better. Once Brian was out of the hospital, his teachers insisted that he, his parents, and his sister Cathy go to counseling. In Brian's and Cathy's eyes, these sessions were worse than useless. In their experience, outsiders always deferred to George, impressed by his aloof bearing, his PhD, and his high-ranking job at the weapons center. In these sessions, too, George duped the counselor by repeating anecdotes about Brian and Cathy that he'd previously rehearsed, the same way he'd memorized facts about them to make people think he was a hands-on dad. This time, the counselor seemed to think Dorothy was to blame for the children's problems, and in turn, Dorothy became angry and defensive. She didn't take kindly to secondhand parenting advice, and although she sat passively in the sessions, she asserted on the way home that she wasn't going to do things differently just because a stranger thought she should.

The counseling sessions came to an end when George got into a car accident while drunk. The crash wasn't life-threatening, but the injuries to his legs meant he couldn't go jogging every day or lift weights. His exercises could be replaced—he soon developed a new, gentler routine that involved swimming and aerobics—but the accident was a wake-up call, and he realized he had to quit drinking. He joined Alcoholics Anonymous and stuck with the program. Brian was relieved that his dad was finally coming to terms with his addiction, but for a while, things got much worse. For the three years it took George to dry out, he became even more aggressive than usual—tense, irritable, and quick-tempered. He'd always had problems sleeping and used to knock himself out with alcohol. Now he suffered from insomnia, which made him even more irascible. His anger was terrifyingly unpredictable, and as the only child still at home, Brian bore the brunt of it.

As George was slowly recovering from alcoholism, his wife's health was rapidly deteriorating. In 1983, she learned she had breast cancer, and that she'd probably had it for some time. Over the next five years, she was in and out of the hospital on a regular basis. She had a lumpectomy and radiation treatment, along with chemotherapy that caused her to suffer fits of nausea and, when she wasn't vomiting, to swell up grotesquely. Eventually, she underwent a double mastectomy. Even after that, she continued with the chemotherapy and continued to need regular hospitalization.

Brian was planning to train as a karate teacher, so he didn't think he needed to go to college. His grades were good, especially in math and science, but after graduating from high school, he continued to focus on karate, working at the pizza parlor to make money for gas. Like any other teenager, he tried to spend as much time away from home as possible, although he had more reasons than most. He dreaded his father's outbursts of rage and felt stifled by the suffocating atmosphere of his mother's sickroom. He preferred to be at the karate studio, especially because a mysterious new girl had started lessons there.

Yasmin came to Master Kim's studio with her two sisters, to whom she kept close. She was the shyest and most guarded of the three, and it was a long time before Brian even got the chance to speak to her. Their first conversations were awkward. Yasmin didn't offer up her thoughts readily, and Brian suspected she kept a lot to herself. But something about her felt familiar to him, as if they were somehow connected. Although their backgrounds were completely different, they bonded over their shared passion for martial arts. He worked hard to win her confidence because he felt it would be worthwhile, and he was right. His persistence paid off. Yasmin became Brian's first girlfriend, and his first sexual partner.

Born and raised in Iran, Yasmin was a Muslim, and Brian learned everything he could about her religion. He listened to the Koran on audiotape, and while he didn't go so far as to convert, he stopped eating pork. He and Yasmin were a couple for almost two years and even began talking about marriage. Brian liked the idea of marrying Yasmin, but without giving him particular reasons, she was reluctant to commit. At first, Brian thought it was because he wasn't a Muslim, but then Yasmin got a new boyfriend, and he wasn't a Muslim, either.

When the relationship ended, Brian was heartbroken. For a while, he didn't want to get out of bed. He didn't want to go to work at the pizzeria, and he definitely didn't want to go to the karate studio, where there was a good chance he'd run into Yasmin. Outside the studio, he still hung out with Kyu, but without the guiding influence of Master Kim, Brian and Kyu began to drift. Instead of going to karate practice, they spent the evenings drinking and smoking pot.

While Brian was suffering, George and Dorothy, at least for a while, seemed almost content. With four of their five children out of the house, and Dorothy's cancer in remission, George, at sixty, felt comfortable enough to retire. He didn't stop working completely, but he began taking short-term contractual jobs abroad, helping construction engineering companies comply with U.S. federal requirements. Dorothy was still undergoing chemotherapy, and her doctors warned her against traveling, but she loved to visit new places and ignored their advice, accompanying George on his foreign assignments. If she was having a bad day, she'd just stay in bed, watch television, and get room service. Three years after George retired, as a tax write-off, the couple purchased a mobile home in Florida, near Daytona, where they planned to spend five months of every year.

Their decision was made without input from Brian, who learned of it only after the fact, shortly after his breakup with Yasmin. While he was relieved that he'd be spending five months of every year free from his father's black moods, he was still hurt not to be included. The family had spent vacations near Daytona when he was a child, and he'd enjoyed exploring the wild swamplands down there. But his parents had made it very clear: he wasn't invited.

One thing took the pain away for a while: smoking pot. Some guys at the pizzeria sold marijuana. Brian quickly picked up the habit. He liked the way it took him out of himself. Soon he was buying his own supply to smoke at home while his parents were in Florida. He made a few bucks from time to time selling it to other kids in the neighborhood. Because marijuana made him feel so good, he started to wonder what other drugs felt like. From the guys at the pizzeria, he bought speed, cocaine, and a kind of PCP called Love Boat, which he began using whenever it was around. He frequently dropped LSD. In fact, he tried everything. "At that time, Brian was doing a lot of drugs," said Kyu. "We drank together, and we smoked pot together, but Brian was doing a lot of other drugs as well, like PCP and cocaine. Brian and I both started to become delusional around that time. We both believed the same things. A lot of it was paranoia, and a lot of it was just due to mental illness. But the drugs made it a lot worse."

Looking back, Brian can see that this was the moment he started to lose his foothold in reality, although at the time, he didn't know he had a mental illness. It was 1987, and he was about to turn nineteen. When he injured his knee while sparring at the YMCA, he found himself unable to fight. Without a girlfriend, without his family, and without karate, he had nothing to focus on and nothing to do. One night in November, while driving home stoned from the pizzeria, he veered off the road and wrecked his car. A cop found an envelope full of cocaine under the passenger seat. It was only a gram, but Brian was charged with possession with intent to distribute.

His boss at the pizza parlor fired him, and the court put him on probation. When George and Dorothy found out what had happened, they sent Brian to rehab at Washington Adventist Hospital in Takoma Park. There, his headaches got worse and were accompanied by a sense of impending doom. He started to grow paranoid, suspecting the other patients were secret agents who'd been sent to gather evidence against him. In moments of great anxiety, his heartbeat would speed up, and he'd find it difficult to breathe. To calm himself, he'd sit in the hallway, away from the others, and rock back and forth until he could feel his pulse slowing down.

The doctors thought he was delusional and diagnosed him with "schizotypal personality disorder and mixed substance abuse disorder." They wanted to transfer him to the psych ward and put him on medication, but Brian refused. From his sisters' experiences, he knew that by law, the hospital could keep him for only three days. After that, as there'd been no court hearing to request longer inpatient treatment, he signed himself out.

Brian's driving accident, like his father's, was a wake-up call, and his New Year's resolution on January 1, 1988, was to quit drugs completely. It wasn't easy, but Brian was the kind of person who didn't do things by half measures. Like George, he was strong-willed and stubborn. It was tough, but he stuck it out, and by spring, he was clean. Now he had to face the rest of his problems: he was single, unemployed, on probation, and living at home—and for five months of the year, he was on his own. While he came off drugs, he stayed in his bedroom all day, sleeping, reading, and listening to music.

He decided he needed company while his parents were away, so he bought two dogs, a female Rottweiler and her male pup. He named them Maxine and Onyx. The pup, Onyx, was a fast learner. Once he got over his natural defiance, obedience came quickly. Master and pup formed a tight bond. Kyu sometimes went along when Brian took the two dogs to Great Falls, a national park on the Potomac River, just across the Virginia border. "We'd go on long walks with the dogs down by the C[hesapeake] and O[hio] canal and climb on the rocks," said Kyu. "Brian was incredibly attached to those dogs."

Brian trusted Maxine and Onyx the way he'd never trusted people. He got into the habit of walking the dogs at night; he didn't want to be seen by the neighbors; he thought they might be spies. Green Forest Drive was a quiet street, populated mainly by families and older couples. It was strictly residential, and there were no sidewalks; it would have been unusual to see someone walking up and down the street during the daytime.

These nighttime walks put pressure on his injured knee, and Brian finally realized that it would never be strong enough for him to work as a karate teacher, so he decided to apply to college. He knew he was smart—his grades in school had been above average, even excellent, when he'd applied himself. His father, who'd paid for Marcia and George Jr. to go to college, seemed pleased when, in 1990, Brian was accepted by DeVry University in Decatur, Georgia, to study electrical engineering technology.

It was a healthy move, in theory. Brian was away from the family home, away from his father's bullying rages and his mother's suffering, and he could spend time with his older brother, George Jr., who was now married and working as an accountant in Atlanta. It seemed as if George Jr.'s delinquent days were behind him, and he'd settled down into a stable life.

But things weren't easy for Brian at DeVry. He was five years older than most of the other students and had trouble making friends. His two housemates found him strange. He went to class regularly, worked hard, and kept on top of his responsibilities, but his increasing paranoia began to show itself in the form of tension and irritation. He started to find himself intensely annoyed by simple things, such as the price of gas at a particular gas station or somebody trying to cut in line ahead of him. He thought one of his housemates was a cop because he kept a revolver in his sock drawer. Brian started to think this housemate—who was, in fact, a computer student from Jacksonville, Florida—was having him followed, and he took to holding a knife behind his back when he answered the door.

Adding fuel to the flame was Brian's older brother, George Jr., who was not, it turned out, living the stable life Brian had imagined. In fact, he was regularly hounding Dorothy to send him money, partly to finance his wife's taste for showy furniture. Instead of helping Brian out when he came to Atlanta, George Jr. would use him as an alibi, telling his wife he was spending time with his brother when he was actually seeing other women. Even worse, he gave Brian's address to people from whom he'd borrowed money, and more than once, during his second trimester, Brian was woken up by someone pounding on his door, looking for his brother.

Brian was living off campus by this time, renting a house with six other students. He'd brought Maxine and Onyx down from Silver Spring with him, though they had to sleep in the car. His housemates accepted him, and his professors seemed to like him. He challenged himself by taking only the most difficult classes, and despite all his problems, he managed to maintain a 4.0 GPA. Gradually, he felt his anxiety starting to ease and grew comfortable enough to let his guard down a little, to trust others, feel connected, and begin forming social bonds. The delusions and paranoia started to dissipate. He made friends with another older student, an electrical engineer in his late thirties.

Then everything fell apart. Brian was still on probation from the drug charge, and when he returned to Maryland after his second trimester at DeVry, his probation officer told him he'd violated the terms of his probation by moving out of state. Instead of helping work things out with the court so Brian could finish college, George simply stopped paying his tuition. Brian knew it wasn't because his parents were broke; they had recently bought the mobile home in Daytona to offset their taxes. He didn't qualify for a loan, so he had no alternative: he dropped out of college and moved back into the family home.

Once he realized he wasn't going to be able to get a college degree, Brian started to fall apart. His parents were in no state to look after him; their own brief respite had come to an end as Dorothy's health declined. Her breast cancer had returned, she was overweight, and her heart was weak. She used an oxygen tank to help her breathe, and a nurse paid weekly visits. Some days, Dorothy seemed to be barely alive, croaking and gasping for air. Brian noticed that she was in the habit of drinking a bottle of cough syrup every day to knock herself out every evening. He could understand why. The sicker she got, the worse George treated her. In the face of his wife's suffering, he resorted to his default mode of mocking cruelty. At one point, Dorothy was in the hospital for a long stretch of time, and whenever George went to visit her, Brian went along. One day, Brian was shocked to hear his father telling Dorothy he'd never loved her and he wished he'd never married her. "You've ruined my life," he said.

Dorothy's condition got worse; she was in a great deal of pain. Her voice got so weak that she couldn't be heard when she tried to speak on the phone. Her own deteriorating condition, and her attempts to numb the pain, meant she was unable to provide a safe environment for Brian or attend to his emotional needs. At this stage, in fact, Dorothy was no longer able to take care of her own needs. Things got so bad that she would sometimes ask Brian to help her kill herself. When Cathy, Carole, and Marcia visited Dorothy in the hospital, she'd ask them the same thing. She put Marcia, who was a nurse, under special pressure. On some days, Dorothy would have such difficulty breathing she'd be in agony all day. Her suffering dragged on and on.

Whenever she could manage it, after finishing work, Cathy, who was now married, would drive to the hospital to visit her mother. When she arrived, she was often surprised to find her father sitting reading a book or gazing absently out the window, ignoring his wife. Dorothy would tell her daughter she was cold, and Cathy would go find a blanket for her, then get her something to drink and find her doctor for an update. She realized her father had no idea what was involved in looking after another human being and didn't seem to care that others were disturbed by his indifference.

That winter, Maxine died. Brian buried her in the backyard. After that, his headaches got worse, and with them came a feeling that he couldn't name. It wasn't exactly depression, but more like a thick fog of boredom that crept over him, taking away all his curiosity, his motivation, his sense of humor, his interest in life. It was like a gas that you can barely smell before it hits you, causing you to drift passively into oblivion. He felt inert and apathetic. He lost his appetite. At night, his sleep was disturbed by bad dreams. He would awaken drained and exhausted. He began staying up all night and slept only when the sun came up.

When his parents went to Florida, Brian left the house during the daytime only to buy groceries, and every time he did, the same car would follow him. Sometimes he'd see it parked outside the house. He installed three locks on his bedroom door and hung blankets over the windows. At night, walking Onyx, he'd notice strange shadows moving under the trees. People seemed to be watching him. He tried to figure out who they were. He'd heard a rumor that one of his German ancestors had been a Nazi, or so he'd been told. Joseph Berchtold had been the first leader of Hitler's stormtroopers, although Brian didn't know whether they were related, since the name was slightly different.

But if they were, he thought, then maybe the people following him were relatives of Jews Joseph Berchtold had killed in the Holocaust. Whenever he caught a glimpse of them, they seemed to be wearing a different disguise. Sometimes they looked like ordinary people; sometimes they were dressed as cops, and sometimes like soldiers.

One night in March, he saw witches on broomsticks flying through his backyard.

By the end of the summer of 1991, the people who were following him had gotten inside his head. They gate-crashed his dreams. They'd set up a device in the attic, a machine with a microphone that picked up his thoughts and a speaker system that sent him subliminal messages. When he realized they were using him as a human guinea pig for mind-control experiments, he knew it was time to fight back.

He drove around the back streets of DC looking for someone on a street corner who'd sell him a gun. He found people dealing in drugs but not firearms. One of them asked him why he didn't just go buy a gun from a store. Brian hadn't even thought about it. In November, he went to the Kmart on Connecticut Avenue in Silver Spring and bought a Mossberg 500 pump-action shotgun and a box of Remington buckshot for just over two hundred dollars.

He sawed off the end of the gun, so he could hide it under his clothes, and took it everywhere with him, even into the shower. He put it down only when he was locked in his bedroom, and even then, he'd position it on his dresser, loaded, with its barrel pointing toward the door.

When his parents returned from Florida, they seemed more bemused than concerned about Brian's behavior. Cathy remembers her father telling her that Brian had been acting oddly and was growing paranoid. He told her Brian had constructed a dummy, dressed it in his own clothes, and propped it up in the window of his room, so that from outside the house, it looked as if he were always home. He also told her that Brian would sometimes talk on the phone without dialing a number, and that he'd bought a gun and was patrolling the house with it. George seemed unconcerned with his own safety. He seemed to think Brian considered himself to be defending the family against threatening outsiders.

By February of the following year, Brian had stopped sleeping completely. At first, he'd stayed awake on purpose, keeping alert in case of attack. In the end, he couldn't sleep even when he tried. Soon, he was desperate for rest, pacing the floor, beating his fists against the walls of his room in frustration.

And then, one morning, shortly after the sun came up, Brian felt his body start to relax. He hadn't slept for a week, maybe longer. Now, at last, he was drifting toward oblivion. Suddenly he was jolted awake by a violent noise. In the kitchen downstairs, his father was yelling in utter rage. The only words Brian could decipher were "my brother Walter."

Without a second thought, Brian stood up, took his loaded shotgun from the dresser, went downstairs, and walked down the hall to the kitchen. George, still yelling, was sitting at the dining table. Behind and to the right, Brian lifted the shotgun and fired, hitting his father in the back. The force of the shot knocked his body to the floor. Blood sprayed over the front of the dishwasher.

Brian turned around to face his mother, who was sitting in her recliner, attached to her oxygen tank. The television was on. Brian didn't look at her face. He lifted the gun and fired, hitting her in the left side of her chest. Then he walked around the recliner and shot her in the back.

At that moment, he realized, his feet weren't touching the ground.

5

Day of Reckoning

Brian was on the run.

He drove eight hundred miles down Interstate 95, heading for the Mexican border, stopping only for gas. He hadn't slept for days, maybe weeks. He thought he was going southwest, toward Texas, when in fact he was going dead south, as he learned when he found himself in Jacksonville, Florida. After stopping to buy a map and dog food for Onyx, he set out again, heading west on Interstate 10. Somewhere around Biloxi, he started seeing what looked like blood on the road. Then he realized there were dead animals all over the highway—unlike any creatures he'd ever seen. Their limbs were torn, their bodies twisted out of proportion. For two hundred miles, he dragged these dead creatures under his car, smearing blood all over the road.

He drove on and on, day and night, through Alabama, Louisiana, Texas. The sun rose and set and then rose again. He stopped only for gas and to buy food. He lost track of time. He could have been driving for three days or three weeks. At one point, he saw a police car in his rearview mirror. Two hundred miles later, it was still there. Brian slowed down and let the car pass. As it drove by, he looked at the driver and recognized him right away. He was one of the detectives from the TV show *Cops*. Brian wondered: Would his arrest be featured on *Cops*?

Finally, just outside Laredo, Brian stopped, pulling up on some wasteland opposite a parking lot. He sat in the car for a while, waiting for a knock on the window, but nothing happened, so he took his dog and his gun and hid in an alley, anticipating a shootout. He thought about shooting himself in the head. He was ready to die. He'd been ready for a long time. But what would happen to Onyx?

He got back in his car and drove to the center of the parking lot opposite the wasteland. After a while, four or five Mexican guys arrived, got into their cars, and started driving in circles around Brian and spitting at his car. The thought crossed his mind that they didn't like him because he was white and this was the Mexican part of town. It made things a little better to think it might be an issue of race—in other words, they didn't hate him because they knew what he'd done. Still, they made him angry. He had to stand his ground. When one of the Mexicans parked and came over to Brian, he got out of his car and prepared to defend himself. But the guy just walked past him. Brian started laughing. He realized the Mexicans had no interest in him at all. Everything that appeared important turned out to be random and irrelevant. The world, it seemed, was meaningless.

Instead of going on to Mexico, as he'd planned, something made him turn back and head in the opposite direction, back east toward Florida. He had the feeling that something was about to happen. He prayed to Jesus for forgiveness. He asked for a sign.

On the outskirts of San Antonio, Brian picked up a hitchhiker, a guy who'd been living on the streets. He said he was going to Houston; he had the address of a mission there. As Brian was driving, the hitchhiker began to talk. He was a Christian, he said, and he had connections with Barbara Bush. If Brian was interested, the hitch-hiker would take him to the mission in Houston. Maybe they'd give him a room, help him find work.

The man also had connections with Nancy Reagan, he said. In fact, he was the person who first came up with the slogan "Just Say No." The hitchhiker asked Brian to pray with him, and Brian prayed. He even agreed to go to the mission in Houston. But when they got to the city and the guy was directing him to the mission, Brian saw him give a secret signal to a man in a passing car who looked like a detective. After that, Brian didn't trust the hitchhiker. When they got to the mission, Brian said he'd changed his mind. He didn't want to go inside, he said, because he didn't have a Social Security card, and anyway, he didn't want to leave his dog.

After dropping off the hitchhiker, Brian drove around town until he found an abandoned building with bars around its broken windows. He parked his car, went up to the building, and shoved his gun through one of the windows. He threw all the shells in after it, then went back to his car and sat there for a while. After an hour or so, he saw people walking toward the building, and not long after that, a cop car pulled up and an officer got out. When everyone had left, Brian went back to the building, looked through the window, and saw that the gun was gone.

It felt like a weight off his chest. After that, he fell asleep. He slept for two days, lying with Onyx in the back of the station wagon. When he woke up, he forgot that he'd killed his parents. When he remembered, he wasn't sure it had really happened. He kept wondering if it was true. At one point, he thought about calling the house to check. He thought it might have been a delusion, a hallucination, or a nightmare. When he replayed the scene in his head, his actions seemed strangely mechanical, as if he'd been sleepwalking or repeating something that had happened before. It was as if he were underwater, no longer breathing air.

After weeks of insomnia, he now had the opposite problem: he couldn't stay awake. Two days of sleep, and he was still exhausted. When he crossed the Florida state line, the voice of a Christian preacher came on the radio. It was the first time Brian had ever heard a preacher whose words made sense to him. About eighty miles west of Pensacola, he came off Interstate 10 and headed south. When it started to get dark, he pulled off the road and checked into the El Governor RV Park and Campground, just outside Mexico Beach. He parked in lot 42A and slept in the car, with Onyx. It was out of season, and the place was almost empty. The next morning, on his way back from the shower in the main building, he noticed a display of tourist pamphlets. Among the brochures was a King James Bible. He picked up the Bible, took it back to his car, and began to read. He read all day and all night. For three days, he stayed at the campsite. Every morning, he took a shower and then, for the rest of the day, did nothing but walk his dog and read the Bible. As he read, he felt his sanity beginning to return.

God was healing him.

"I fled the scene of a crime, and I want to turn myself in," Brian told the cop at the front desk. He'd driven from the campground to the nearest town, Port St. Joe, and asked for directions to the police station.

"Okay," the cop said. He took down Brian's name. "When did this crime take place?" he asked.

Brian was unsure. "I guess it could have been ten days ago, or seven days ago," he said.

"Okay," the cop said. "Where were you at seven days ago?"

Brian gave his Maryland address and telephone number.

"Are there any relatives or anyone at home there we could call?" the officer asked.

"That's who I killed," Brian told him. "I killed my parents."

The officer led him down a hallway to a small room, invited him to take a seat, asked if he was comfortable, asked if he wanted a glass of water, then left. He returned fifteen minutes later with an older cop. The two told Brian they'd be recording the interview.

The first cop sat opposite Brian across a table, and the older cop sat on a chair to the side of him. They both looked serious and intense.

"Now," the first cop said, "you want to go into the details and tell me what led up to this, Brian?"

"All I can say is that I was insane for six or seven years," Brian said.

"Who said you were insane?"

"I know I was insane," he said.

"Was there something that happened at home to cause you to kill your parents?" the cop asked. Brian could tell the man didn't believe him.

"I'm not sure exactly," he said. "There were a lot of things going on at the time."

"Okay. Let's go back real quick to where your home's located," the officer said. "What was the name of the town again? What city?"

"Hillandale, Maryland." Brian said.

"Hillandale, Maryland. And what county would that be in?"

"Montgomery."

"Montgomery County. Okay. And how old were your parents?"

"I'm not sure."

"You're not sure?

"Sixty-seven, sixty-six."

"And you've been living at home with them?"

"On and off, yes."

"Do you know your neighbors' names, that live next door to your parents?"

"I know a few of them," Brian said. "The Carters, the Kleins."

"Okay," the cop said. "And they live right there, next door?"

"The Carters live across the street," Brian said. "The Kleins live to the right."

"What's your address again?" the older cop asked. "I mean the address of your parents in Maryland?"

For the second time, Brian gave the cops his address and telephone number. This time, the older cop jotted it down on a notepad, nodded to his colleague, and left the room. The other cop continued to question Brian.

"You want to tell me how you committed the offense, how you committed the act?" he asked.

"I shot them," Brian said.

"You shot both your parents?"

"Yes, sir," he said.

The officer asked Brian what kind of weapon he'd used ("twelve-gauge shotgun") and what kind of shot ("double-aught buckshot"). He asked where Brian's parents were when he killed them. ("My father was eating breakfast. My mother was sitting down in a recliner chair.") The officer kept asking him to repeat the same details. He seemed to think Brian was on drugs and hallucinating.

"Step by step, as best as you can remember," the officer said, "tell me what took place from the time you left your room and started downstairs. Close your eyes for me and try to picture being in your room and then walking down the stairs, and give me a verbal description of what you remember and what you see."

"I'm not sure about what I remember and what happened," Brian replied. "I don't know whether I did something or whether it happened, or what the difference is. I just remember being down there, and it didn't seem like it was me. It seemed like I was possessed. It seemed like I wasn't alive, like I wasn't there or something. It seemed like, I don't know, it just seemed like something on TV or something like that, like I wasn't there, like it wasn't going on or something. It was like I didn't have anything to do with it."

"Okay. So, we're in the room and we go downstairs. Once we go down the stairs, describe to me how we have to go. Give me directions how we have to go."

"It's a straight line down to where I was."

"Okay. And where was your father located at?"

"He was in the dining room."

"Okay. What about your mother?"

"I didn't really look at her when I shot her. She was sitting straight in front of me. I just turned the gun and that was it . . ."

"How did you leave the body?"

"I moved my father's body into the kitchen. It was in the kitchen. I shot him. And somehow, he got up. I don't know how. It was, like, instant death. But somehow—he's real strong; he was real strong, he was real athletic—somehow, he, like, just sprung up and jumped into the kitchen ten feet away or twelve feet away."

"Where was he when you shot him?"

"He was sitting down in the dining room."

"Okay. Where was your mother at?"

"She was in the living room."

"Okay. And what did you do with her?"

"I just left her there."

"You didn't cover the bodies or anything?"

"No. I moved my father. His legs were sticking out . . ."

"Do your mother and father work?"

"My father is retired."

"Do they normally stay at home or do they travel, go out? Do they go on vacation?"

"They vacation a lot. My father has got a mobile home in Florida."

"A mobile home where in Florida?"

"Deland."

"Can I ask you a question, Brian?"

"Yes."

"Are you sure you killed them, or did they make it to the mobile home in Florida?"

"I'm sure. I'm sure it happened."

"Is there a possibility you dreamed it or thought it?"

"Yes, there is."

"Where did you take the car from? Did you take the car from the house or from the mobile home in Florida?"

"I took it from the house."

"Okay. Why are you reporting this stuff? What made you come in and decide to tell us and get it off your chest?"

"It seemed like Jesus wanted me to do it."

"Are you sorry, Brian?"

"I don't know."

"You don't know if you're sorry? Are you sure this happened? Do you think it occurred, or is there a possibility that your parents could be ..."

"... I don't want to hear you! Don't ... don't say that. It's ..."

"Okay, okay."

"... it's kind of like ... it's kind of like ... making me kind of ..."

"... I don't mean to ..."

"... making me feel strange when you say that."

"But it's a question I have to ask. Okay. I don't mean to make you feel strange."

"It feels like maybe I'd wish or hope, and I don't ... I don't ..."

"Well, I don't mean that at all."

"I don't want to feel like that, like this didn't happen or something."

"Okay. I have to ask you. That's my job, okay? Is there a possibility that they may be at the mobile home?"

"No. No. I don't know. You know, I wish it didn't happen. I wish, I wish that something else happened. But I don't know. I don't think so. I think it happened."

"Okay. And in your mind, it occurred. To the best of your knowledge, it happened."

"Yes. Something happened. Something bad happened. But it didn't seem like it was happening," Brian said. "It seemed like a nightmare. It was like I was going to sleep or something. I was going to sleep, and the next thing I knew, I was downstairs. It didn't seem like it was me doing anything."

Had Brian been using drugs? the officer wondered. Brian said he'd quit drugs five years ago and hadn't used any since then. The officer didn't seem to believe him. He kept asking the same questions over and over again. Finally, the older cop came back and said no one was picking up the phone at the number Brian had given them. Both officers left the room for a few moments, then returned.

"Brian, you said earlier that you felt like you had a mental problem. Why do you feel that way?" the older cop asked.

"Up until I guess about five days ago, I thought people were following me," Brian said. "I thought the community was out to persecute me or something. I felt that wherever I went, people were following me. I thought that no matter what I did, I was going to be put down for some reason. Society was out to get me. It was some kind of group of people that were watching me."

"Did you feel that your parents were a part of this society that was persecuting you?"

"No," Brian said.

The younger officer asked him what kind of car he was driving, and Brian said he was driving his father's car, a blue Subaru station wagon. It was parked outside the police station, he told them, adding that his dog was in the car.

The cop then asked him whether he thought anyone had found his parents' bodies, whether anybody knew about the crime.

Brian said the bodies must have been found by now. He thought the police had probably come not long after he left. Their neighbors must have heard the gunshots, he said, because their house was only twenty-five feet away, and he knew they were home because their car was in the driveway. It would have taken the police only two or three minutes to get there.

"Somebody would have to know about it," Brian said.

"Are you sure?" the cop asked.

"Somebody would have to know by now," Brian repeated.

The other cop asked Brian, again, why he had killed his parents.

"I've been crazy and possessed," he said.

"How do you mean 'crazy and possessed'?" the officer asked. "What do you mean? Can you tell us in a little more detail what you mean by 'crazy and possessed'?"

"People have been following me around," Brian told him. "People have been making fun of me and following me around, and I've been hearing voices, and I felt there were people in my attic."

"Are you religious?" the officer asked.

"Yes, I am," Brian said. "It was about five days ago that I realized it was the devil in my life."

Later, in his incident report, Officer Timothy Hightower wrote:

> He could not stand it anymore and had to tell someone that he had killed his parents.... He could offer no explanation as to why he shot his parents, other than that the devil made him do it, and Jesus made him confess.... He further reported that he believed he had been followed by a group of conspirators who were agents of the devil.... He believed the incident took place about two weeks ago. He said he used a shotgun loaded with 12-gauge buckshot. He said he had been possessed by the devil. He noted he believes that he has committed a sin by killing his parents, but now he believes that he had received forgiveness by the angel who speaks to him.

Hightower placed a call to the Maryland police. Within the hour, Maryland returned the call. They asked Port St. Joe to hold the suspect until they could get a warrant for extradition. Brian's car was secured in the fire station, and a dog handler came for Onyx. Their separation was traumatic for Brian. Onyx had bonded to him at a very young age and was his closest friend. The dog had been with Brian through everything.

"At the time," Officer Hightower wrote in his report, "it was noted that he was more upset that police officers were taking the dog to the pound than the fact that he had killed his parents."

Brian spent four days in the jail at Port St. Joe. On the fourth day, because Maryland, like most states, outsources its long-distance transport of prisoners and fugitives, Officer Hightower handed Brian over to two representatives of a private, for-profit extradition company. After leading him outside, the two men handcuffed Brian, shackled him by the waist and ankles, and made him climb up into a cage in the back of a van with darkened windows. There were five other prisoners in the van already, sitting tightly packed in the suffocating heat. There was no air-conditioning, no way to get comfortable or to sleep, and no way to go to the bathroom. The trip to Maryland took two weeks. First, they drove north, picking up and dropping off prisoners in Mississippi, Alabama, Tennessee, Illinois, and Michigan. Then they headed east, to Ohio, then north again, to New York, then south to Maryland by way of Pennsylvania and Delaware.

Twice a day, the van would stop at a McDonald's restaurant. The men in the back would be unchained, taken inside, allowed to use the bathroom, and given two cheeseburgers and a large soda. At night, they'd be housed in local detention centers. One of the prisoners was very young and good-looking, and the security guards advised him, with a grin, to buy himself a jar of Vaseline.

At night, in the detention centers, they all slept together in a large single cell with an open toilet. The worst one was in Mississippi. It was underground, like a dungeon, and about forty feet square, the size of a residential garage. There was a black-and-white television in a cage attached to the wall; it played only one channel. A prisoner down there said he'd been living in that dungeon for ten years without ever getting to see an attorney. He begged Brian to help him. He was terrified of dying down there. Brian wanted to help, but there was nothing he could do. He didn't even have a pencil to write down the guy's name.

When they got to Maryland, they took Brian to the Montgomery County Detention Center in Seven Locks, near Rockville. Here, guards removed his handcuffs and gave him an orange jumpsuit to wear. As he was led down a long row of prison cells, the news was playing on a television. Brian heard the announcer mention his name; he looked up and saw his face on the screen. His arrest and extradition had made local headlines. He wasn't sure what the other inmates would make of this. Would they be impressed, he wondered, or would it make him a target?

In the end, it made little difference. Prisoners arrived at the detention center so regularly, and were taken away so often, that he didn't get the chance to make either enemies or friends. He was there for three and a half months, which was longer than anyone else, but it was difficult to get the wheels moving on his legal case. Personally, Brian didn't think he needed an attorney. He knew what he'd done. He knew how serious it was, and he knew he was responsible. He was ready to go to prison and serve his time. But others disagreed.

When the news of their parents' murder was broken to Brian's siblings, their reactions were mixed. George Jr. and Carole were extremely shocked and angry with Brian, but Cathy and Marcia, although they were both upset, understood that Brian was seriously ill. They knew that if he'd been in his right mind, their brother would never have been capable of such an act. They also wondered whether the shooting, although it made no sense, was some kind of mercy killing. Perhaps Brian wanted to put Dorothy out of her misery, and because their father would have tried to stop him, he'd had to go, too.

As they tried to make sense of what Brian had done, the sisters both acknowledged that their feelings of enormous grief and loss were complicated by the fact that George and Dorothy had abused them all, both physically and emotionally. In many ways, they'd been terrible parents, and none of the children had escaped unscathed. They'd all grown into damaged people. It was as if Brian had been standing in for all five siblings, acting out their long-repressed rage. At the same time, however, Cathy and Marcia knew their parents had loved them. George and Dorothy hadn't been awful people—they'd just been confused, overwhelmed, and ill-equipped to deal with the demands of parenthood. It wasn't a simple question of good versus evil. It was more complicated than that.

Marcia, who was living in South Carolina at the time, drove up to join Cathy, and the two sisters tried to make sense of what had gone wrong at home, and why nobody had alerted the authorities about Brian's behavior. They discussed how Brian's crime had been an acting out of the four older siblings' joint anguish growing up. They wondered about the hospice worker who'd been coming to visit Dorothy every day. Hadn't they realized that things were terribly wrong—that the house was in chaos, that Brian was walking around with a shotgun?

The sisters hired a seasoned defense attorney, Mark Van Bavel, who remembers Brian, when they first met, as being "a very pleasant young man," but "obviously insane." Van Bavel consulted with Brian in a private room at the detention center reserved for lawyers' visits. "He told me he killed his parents because he'd been possessed by the devil," Van Bavel said. "He'd been behaving bizarrely, walking around the house with a shotgun. I couldn't imagine why his parents didn't see this as a terrible crisis on the verge of exploding. At the detention center, I was able to have a conversation with him, but I remember he was constantly aware of sounds and noises in the building and gave them sinister motivations. Air-conditioning, doors closing, and things like that—he thought they were people watching him, or devices that had been set up to observe him."

Brian's friend Kyu was working in his father's restaurant when Master Kim came into the kitchen to tell him what Brian had done. "We were all trying to figure out what had happened," Kyu said. "I was pretty shocked. I didn't believe it at first. I thought there must have been some kind of mistake. The guy I knew couldn't carry out this act."

Statistics show that children who kill their parents almost never kill again; the objects of their fear and anger are dead. The research of criminologist Kathleen M. Heide, who has undertaken extensive empirical analysis of homicides in which adolescents killed their parents, shows that Brian's crime was an archetypal parricide. "Murder in the family," Heide writes, "although shocking and unsettling, is not uncommon." In the United States alone, there are at least three hundred cases of parricide every year. Almost all occur in dysfunctional and codependent families like Brian's, after years of physical, verbal, and sometimes sexual abuse on the part of one or both parents. Parricide usually occurs when a child feels cornered, engulfed, desperate, or lost, pushed beyond their limits. It's a desperate reaction to an unendurable situation.

Typically, the perpetrator is a male in his late teens or early twenties, is from a white middle-class family, and may be acting out the unconscious wishes of his siblings or, in cases where only one parent is killed, of the surviving parent. Most are of above-average intelligence. They tend to be isolated, without many friends, and the typical weapon is a gun kept in the home.

In such cases, people will often wonder whether the perpetrator was a victim of abuse or is mentally ill, as if the two can't exist simultaneously. In many of the examples Heide studied, the child's attempts to get help or to escape from the situation failed or were ignored. Most perpetrators of parricide are isolated from other individuals and have few, if any, friends. There's usually a history of alcoholism or drug abuse in the family, and in most cases, the victims' deaths come as a relief to the perpetrator, at least initially. Often after the fact, the perpetrator will be diagnosed with a mental illness, most often schizophrenia. In fact, the two are so intertwined that parricide used to be known as "the schizophrenic crime."

Though some children murder their parents during an episode of brutal abuse, Heide has shown that most such killings occur when parents are in a vulnerable position: coming in the door, watching television, cooking dinner with their back turned, or asleep in bed. The average age of the parents in such cases is midfifties. In most cases, when the murder occurs, the perpetrator reports being in a dissociative state; afterward, if they can remember the crime at all, it seems unreal, dreamlike, or vague, as though it happened to someone else. They often express the belief that the parent isn't really dead, and they either remain afraid of the parent or are unwilling to speak about their act. This is a symptom of PTSD, often mistakenly interpreted as a lack of remorse or an indication of callousness.

The state's attorney for Montgomery County, John J. McCarthy, requested that Brian submit to a psychiatric evaluation, and Mark Van Bavel agreed. The evaluation was performed by psychiatrist Lawrence Raifman in July 1992; it consisted of a three-hour structured interview followed by a number of psychological tests. Dr. Raifman's final report, written on July 29, 1992, contained the following observations:

> [Mr. Bechtold] noted [that] agents had infiltrated the attic of his parents' home. . . . He commented that beings from other planets could analyze people's thoughts and take control. . . . He was spending much of his time in his room. He seldom came out. . . . He lived in filth and practiced bizarre rituals such as surrounding himself with containers of urine to ward off evil. . . . He reported his belief that his parents became aware of the content of his dreams. . . . He considered himself to be in conflict with the devil, who was continually playing tricks on him. . . . There were rituals involving water and placing wax on the mirror to avoid voodoo. . . . He recalled in

the days following his arrest, he believed that "something bad would happen" to him if he did not remain awake.

According to Dr. Raifman's report, Brian was suffering from "a psychotic illness, namely Schizophrenia, Paranoid Type," which, at the time of the alleged offenses, "substantially impaired his ability to appreciate the criminality of his conduct and his ability to conform his conduct to the requirements of the law."

In 1992, being diagnosed with schizophrenia was a little like being diagnosed with cancer. It was regarded as a chronic brain disease that reduced life expectancy by at least twenty years. Over time, however, researchers have realized that "schizophrenia" is not a single disease, but a clustering of several different malfunctions in the brain—genetic glitches that are unlikely to produce schizophrenia unless stimulated by environmental conditions, particularly stress during early childhood and adolescence, when the brain is still developing. More recently, researchers in the field have begun to question the idea of schizophrenia as a distinct disease, reframing it as a "psychotic spectrum disorder." From this perspective, milder forms of the condition are characterized by confused thoughts and pressured speech; severe forms, like Brian's, usually involve delusions, hallucinations, and mania. More recently, the usefulness and validity of schizophrenia as a diagnosis have been strongly challenged by patient activists and mental health professionals, who've argued that the concept is neither valid nor reliable, and that *schizophrenia* is simply a catch-all term for serious mental disorders that don't fit into any other category.

As far as Brian was aware, none of his siblings or parents had ever been diagnosed with a psychotic disorder, although there was a history of mental illness on both sides of the family. But although heredity can play a role, schizophrenia isn't caused solely by genetics. It can have any number of causes, including birth complications, childhood viral infections of the nervous system, trauma, habitual cannabis use, high levels of stress, and even exposure to a parasite found in cat feces. For Brian, as for most people diagnosed with schizophrenia, the cause remained unclear.

In light of his diagnosis and Dr. Raifman's report, Brian was found "Not Criminally Responsible at the time of the commission of the offense." As a result, there was no need for Mark Van Bavel to hire a private psychiatrist. "The state psychiatrist found [Brian] NCR, and we just proceeded on those grounds, because it was pretty obvious that was the situation," Van Bavel recalls. The hearing took place on October 8, 1992, in the Circuit Court for Montgomery County; Brian voluntarily waived his right to a jury trial. On November 30, the judge, James McKenna, issued a court order committing Brian Bechtold to the Maryland Department of Health and Mental Hygiene at Clifton T. Perkins Hospital Center, Maryland's only maximum-security forensic psychiatric facility, "for institutional, inpatient care and treatment."

6

Focus on Fiction

Named after an influential psychiatrist who helped bring about the desegregation of Maryland's psychiatric hospitals, the Clifton T. Perkins Hospital Center—usually known simply as Perkins—has beds for 350 patients and is usually at capacity. Some of the hospital's patients have committed serious felonies and are being held for competency evaluations, to see if they have the capacity to stand trial, and some are inmates who've been sent to Perkins from prisons or other psychiatric facilities in Maryland because their behavior has been violent or aggressive and they meet the criteria for involuntary commitment. Most, however, have been found incompetent to stand trial or have been convicted of a crime committed when they were under the influence of a mental illness.

Built in 1959, Perkins is a nondescript redbrick structure set back off a highway on a forty-five-acre tract one mile south of Jessup, halfway between Baltimore and Washington, DC, in a hinterland of freight warehouses, lumberyards, and industrial storage facilities. Like all maximum-security psychiatric hospitals, Perkins was designed so that staff are able to constantly observe all activity everywhere except for in the patients' rooms, which are built to minimize the risk of suicide by hanging. The threat of escape requires a well-designed perimeter and a limited number of entrance and exit points.

In April 2013, as a volunteer, I began to lead a reading group for patients at Perkins. The group was called Focus on Fiction (invariably misheard as "Addiction"). Designed for patients with a "medium to high" level of functioning and intended to "normalize patient life, help promote a calming atmosphere and reduce boredom and violence," Focus on Fiction ran every other week from early 2013 until mid-2016.

Focus on Fiction was a nonclinical group, and participation was voluntary. Still, many of the patients were convinced that I had the ability to, as someone put it, "drop a note in our files." I assured them I did not, but I wasn't convinced they believed me. When, for example, I suggested that Peter, a smart and imaginative young man, write a short story for us to discuss the following week, he was appalled. "You've got to be kidding me," he said. "If I did something like that, I promise you, it can and *will* be used against me. You don't get it. They read into *everything* here." Others also admitted to me that they stayed out of the group's discussions because they were afraid to say things that might get them into trouble, no matter how often I promised them I wasn't taking notes.

Some of the patients in my group had been college students when their crisis occurred and were obviously intelligent and articulate. At the other end of the spectrum were patients who sat with vacant eyes and slack jaws, never saying a word. I was never sure why these patients kept coming back to the group, but most of them did. Nonetheless, participation was inconsistent; the group changed its members over time. Even the most enthusiastic participants sometimes had to drop out for a while, depending on their work assignments, ward groups, court dates, medications, and other variables.

Every week, I'd hand out photocopies of a short story for the patients to read in preparation for our next meeting, but out of the fifteen or so members of the group, only three or four would do the reading. The rest would either forget, tell me they didn't have time, or lose the photocopies (not as implausible as it sounds, as I wasn't allowed to staple the pages together). Ordinary writing instruments weren't permitted, although we were allowed to use small, flexible ballpoints known as "shorties." As a result of these and other impediments, we did not, in the end, focus very much on fiction.

Brian was a member of the group from its very first meeting. He struck me as smart, well-spoken, and politely deferential. Although he was friendly, I got the impression that, given the choice, he would have preferred to stay in the background. In his late forties at the time, he was solidly built, with thick brown hair parted down the middle and shaved cleanly above the ears. His eyes were bright blue and engaging; his gaze, level and serious. I was drawn to his enthusiasm, his intelligence, and his sense of humor. I also admired the way he encouraged the participation of other, less confident patients in the group. He was especially kind to Tia, a nineteen-year-old Hispanic woman who'd been brought to Perkins for a competency evaluation.

Tia was a delight. She always did the reading and always had things to say. Chatty and bouncy, she seemed younger than her age, partly because she could be disarmingly open. She talked about struggling with her weight, her looks, and the hospital's clothing restrictions. (She was particularly indignant when told she couldn't have her favorite Ugg boots.) Despite all constraints, Tia kept up her appearance; she wore her hair in a different style every time we met, explaining the ingenious method she'd developed of wrapping it in wet paper towels at night, to make it curl.

On the surface, Tia was optimistic, lively, and gregarious, but this was obviously not the whole picture. Her bubbly disposition was real, but it was also clearly a cover for pain. Tia, like many other patients at Perkins, was being evaluated to see if she was fit to stand trial for a terrible crime. In a fit of postpartum depression, she'd taken the life of her newborn son. Eventually the strain began to show. One day, she was accompanied to Focus on Fiction by a nurse, whom she introduced as "my one-on-one," referring to an arrangement in which a patient is monitored every hour of the day. (I also heard of two-on-ones and even a three-on-one.) In other words, Tia was effectively on suicide watch. Still, her "one-on-one" was no hard-liner. When class began, Tia's chaperone pulled out a celebrity gossip magazine and a stick of gum, swung back in her seat, and made herself at home.

In one meeting of the group, after we'd been discussing a short story in the form of a fictional memoir, I asked each of the patients to write a memoir of their own. There was a catch: they only had six words. Tia's was poignant and revealing: "Dream Big: Dancer, Actress, Cosmetologist, Nurse." A few weeks later, she was found competent to stand trial for murder. She was sentenced to fifty years in prison.

One day after Tia had left, I stayed behind at the end of Focus on Fiction and chatted for a while with Brian. At this point, all I knew about him was his name and his ward. We talked about Tia and how much we both missed her. She'd brought so much energy to the group; it wasn't the same without her. Brian admitted that he'd had a crush on her. In fact, he said, he was going to ask her if she was interested in being his girlfriend, until he learned she was only nineteen. Brian was forty-eight at the time.

"She was way too young for me," he concluded, with regret. "She was born in nineteen ninety-four. That's hard to believe."

"Where were you in nineteen ninety-four?" I asked him.

"I was here at Perkins," Brian said. "And closer to being released than I am today."

What this meant, I realized, was that Brian had been at Perkins for over twenty years. I was surprised, because he seemed so stable, sensible, and intelligent. I wondered what he'd done that had caused him to be kept locked up for over two decades, but I was hesitant to ask. Patients rarely discussed their crimes, even with one another. They'd talk about what ward they were on, their security level, the medication they were taking, and how long they'd been at Perkins, but I never heard a patient ask another patient about their crime. For most, the subject was too perilous to be broached except in the vaguest of terms—nor were their offenses even mentioned in therapy sessions, I gathered, which were focused mostly on current symptoms and medication adjustments. This confused me at first, given that some of the patients at the hospital, even those in my group, had committed high-profile crimes that had been covered extensively in the local and sometimes national media, and that watching television seemed to be everyone's main activity. Perhaps the other patients simply hadn't connected the events described in the media to the newcomers on the ward. This wasn't impossible; it was often difficult for me to connect the police mug shots I saw online, of mad-eyed, disheveled, dangerous-looking berserkers, with the quiet, polite, good-natured patients in my group.

At first, when I talked to patients in private before or after Focus on Fiction, I'd sometimes ask what brought them to the hospital, but I quickly discovered this wasn't the best way of finding out. They'd answer in shorthand, in a few brief words that encapsulated their story without particulars: "I had a serious drug problem"; "I had a psychotic break"; "I was suffering from postpartum syndrome"; "My father tried to kill me"; "I went off my meds and got arrested by the cops."

These summaries, I learned, were a way of warding off further questions. Like Tia's optimistic six-word memoir, these abridgements were alternate versions of their psychiatric case files (in which they were described as dangerously sick) or the arguments of prosecutors (which depicted them as evil monsters). In the patients' revised narratives, their once-promising life was interrupted by the onset of a terrible illness. At first, I was taken off guard by these censored and self-justifying accounts, but I later came to understand they were a natural, even a healthy way of looking at things. Don't we all construct a picture of ourselves, especially of our past behavior, that selects, abstracts, and distorts in order to minimize our failures and foreground our achievements? And once we've constructed this image, we have a strong interest in defending it, even if other people don't see us in quite so favorable a light. In fact, the further our situation from the social consensus on what constitutes "a successful life," the more pressure we may feel to defend our self-image.

Which makes it all the more unusual that when I asked Brian about his crime, he told the flat, simple truth: "I killed my parents," he said.

After a year or so, Brian got a job working in Clifton's Corner, a communal area in the hospital where patients could hang out, drink coffee, watch television, and play board games. His work hours meant he could no longer attend Focus on Fiction, so I'd go and find him in Clifton's Corner after the group meeting was over. He'd make coffee, and we'd hang out and chat for a while. My impression of Brian never changed. He never said or did anything to suggest he was less mentally stable than anyone else I knew, either inside or outside the hospital. Later, we began talking on the phone, and when I was no longer running the group, I'd continue coming to see Brian as a visitor. We talked mostly about his current situation, his friends and fellow patients, the absurdities of hospital life. Sometimes I'd tell him what was going on with me. Sometimes we'd talk about his childhood and memories of the past. His conversation was always focused and rational, and he had an amazing memory for names and details. He was always lucid. He had a strong sense of irony and a lively, fertile mind. I never saw any sign of mental illness—certainly none of the florid psychosis, hostility, paranoia, or simmering violence described in some of his risk assessments and psychological evaluations.

Mental illness is often associated with creativity, at least in cultural myth; Brian is certainly creative, but not in the sense normally associated with the unleashed imagination. His intelligence, which has been tested many times, is "above average," but he isn't artistic or poetic. He's not an enthusiastic reader or writer. He's creative when it comes to practical, tangible real-world inventions he hopes someday to patent.* He is also genial, polite, and good-natured, although he often struggles to remain civilized when dealing with his psychiatrists, to make his way through conversations that seem devoid of reason, and to jump through hoops for a reward that never comes.

At first, I assumed the reason Brian had been at Perkins for so long was that his crime was such a shocking one. He killed both his parents in the family home, during their daily domestic routine. Symbolically, this isn't twice as bad as killing one parent; it's far worse. The family, despite its changing profile, remains sacrosanct in American life, and it's always shocking to hear of a child taking the lives of the people who brought them into the world. Partly, parricide is shocking because, like other taboos, it reminds us of our own uncomfortably ambivalent feelings toward our parents. Taboos, after all, are directed against our strongest desires.

But I soon learned that Brian was far from the only patient at Perkins who'd killed members of his family. In fact, it was a pretty common crime among patients in the hospital. In 1982, H.H., twenty-one, diagnosed as a paranoid schizophrenic, killed his mother, aunt, uncle, and grandmother, then went to the movies. He was released from Perkins nine years later. In 1990, R.S., nineteen, killed his father with a rifle; he was released after ten years. In 1991, also in Montgomery County, J.K., twenty, killed his father and stepmother, both prominent physicians,

---

* I noticed that a disproportionate number of the men diagnosed with schizophrenia at Perkins had fathers who were engineers or engineering professors; some of these patients had, like Brian, been studying engineering themselves before their lives were interrupted by mental illness. As G.K. Chesterton writes, "Imagination does not breed insanity. Exactly what does breed insanity is reason. Poets do not go mad, but chess-players do. Mathematicians go mad, and cashiers."

while they were making dinner in the family home. He was released after fourteen years. Twenty-two-year-old T.S. bludgeoned his mother to death in January 1994 and was released from Perkins after only three years. In 1996, D.L., forty-nine, shot and killed his elderly parents in their Bethesda home, an act that led to an eight-hour standoff with police. He was released from Perkins six years later. In 2003, G.O., twenty-five, killed his stepfather with a handgun and was released after thirteen years. B.H., also twenty-five, bludgeoned and stabbed his mother and a family friend to death in 2001; he was released from Perkins after twelve years. In 2008, C.T., twenty-two, killed his stepfather with a baseball bat while he was lying in a recliner reading a newspaper; he then used the bat to kill the family dog. He spent eight years at Perkins. I'm not suggesting the release of these patients was unwarranted, or that they were released too early, just that Brian's crime, at Perkins, is hardly unique.

Brian always maintained to me that he was not mentally ill. Not everyone who claims to be mentally stable is correct, of course. In fact, about 50 percent of schizophrenics suffer from the false conviction that there's nothing wrong with their minds. This condition is called anosognosia, and it stems from a physiological by-product of psychosis. Still, I wasn't alone in my belief that Brian was cogent and reasonable. In 2016, he was evaluated by Leonard Hertzberg, an experienced forensic psychiatrist hired by Brian's public defender with a view to possibly testifying on Brian's behalf at an upcoming release hearing. Dr. Hertzberg met with Brian twice in 2016 and twice again in 2018. He found him to be "free of psychotic thinking," neither paranoid nor delusional, and with no signs of schizophrenia or schizoaffective disorder. "It is my profession, with reasonable medical certainty," Dr. Hertzberg wrote, "that Mr. Bechtold would not be a danger to himself or others if released into the community. He has basically been behaviorally stable for almost the past 12 years."

At one point, Brian's black-market supply of coffee dried up, and he had to wean himself off caffeine. This, he figured, probably wasn't a bad thing. When he'd been without caffeine for two and a half months, he told me that his head was starting to clear. But in a situation like this, he realized, having a clear head wasn't necessarily an advantage. It forced him to face up to the real-life nightmare he described to me as "playing musical chairs with the invisible man." He was close to fifty now. Every day, or so it seemed, patients who'd committed high-profile crimes were allowed to move on from Perkins, while Brian was told, after twenty-seven years in the hospital, that he was still not even a candidate for release. He was utterly and absolutely at a loss. He could not understand why he was being treated, as he saw it, so unfairly, and neither could I. I wanted to make sense of the puzzle, and in order to do so, I needed to learn everything I could about Brian's crime, his illness, and his life in a maximum-security psychiatric hospital.

7

Ward 8

Contrary to popular opinion, the "insanity" defense is rarely used, and it definitely isn't an easy way to get out of going to prison. According to an eight-state study, it's used in less than 1 percent of all court cases, and when used, it has only a 26 percent success rate. (Also, of those cases that are successful, 90 percent of the defendants have been previously diagnosed with a mental illness.) Once they've been committed to a psychiatric hospital, according to the law, these defendants must remain confined until they're considered safe to be released into the community—no matter how long that takes. Many remain in forensic psychiatric hospitals indefinitely. No federal agency is charged with monitoring them; no registry or organization tracks how long they've been incarcerated, or why. "The worst thing about this place is that you're here indefinitely," a patient named Dean told me. "You don't know when you'll get out, if ever."

Although people still talk about the "insanity defense," most states no longer use the phrase "criminally insane." (As a general rule, the word *insane* has fallen into disuse.) A person who once would have been found "not guilty by reason of insanity" is now, in Maryland and many other states, referred to as "not criminally responsible," or, simply, "NCR."

But being found "not responsible" for a crime isn't the same as being found "not guilty." The latter suggests exoneration; the former does not. In effect, "not criminally responsible" implies that a person is culpable of the crime in some other way—morally, perhaps, or literally. Even if a court has resolved that the concept of "guilt" doesn't apply to those who commit a crime while in the grips of a mental disease—"out of their mind" is a good way of putting it—most people still think in terms of good and evil, right and wrong. We can't help judging people on the evidence of their actions, both present and past. If they've committed a crime of violence, we can't help thinking, *When will it happen again?*

In other words, crime contaminates. Perkins, then, at least symbolically, is a place of quarantine, confounding physical and psychological "health." It's regulated by a body that, until 2017, was known as the Maryland Department of Health and Mental Hygiene (the old name is still in use on court documents and websites and in logos and letterheads), a name that implies that psychological problems can be transmitted by infection and that it makes sense for those whose behavior is "unhealthy" to be sent to a hospital—or, in the case of Perkins, a "hospital center." This sounds like something more than a hospital when, in fact, it's something less—neither hospital nor prison, but something in between the two.

Perkins doesn't contain any of the facilities you'd expect to find at a regular hospital. (In fact, if anyone gets really sick or injured at Perkins, they have to be taken elsewhere.) It has a medical ward and a small medical clinic for physical illnesses, which is staffed by family practice physicians but contains no equipment for X-rays, ultrasounds, or CT scans and no operating theater. It doesn't have the buzz and hum of a hospital, or even the smell of disinfectant. A hospital is an active place, where patients come and go. Perkins, where the average stay is more than six years, should more properly be called an asylum or an institution. It's a place where things move very slowly. Every day is the same as the one before—except when it's not.

Patients sent to Perkins after being found not criminally responsible are not criminals; it isn't a prison, although from the outside, it might easily be mistaken for one. The hospital is surrounded by inward-curving, anti-climb perimeter fencing and is divided into minimum-, medium-, and maximum-security wings, each containing a number of wards. Maximum-security wards are constantly locked, medium-security wards are locked part of the time, and minimum-security wards are left unlocked. The original part of the hospital, built in 1959, was constructed on two levels, with six maximum-security wards jutting into a recreation yard and surrounded by a large wall. Between 1972 and 1984, more buildings were added: an administration center, a rehabilitation ward, and an eighty-bed medium-security wing.

Some of the patients at Perkins have been found "incompetent to stand trial." Jeremy, a patient in my group who was born and raised in Puerto Rico and who worked as a gardener before his arrest on two counts of murder, explained to me what that means:

> If a patient comes here after being judged incompetent to stand trial, they have to be found competent first. Part of being found competent is being compliant with meds. You also have to show that you understand the charges, and who the different people are in the courtroom, from the judge and the jury to the bailiffs and the sheriff's deputies. Once you've shown that you understand all that, you can go to court to be charged.

If a patient is found competent and responsible for their crime, they go to prison. If they're found not criminally responsible due to mental illness, their stay at Perkins then becomes long-term, Jeremy explained.

> A certain amount of time after your court case is behind you, if you've exhibited good behavior, you can move from maximum security to medium. On medium, if you keep behaving yourself for a while, and going to groups, and being compliant with your meds, you can move to minimum. On minimum, they start you out with two hours where you can go and visit family and come back. As long as you don't break curfew, and your behavior patterns don't change, and you're compliant with medication, you can work your way up gradually until you can even spend 72 hours out of here; then you come back. You stay on minimum until the doctors think you're ready to go to supervised housing or go back home.

After his initial evaluation, in the summer of 1992, Brian was sent to Ward 3, the Admissions Unit. Before his crime, he'd never talked to anyone about his problems; now he talked about little else. His life so far had been very difficult, but he told himself he had lots of time ahead. He was still young, physically fit, and motivated to recover. He hoped to put the mental illness behind him and move on. He wanted to finish his education, build a career, travel, marry, and have a family. Despite his guilt, Brian felt optimistic. He wanted to feel pleasure in the course of his life and look back on his achievements with pride.

But it wasn't easy to feel optimistic on the Admissions Unit, which was colorless and functional, with tile and cinder block walls, linoleum floors, and very little natural light. Patients hung around the hallways with nothing to do, but there was one redeeming factor: it was a coed ward. There were hardly any female patients at Perkins—certainly not enough for them to have their own admissions ward (which the staff was thankful for, as most of them agreed that the female patients usually caused more trouble than the men).

Not long after his arrival, Brian got to know a fellow patient named Tracy, a pretty blonde. He took a liking to her right off the bat, and the feeling was mutual. They used the time between therapy groups to get to know each other, and Brian discovered that he and Tracy had a lot in common. They started to visit the library together, but not necessarily to read. Brian had learned from other patients that the library could be used for more than just checking out books: You could hook up behind the shelves, too. Miss Chong, the librarian, turned a blind eye, apparently.

And for a month or so, that's what Brian and Tracy did. He would meet her in the library twice a week, and they'd find a quiet corner to make out. But Admissions was a temporary ward—no one stayed there for long—and too soon, the pair was separated: Tracy was sent to medium security, and Brian to maximum. Of the eight maximum-security wards, they sent him to the most restrictive: Ward 8.

A guard led Brian through two sets of doors into the dayroom. The noise was disorienting. A television, perched on a stand and protected by an iron cage, was playing at full blast. Patients were yelling, arguing, talking to themselves. One man was sleeping on the floor; another was gazing blankly at a wall. One danced to music from a small radio he held up to his ear; another paced in circles like an unhappy zoo animal. A delicate-looking man was walking back and forth, whispering to himself, making odd gestures with his hands. From behind the protective glass of the nurses' station, a gap-toothed nurse in white scrubs eyed Brian skeptically. A sign taped to the glass read: "Do Not Approach Without Asking for Permission." On the wall beside it, a poster listed five rules:

No Sexual Contact
No Horseplay
No Touching
Shaking Hands or a "High Five" may be permitted under Certain
    Circumstances and During Mass Transportation
A Brief Kiss may be permitted at the End of a Visit

Suddenly, a heavy-set man attacked the trash can with a series of body slams. In his wake, another man, his face covered by a white mask of Noxzema cleansing cream, ran across the dayroom, jumped in the air, and aimed a karate kick at the television stand, causing it to shake precariously.

Nobody seemed to acknowledge the pandemonium—neither the staff at the nurses' station nor the three or four patients slumped in front of the trembling television like tired passengers at a bus station. One of them, an elderly fellow with a thick white beard, was sprawled out with his head tilted back, his mouth wide open. Later, Brian learned that the patients sitting placidly were among the most disturbed in the hospital. When they weren't in a stupor from medication, they were far more dangerous than the kickers and screamers.

He also learned that more than half the patients at Perkins had been diagnosed with paranoid schizophrenia, which, although it can occur at any age, tends to emerge first in young adulthood and is found more commonly in men than women. This meant that the hospital had a large population of patients like him—bright, serious young men in their late teens or early twenties who'd recently left home, perhaps to start college or join the military, and had committed a baffling crime during their "first break," the initial episode of psychosis that often heralds the onset of schizophrenia.

Like all the wards at Perkins, Ward 8 was arranged with two hallways branching off from a central nursing station and dayroom at the hub. Each hallway contained eight patient dormitories, one shared bathroom, and a "quiet room" for patients who needed to be secluded and restrained. This "quiet room" contained a special bed with bars at the sides, straps to bind the wrists and ankles, and a belt that fastened across the stomach. There was a steel grate in the door for food to be passed through.

A guard led Brian down one of the two corridors, whose vinyl tiles were soiled with ancient stains, and showed him to his dorm, which was shared with seven other patients. Each patient had a bed, a small chest of drawers, and a locker that didn't lock. The walls were bare cinder block. It was early summer, and the heat was stifling. The only air-conditioning was a small window unit in the dayroom and two giant standing fans, one at the end of each of the two hallways. Brian put his things down on his bed and went to use the bathroom. Under the door of a toilet stall, a man was lying asleep on the floor in a puddle of piss.

The daily routine wasn't complicated. Patients were woken at six by a guard (or "psychiatric service technician," as they were known at Perkins) who walked up and down the hallways rapping on the doors with his keys. They had to be up and out of their rooms by 6:30 a.m., even though there was nothing to do until Goals Group an hour later, in which they had to set a goal for themselves for the day. (Typical goals set by the other patients included "not losing my temper," "writing to Mother," "reading a chapter of a book," "writing in my journal," and "trying not to cry.") At 8 a.m., they were taken to the cafeteria—or, at least, they were taken to stand in line outside the cafeteria, as there was often a fifteen-minute wait before the food was ready. Eventually, they'd file in, sit at a designated table—socializing with patients from other wards wasn't permitted during mealtimes—and receive a small box of cereal, a carton of milk, and some toast or scrambled eggs. The tableware was plastic, and so were the utensils—or, to be more precise, the utensil. Neither knives nor forks were permitted, "for safety reasons," and everything had to be eaten with a plastic spoon. This was fine for cereal and scrambled eggs, but not so easy for spaghetti, fish, or salad, especially for patients with tremors. Some of them were very messy eaters.

After breakfast, they returned to the ward. At 8:30 a.m., medication was dispensed. This was the only time the ward was quiet. For some reason, the handing out of drugs was treated like a sacred ritual; conversations at this time were whispered and brief, as if any unexpected noise would break the spell. After medication had been dispensed, the inmates were allowed to go outside into the court-yard for a cigarette. (At this time, smoking was still permitted.) After breakfast, they were locked out of their rooms but not allowed to leave the ward. At 10 a.m., there was a ward meeting—the television was finally turned off for an hour. During the meeting, staff reminded everyone of the ward rules: no coffee, tea, or anything else that contained caffeine; no food in the bedrooms; no touching the other patients; no hardback books. Phone conversations were limited to ten minutes. Nothing was allowed on the ward that could conceivably be used as a weapon or to attempt suicide—no belts, straps, rosary beads, bathrobe cords, or bath towels. Nor were the patients permitted cell phones, laptops, backpacks, knives, pens, purses, or wallets. Other things included on the contraband list were umbrellas, screwdrivers, cleated shoes, and fishing rods. (Brian wondered why they didn't just come up with a list of the things the patients *could* have.)

Lunch was served at 12:30 p.m., followed by another smoke break at 1 p.m. After that, the patients were left to themselves until 3 p.m. Most of them slumped in front of the television; many nodded off. If you had a question for any of the nurses, you had to stand by a line painted on the floor two feet away from the nurses' station and wait until the nurses had finished their paperwork and were ready for you. While Brian could understand that the nurses were busy and didn't have time to answer questions all day, the procedure seemed patronizing and undignified.

In the downtime, there was little to do. There were some books, board games, and puzzles available, but they didn't get much use. Brian tried to break up the monotony by talking on the phone to Kyu or Cathy, reading the Bible, or playing cards. He soon became the king of partner spades. When the weather was fine, the patients could go outside into the small paved courtyard adjacent to the ward, though there wasn't much to do out there, either. It was difficult to hold a conversation when you were surrounded by people yelling, singing, running around, and holding each other in headlocks.

From 3 p.m. to 4:15 p.m. was "quiet time," when patients returned to their rooms and were encouraged to take a nap. At 4:15 there was another smoke break, and at 4:30 there was group therapy for those capable of engaging in the back-and-forth of conversation. At first, Brian found group therapy helpful. He liked the two psychologists who led the group, Julie Sasscer-Burgos and Kevin Richardson. He could tell they really wanted to help him, and he tried not to let them down. Group sessions could be intense. In the early days, patients would speak openly about their crimes and what had led up to them. It was tough, but it helped Brian feel less alone.

At 5 p.m. the patients were locked in their rooms for half an hour, then allowed down to dinner at 5:30 p.m. At 6 p.m., they had to shower and brush their teeth, and at 7 p.m., those who had money to spend were allowed to visit the canteen, where they could buy snacks and cigarettes. Everyone was encouraged to be in bed by 8 p.m., in order to get up early the next morning and start the routine again.

At some point during the day, usually in the afternoon, the ward psychiatrist, Hanif Gopalani, would meet with patients one-on-one in his office for around ten minutes each. He was always busy. Brian gathered that some of the psychiatrists at Perkins also had private practices outside the hospital, and others had teaching appointments at Johns Hopkins or elsewhere. At first, Brian was disappointed that he got so little time with his psychiatrist, but he soon came to see this as a blessing. When Dr. Gopalani was on the ward, patients weren't allowed to approach him or speak to him. Even then, the doctor usually ducked out as soon as he could, locking himself in his office to complete "paperwork" or "research."

During his scheduled appointments, Brian felt, the doctor never seemed to listen to what he was saying. All Gopalani focused on (as Brian learned when he later saw the notes in his chart) were physical signs like eye contact, tone of voice, and facial expression, which he always found "symptomatic." If Brian had been late to the ward meeting, or kept to himself, or skipped a meal, or seemed impatient, it all went down in his chart and was interpreted by Dr. Gopalani as further evidence of pathology. Brian came to see his meetings with the psychiatrist as more than pointless—they were actually damaging his chances of release.

Fortunately, the psychiatrist was only one member of Brian's treatment team (albeit the most important member), which comprised everyone involved in his care: nurses, social workers, psychologists, therapists, counselors, ancillary staff such as those who ran activity groups, and sometimes even security guards. He met with his treatment team twice a month to discuss his "individual treatment protocol"—his schedule, groups, plans, goals, emotional stability, progress in therapy, and most important, his medication, or lack of it.

At this time, it was a policy at Perkins that while patients were very strongly encouraged to take whatever medication their psychiatrist had prescribed, they couldn't be forced to do so as long as they were calm on the ward. And Brian was calm. Right from the start, he'd told the doctor he didn't want to take any sedatives or antipsychotics. His mind seemed clearer than it had been in years, and he wanted to keep it that way. Brian sometimes suspected that Dr. Gopalani was annoyed by this, though he wasn't sure why.

While Ward 8 had its own psychologist, social workers, and an art therapist, only nurses and security guards remained on the ward after hours. Often, in the evenings, the duty staff would go off somewhere together (to get drunk, Brian heard), leaving the ward in the charge of a heavy-set patient who enjoyed inflicting swift and violent punishment. Even when staff were present, violence was disturbingly commonplace. The guards just sat back and let the patients fight their issues out. People would attack one another at random. A patient named Lee Trotter once pulled a large wooden leg off a table with his bare hands and started brandishing it like a weapon. Dante Vanable, the man who liked attacking the trash can with body slams, once drank boiling water directly from a kettle, burning his face and mouth and claiming to have "swallowed the lake of fire."

Hector Craven, the patient Brian had seen sleeping in the bathroom, was particularly dangerous. He claimed to be a cat that had been turned into a human being by a witch. When the guards were out of sight, he'd climb over the glass barrier and piss behind the desk in the nurses' station. He also liked to rub baby oil into his skin and then run through the ward naked and slippery, sliding out of the clutches of the guards when they tried to restrain him. Hector suffered from involuntary tooth grinding and jaw clenching, which might have been caused by stress but was probably a side effect of his medication. His outbursts of violence were always preceded by a particularly intense bout of jaw clicking. Once, he bit a guard's hand so hard that the guy lost his finger.

Each patient had a different schedule, depending on whether they had a job and when they met with hospital staff for treatment. Clinical meetings, held mostly on the ward, were mandatory, and so was outdoor time. Other, nonclinical groups (choir, cooking, art, debate, music, and tai chi) were voluntary, but these were offered only when staff or volunteers were available to lead them, and even then, they were available only to certain patients. The rest of the time was spent on the ward but out of bedrooms, which meant the patients could watch television, sleep in a chair, play cards, talk on the phone, or read. Although, in principle, they were supposed to be occupied with some activity most of the time, in practice, there were long stretches of empty time when they had nothing to do except sleep in a chair or slump in front of the television.

Perkins worked according to a privilege system that resembled a game of Chutes and Ladders. Being admitted to the hospital meant sliding down a long chute that took you from person to patient; your task was to work your way back up from patient to person. As your security level decreased, you gradually acquired more privileges. How long this took depended on a number of factors, including your diagnosis, the seriousness of your crime, your age, your risk assessment level, and your connections to family and friends outside the hospital.

It could take just a few months, or it could be upward of thirty years. Some people never got out. Privileges that could be lost or acquired along the way included the opportunity to receive visitors, order take-out food, attend off-ward groups, go to the gym, go outdoors, and get a hospital job. If you did well, you could look forward to the eventual prospect of supervised trips outside the hospital, then unsupervised home visits, and finally, conditional release.

Brian was surprised to learn that most of the patients on Ward 8 had plenty of money, too much, really—but there was nothing to spend it on except junk food from the canteen or the weekly takeout meals. One of the big differences between Perkins and prison was that at Perkins, almost everyone got Social Security checks of between four hundred and nine hundred dollars a month. Some also got checks from the Veterans Benefits Administration. Many received another five or ten dollars a week from home, sent to assuage the guilt of family members who'd stopped visiting long ago. Some patients saved their money until they had enough to hire a lawyer who specialized in competence and mental capacity, who could then pay a private psychiatrist for an evaluation. Once you had the thumbs-up from a shrink, getting out of Perkins was a lot easier, though it was always a gamble.

In some ways, the lack of supervision had benefits. Every week, all 150 patients from the maximum-security wards shared outdoor time together, along with staff and guards. This weekly recess was held not in the small courtyard adjacent to the ward, but on the grass inside the hospital fences, a giant space the size of three football fields. Here, you could practice basketball shots; take a walk or a jog; play volleyball, baseball, pinochle, or backgammon; or work on your dance moves. Even patients in restraints would be taken out for some fresh air. The shared breaks from routine led to a feeling of togetherness, even if what brought them all together was their suffering.

At the end of each week, a list was pinned to the notice board naming patients on the ward in order of their readiness for promotion. Eager to make progress, Brian followed the rules. A psychiatrist named Dr. Joanna Brandt observed at the time that "He asks about being allowed to participate in programs. He expresses interest in mental health class and all the groups he can. He'd also like the ward cleaning program as long as it doesn't interfere with group attendance. He asks intelligent questions." As a result of Brian's "positive adjustment," his name moved slowly up the ranks. In August 1993, when he'd been at Perkins for just over a year, he was moved to a medium-security ward.

For many months, medium security had been the promised land, and it didn't disappoint. Brian's new ward had air-conditioning, real mirrors, soft beds, and clean bathrooms. Now he could drink coffee and wear street clothes. Right away, he made some close friends. One of them was Roland Drumgold, a Vietnam veteran with a genius IQ who loved to play board games. Another was Curtis Belton, a guy who'd tried to kill an unpopular coworker with a handgun. (He missed.) One day, Curtis called his former boss from the hospital ward and asked if he could get his job back when he got out. According to a doubtful story going around Perkins, his boss not only agreed but offered to give Curtis money to pay for shooting lessons.

There was a female ward across the hall, and Brian got to know some of the patients there as well. While they couldn't leave their wards unescorted, patients could chat briefly in the library, at church, and during activity groups. Brian had been on the lookout for a new girlfriend ever since Tracy left him after hooking up with another patient. Her rejection had come as a blow for Brian. His unhappiness increased when he learned from Kyu that their former mentor, Master Kim, had passed away. To help Brian through his depression, his new psychiatrist, Faramarz Mokhtari, put him on a low dose of an antidepressant.

For a new girlfriend, Brian had his eye on Hattie Cramblitt, a slim, red-haired ex-prostitute who'd set her mother's house on fire. Hattie gave Brian chilling accounts of being molested by her father, a big-deal editor for a major magazine. Hattie was unabashed, turning everything into a big joke. She thought of Brian as a friend, even though she'd flirt with him constantly. He got into mock fights with her all the time. Hattie would aim blows while Brian ducked and dodged. They had the same sense of humor. Brian cared about her and wanted to reach her, but she never let him get serious. "I think everybody has some kind of pathology when it comes to relationships," Brian told me. "I think most of it's based on your family."

After Hattie was released, he got to know her friend Eloise Dixon, another ex-prostitute. Eloise was Hattie's opposite: always run-down and miserable. Her price for sex was a pack of cigarettes, but Brian declined the offer. Other guys who'd taken her offer had ended up in the clinic, and Brian had enough problems without a dose of gonorrhea.

8

Rehab and Risperdal

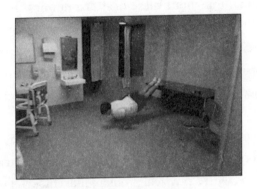

At Perkins, patients received full psychological evaluations, including a risk assessment, whenever their security level was reconsidered, which was supposed to be once every year—although Brian soon learned that things didn't always happen the way they were supposed to. Still, he was making excellent progress. Two years after his admission to the hospital, in June 1994, a psychological evaluation was performed on him by Stephen Lucente, a psychology intern from nearby Crownsville Hospital Center.

The results, for the main part, were good. Brian was described as "a 25-year-old single white male, appropriately dressed and groomed." According to Dr. Lucente, Brian's overall presentation was "marked by relative clarity." His intelligence tested "solidly in the average range," and his Rorschach performance was "demonstrably superior to that of two years ago." As a result of Dr. Lucente's evaluation, Brian's original diagnosis of paranoid schizophrenia was modified to "Single Episode in Substantial Remission." The doctor also noted that Brian "was not clinically depressed," he didn't exhibit a "formal thought disorder," and he was "currently stable and not presently psychotic."

A diagnosis is a double-edged sword. When it comes to something as inchoate as mental illness, it can be a huge relief to learn that your pattern of experiences has a name, that others share it, that there's a protocol for treating it, perhaps even a cure. Still, there's something unnatural about these neat taxonomies. There's no blood test or genetic marker to prove a person has schizophrenia. Mental illnesses, especially personality disorders, are so interwoven and bound up with a person's life history, disposition, and temperament that no one experiences them in the same way or shows precisely the same symptoms.

The primary tool for diagnosing a person with a mental illness is the judgment of the clinician, a fact that gives psychiatrists enormous power. Someone with a physical problem like chicken pox or a broken arm will receive pretty much the same diagnosis whichever doctor they consult, but the same isn't true of mental illnesses. Anyone who's spent time in the mental health system will know that it's common for a patient to accumulate a series of psychiatric labels depending on how many different doctors they've seen. Of course, diagnoses aren't completely arbitrary—they're names for clusters of human experiences that often occur together. But these clusters of experiences aren't "diseases"—at least, not in the medical sense.

This failure to deliver consistently reliable diagnoses has long been something of an embarrassment for psychiatry. Some people even consider diagnosis to be an impediment to meaningful recovery, partly because unlike physical illnesses, mental illnesses can carry personal, legal, and social stigmas.

David L. Rosenhan, a professor of psychology and law at Stanford University, was of the opinion that "psychological categorization of mental illness is useless at best and downright harmful, misleading, and pejorative at worst." In an article published in *Science* magazine on January 19, 1973, Rosenhan described how he and seven other people with no history of mental illness got themselves admitted into twelve different psychiatric hospitals across the country, both state and private. Here, the researchers found that their most common-place actions on the wards were interpreted as pathological symptoms. When one of them made notes for the article, for example, this was classed as "compulsive writing." Rosenhan explains how the hospital itself imposes a special environment in which the meanings of behavior can easily be misunderstood. The researchers were all released (between seven and fifty-two days after their "hospitalization") as "schizophrenics in remission," despite their best efforts to convince hospital staff of their sanity.

Evidence has shown that American psychiatrists in particular have a special fondness for diagnosing schizophrenia because the cluster of experiences covered by the label is very broad. On the milder end of the spectrum, these include social isolation; general discontent; a loss of interest or pleasure in life; anxiety; apathy; and agitation. At the other end of the spectrum are things like repetitive movements, delusions, aural and visual hallucinations, frenzied speech, memory loss, and catatonia. Once a person has been diagnosed with schizophrenia, the label remains for life. The schizophrenic is never "cured," "recovered," "mistakenly diagnosed," or "sane," but always "in remission."

Brian was acutely aware that he'd been mentally ill in the years leading up to his crime; he'd accepted that many of his symptoms fit the category of schizophrenia, although he believed he'd been restored to sanity while reading the Bible in the campground at Port St. Joe. His psychiatrists, however, didn't agree. They believed he was still schizophrenic, paranoid, and delusional. Because they regarded almost everything he said and did as a validation of their original diagnosis, Brian became gradually less eager to talk about his feelings, at least during group therapy and community meetings, when there were staff members around. While he'd always been guarded, he now found himself growing increasingly defensive and started to stay in his room, avoiding social contact.

Considering Brian's behavior on the ward, Dr. Lucente concluded that although he seemed stable and well adjusted on the surface, he was strategically hiding his emotions and avoiding situations in which he'd be forced to face up to his crime. Lucente believed that Brian was unconsciously projecting his negative emotions onto others. He thought Brian wasn't really engaging in treatment activities but was just going through the motions, keeping his real thoughts to himself. "This defensive style helps to protect his fragile sense of self," the doctor wrote. "It will be more difficult than usual to get him to 'open up' and discuss exactly what he's defending against." The doctor thought Brian was hiding his problems even from himself. "It may take months or years before he feels safe in a therapeutic relationship," Lucente concluded, adding that "attempts to push him to 'open up' will merely delay his doing so."

Brian found this annoying. He'd been following all the rules and felt he deserved to move to an open ward, but the doctors didn't believe he was ready. After reading Dr. Lucente's evaluation, Dr. Mokhtari decided that before Brian was moved to minimum security, he had to come to terms with his crime and the mental illness that had led up to it. The first step, the doctor believed, was for Brian to confront his drug use and his addictive personality. Habitual marijuana smoking is known to increase the risk of schizophrenia in people who are genetically vulnerable, and it makes psychotic symptoms worse. Brian had used marijuana regularly in his teens, as well as PCP, which has also been linked to schizophrenia. Dr. Mokhtari decided to send him to the rehab ward, where he'd get help understanding his history of drug use.

Brian accepted the condition—he had no real choice—but he found the idea absurd. Apart from his antidepressant medication, prescribed by Dr. Mokhtari himself, Brian didn't use drugs. He'd quit completely four years earlier, of his own volition. Going to rehab, he figured, was just another hoop he had to jump through to prove he was sane.

The rehab ward housed patients with addiction problems. Brian arrived there in September 1994 and did his best to stay positive. He added extra activities to his already full schedule: art therapy, gardening, an affective disorder group. He exercised whenever possible—his goal was a thousand push-ups a day. As always, he drew strength from the camaraderie of fellow patients, who shared tales of their own frustrations and setbacks. The gardening group was especially close. Along with Kenny Ross, another patient from rehab, Brian was given a little plot of land to cultivate. The two of them laid down soil and a thick bed of mulch and then, in the spring, planted tomatoes, hot peppers, honeydew melons, and a papaya tree. That summer was hot and wet. All their seeds grew. The papaya was over a foot tall when Hector Craven stepped on it by accident.

It was a time of upheaval at Perkins. Ever since Brian arrived, the hospital had been undergoing construction, and finally, in October 1996, the new building was completed. Named the Silver Wing after Stuart B. Silver, a past director of the Maryland State Mental Hygiene Administration and a former superintendent of Perkins, it contained a twenty-bed admission ward, five thirty-bed maximum-security wards, a medical clinic, a dining facility, a chapel, a library, a conference center, family visiting rooms, and even a small gym.

The Silver Wing was open and welcoming. A plant-lined hallway, its walls hung with framed patient artwork, opened onto a glass-roofed atrium two stories high. The place had an airy spaciousness reminiscent of a shopping center. (It was, in fact, referred to as the "treatment mall.")

While Brian spent plenty of time in the Silver Wing, he didn't live there, as he was no longer a maximum-security patient. In fact, by October 1995, he'd completed his stint in rehab and was finally recommended for minimum. He was elated. The next step would be a release back into the community, and he figured his chances were excellent, as his record at Perkins was clean. But the changes at the hospital weren't all progressive, as far as Brian was concerned. Just as he was starting to make some real advances, a new superintendent was hired. Dr. M. Richard Fragala was a military psychiatrist, and it showed. The tight-lipped, smartly dressed doctor imposed a strict new regime at Perkins. The first thing he did was introduce a system of demerits that could be given for any infraction, however minor; this led to the loss of privileges like snacks and cigarettes. Demerits could also be given for not being "re-directable"—in other words, for not joining in the day's activities with a positive attitude.

Brian was disturbed by this change of events and even more dismayed by Dr. Fragala's new rule that before they could move to a different security level, patients had to appear before a committee called the Clinical Forensic Review Board, which would consider their progress, assess risks of violence, and approve them for higher privilege levels or, alternatively, revoke privileges and demote patients to wards with more rigorous security. The CFRB wasn't a particular group of people, but a panel made up of everyone at the hospital involved in a patient's case, plus any other members of staff who wanted to be there. Dr. Fragala said that every patient would be assessed by the CFRB each year on the anniversary of their admission to the hospital. Membership of the board wasn't made public, but Brian assumed it included all the hospital's top players: the head of social work, the head of psychology, the director of forensic psychiatry, and of course, Dr. Fragala himself.

Another unhappy change was the end of meaningful group therapy—fallout from the 1996 Health Insurance Portability and Accountability Act (HIPAA) regulations on patient confidentiality. On Ward 8, Brian had found these sessions surprisingly helpful.

Now, under the new HIPAA climate, this kind of open discussion no longer occurred; it was all about present-day symptom reduction. Therapists and psychologists no longer seemed interested in talking about a patient's background and upbringing; the "family dynamic" model of mental illness had been replaced by the idea of mental illness as an organic disease. Origins were no longer considered relevant. Consequently, patients were no longer encouraged to talk about their childhood, their history, their parents, or their crime. "Group therapy" continued, but in name only. Discussions never went below the surface; it was just small talk.

Others disagreed. Jeremy, one of the patients in Focus on Fiction, said he thought group therapy was still useful even if it didn't necessarily get very far beneath the surface. "It's helpful to know other people are feeling the way you're feeling," he told me. "If I'm hearing voices, or if I think I've been dealt a bad hand in life, or I think there's some kind of conspiracy against me, when I hear other people saying the same thing, I realize it's not only me. I can find out how they cope, how they deal with it, how they move on."

Brian felt differently. He noticed that individual therapy, too, involved less digging into the past; mostly, the focus was on tweaking the patient's medications. The *Diagnostic and Statistical Manual of Mental Disorders* had recently been revised, and now, to be diagnosed with a mental illness, a patient had to display a certain number of symptoms. This meant therapy could be streamlined and standardized for every patient, its success or failure measured in charts, graphs, and statistics.

At the same time, various symptom-targeted medications hit the market that were safer than earlier ones, with fewer side effects. First came the SSRIs: new antidepressants like Prozac, Zoloft, and Wellbutrin. Next came a new generation of "atypical" antipsychotics: medications like Risperdal, Clozaril, and Zyprexa. These were particularly useful at forensic hospitals like Perkins, where large numbers of patients had been diagnosed as psychotic. This increasing reliance on pharmaceuticals and the new focus on symptom reduction brought psychiatry into line with other branches of medicine, disguising the turmoil of mental illness as something that could be managed, even cured, with the right course of drugs.

When the new antipsychotics hit the market, they were advertised (to psychiatrists) as inducing a "twilight state" in patients. In fact, their main effect was to reduce sensitivity to external stimuli. Under the influence of these medications, patients' conscious awareness and intellectual faculties remained intact, but they lost initiative and agency. Patients who'd been preoccupied by delusions and hallucinations became calmer and less tense, but they also became emotionally flatter and less responsive. Essentially, these medications were like a blunt instrument that dulled all mental activity. And while patients often resisted them at first, one of the effects of the drugs was to soften the edges of resistance until the patient no longer realized, or didn't care, that their emotions had been flattened out.

Then there were the side effects: anxiety, sleepiness, blurred vision, tremors, sweating, nausea, dizziness, depression, headache, vomiting, drooling, hunger, restlessness, rash, stomach pain, insomnia, weight gain, and, most disturbingly, cerebral atrophy.

Dean, who'd been a student at Johns Hopkins University before his arrest, believed that although there were positive things about Perkins, taking medication wasn't one of them. "The people have been awesome," he said. "The best thing about being here is that you get lots of time to heal." Like Brian, Dean had been diagnosed with paranoid schizophrenia. "The worst thing about being here," he said, "is having to take medication that affects you in ways that you can't control. I'm taking about six medications now. They gave me Bell's palsy. One side of my face went numb, and I couldn't open one side of my mouth or open one of my eyes. Haldol is the worst. That's the one that causes the most side effects."

Jeremy had also suffered terrible side effects from the medication he was forced to take. He was on a high dose of Seroquel (an anti-psychotic) and Depakote (to prevent mania), as well as Cogentin (to combat tremors). "There's a range of medication levels they can give you, from the minimum to the maximum, and anywhere in between is on staff discretion, based on your behavior," he said. "I've had times when they gave me so much medication that my hands were shaking. I couldn't open a book. I was constantly distracted by the fact that I couldn't keep my hands from moving. It's difficult for me to feel like that when, on the outside and in society, I was so functional and normal."

Cliff, another of the patients in my group, was a former teacher in his early fifties who seemed healthy and smart. When I first met him, he'd been at Perkins less than a year, and I could easily imagine him in front of a classroom. But Cliff, who had a diagnosis of bipolar disorder, went rapidly downhill. He had all kinds of problems with the medication he was taking. "They were trying to get me to take Klonopin, which is a Valium type of drug that's highly addictive," he told me. "I disagreed completely. That's a drug that I used to pay for on the street." Cliff had been an alcoholic, and his reluctance to take an addictive drug was one complication with his treatment; another was his heart condition. The doctors were trying to get him stabilized on a medication that didn't cause him debilitating side effects.

When I returned to Perkins one summer after a vacation, I was shocked to see how much worse Cliff's illness had become. I asked him to read aloud from a short story. He'd done this readily in the past, but now his speech was slurred, his eyes unfocused. The following week, he arrived late, sat beside me, and shifted in his seat restlessly. The last time I saw him, he was walking on crutches and one of his front teeth was missing. He told me he'd lost his balance (a side effect of his latest drug, Depakote), fallen, and broken some toes. He couldn't remember what had happened to his tooth.

Brian had witnessed similar changes in his fellow patients: clumsy

movements, sedation, incontinence, and weight gain. Taking antipsychotics caused them to slump on the sofa all day in front of the television, mumbling and drooling. To Brian, these patients had crossed
over from consensus reality into a spirit world—their bodies were
here, but their minds were elsewhere. He didn't want to join them.
His head felt clear; he didn't understand why he needed medication.
He'd been at Perkins for three years now—at the time, this was the
average length of a patient's stay—and he'd managed to remain stable.
When he agreed to take Zoloft, he'd stayed on a very low dose. But
while Brian considered this a sign of strength, Dr. Mokhtari believed
it increased his level of risk, and the psychiatrist regularly talked about
sending him back to the most restrictive, maximum-security ward.
The violence of his original crime, Brian discovered, meant his "risk
factor" would always be high, no matter how quiet and peaceful he
was on the ward.

In 1996, after completing his stint in rehab, Brian faced the CFRB.
As he feared, they gave him the thumbs-down. The board decided he
wasn't ready for minimum security. They agreed with Dr. Mokhtari:
Brian was paranoid, they said, and should be taking more medication. They recounted various incidents of guarded and threatening
behavior, anxiety about staff making notes in his files, and mistrust
of doctors. An antidepressant wasn't enough; they wanted him to be
on an antipsychotic, like most of the other patients at Perkins. They
told him that if he continued to refuse, it would be a hindrance to his
progress, and he'd have his first infraction on an otherwise spotless
record.

After spending so long at Perkins, Brian had learned to wear a
mask; he'd become fearful and sensitive, and his anxiety sometimes
became overwhelming. It would hardly be surprising if he had also
become paranoid. Of course, he didn't think he was paranoid, but
this is true of virtually all paranoid people—and a patient who fails

to recognize his own illness is especially difficult to treat. Paranoia is inflexible and not amenable to reason. Paranoid people have a tenacious belief in their own truth that makes it impossible for them to see things objectively or in a nuanced way. Unable to accept that they're in the same boat as everyone else, facing the daily problems of life, they feel incessantly victimized and insulted; they harbor deep grudges and relate to the world by relentlessly searching for evidence that validates their fears. In ordinary conversations, they may find hidden threats or affronts that are often indiscernible to others. Sometimes these false beliefs are so overwhelming that they might better be described as delusions.

In situations like these, antipsychotics can be useful because they cause patients to distance themselves from their thoughts. In short, antipsychotics induce doubt, which is enormously helpful when treating patients whose confidence has become pathological. It makes them less suspicious and apprehensive, more amenable to therapy—although, again, the effect is achieved only by the dampening of all positive emotions, leading to a general numbing of affect and a reduced sense of self.

To his doctors, reducing Brian's sense of self seemed like a good idea. "He puts people off by making outrageously threatening statements," someone had noted in his file, and it was true that when Brian felt disrespected, he liked to remind people of his martial arts training. He'd never had to use it at Perkins, but he tried to keep in shape should the need arise. When Dr. Mokhtari said he needed to go on antipsychotics, Brian grew frustrated. He told the doctor he'd been clearheaded and healthy for the last three years.

They argued back and forth for a while. Finally, Brian, who'd developed an intense dislike of Mokhtari, reminded the psychiatrist that he was a trained fighter. He could do some serious damage to the doctor, he pointed out. This was a mistake. It led Dr. Mokhtari to believe that Brian was still agitated, paranoid, and dangerous—and perhaps he was. Mokhtari prescribed Risperdal, a widely used anti-psychotic, and sent Brian to a different ward.

Realizing he had no choice, Brian tried to see this as a step back to gain more traction, but he knew he was deceiving himself. Within weeks, he'd entered a dark world. When he walked, his arms hung stiffly at his sides. His face felt like a leather mask that refused to make expressions.

At first, he tried to fight the fog. He asked another patient to wake him up every couple of hours so he could go to the bathroom and so he wouldn't be too sluggish to fight back if he was used as a punching bag by the ward sadists or by those who were simply bored. But he lost the battle, and then the will to fight. Soon, each day was the same, and the days were hardly different from the nights. He'd sleep in a chair until breakfast, go back to bed, get up again briefly for lunch, then sleep in a chair again from lunch until dinner. He'd manage to stay awake after dinner until eight o'clock, when it was time for evening meds. Then he'd be knocked out again.

His body betrayed him. He became impotent, then incontinent. He'd turned into a shuffling beast, half man, half corpse.

Brian hated being on Risperdal. Apart from the general dullness and mind fog, it caused a pounding in his ears, a dead feeling around the edge of his skull, depression, vertigo, and constant drowsiness. Sometimes, late at night, he'd start to think that pleading not criminally responsible had been a terrible mistake. Yes, he'd been out of his mind when he shot his parents, but if he'd been sent to prison instead of Perkins, he wouldn't have to take numbing doses of medication. He wouldn't be impotent and incontinent. Convicted criminals might be looked down upon, but the criminally insane, he was beginning to realize, were downright untouchable.

One morning, a new psychiatrist arrived on the ward. Brian's previous doctors had been authoritative and closed off, but the new resident,

Jonathan Briskin, was open and friendly. The first thing he did, at Brian's request, was reduce his meds. Like an animal coming out of hibernation, Brian gradually emerged from his stupor.

In his midthirties, Dr. Briskin was younger than most of the other doctors at Perkins, and just talking to him about ordinary things made Brian feel better. He realized it had been months since he'd had a real conversation with somebody who seemed interested in who he was as a person, someone who didn't see him as just another "paranoid schizophrenic." Part of what made these conversations so unusual was that Brian felt as if he were being treated as an equal. He felt comfortable enough to ask Dr. Briskin questions, and the psychiatrist would respond honestly, opening up to him in return. Their conversations were so interesting that Brian sometimes forgot he was a patient in a psychiatric hospital. Dr. Briskin was forthcoming and undefended, sharing details of his personal life outside the hospital fence. The young resident told Brian that in his spare time, and under his middle name, Kalonymus, he entertained audiences as a juggler, magician, unicyclist, and acrobat. In personality, he was the opposite of the cold, pompous Dr. Mokhtari and the formal, guarded Dr. Fragala.

Under Dr. Briskin's advisement, Brian's Risperdal was replaced with five milligrams of a different antipsychotic, called Stelazine, a prophylactic dose intended to prevent the return of any psychotic symptoms. With the reduction in medication—and plenty of real coffee—the fog soon began to clear. Taking a long, hard look in the mirror, Brian realized that months in a haze had left him out of shape, and he started working out again. At first, he could manage only five push-ups at a time, a pitiful fraction of his former routine, but by early the following year, 1997, most of his old strength had returned.

That year, Brian saw Dr. Briskin almost every day, and he came to rely on the young doctor's honesty, enthusiasm, and compassion. Even better, when it was time for Brian's annual evaluation, Dr. Briskin agreed he was no longer psychotic, had "virtually no remaining symptoms of schizophrenia," and was "highly treatable." The report couldn't

have been better. Compared to the patients around him, Brian realized, he was in pretty good shape. According to Dr. Briskin, he'd soon
be doing well enough to be moved to minimum security, where he'd
be allowed to take accompanied trips out of the hospital. "A year on
minimum," said Dr. Briskin, "and in my opinion, you'll be ready to go
home."

9

"Untying the Straitjacket"

In mid-1997, Perkins authorities made the decision to admit a television crew inside the hospital for an episode of the A&E television show *Investigative Reports* titled "Untying the Straitjacket." The documentary was meant to educate the public about the insanity defense, which had been a source of public outrage since 1982, when John Hinckley Jr. was found not guilty by reason of insanity for his attempted assassination of President Ronald Reagan. Hinckley was clearly delusional, driven by an obsession with the actress Jodie Foster. Yet people claimed the legal system made it too easy for juries to return "not guilty" verdicts in insanity cases. The Hinckley verdict had led to changes in the law that made it much more difficult for a defendant to plead insanity. Within three years of the verdict, thirty-four states, in addition to Congress, had shifted the burden of proving insanity to the defense, eight states had adopted a separate verdict of "guilty but mentally ill," and one state (Utah) had abolished the defense altogether. Congress had also narrowed the terms of the defense itself. The Insanity Defense Reform Act of 1984 required the defendant to prove the existence of a "severe" mental disease that made him "unable to appreciate the nature and quality or the wrongfulness of his acts" not just at the time of the crime, but in general.

By the time "Untying the Straitjacket" was filmed, however, these concerns were less imperative, and the pendulum was swinging back in the other direction. Hosted by Bill Kurtis and filmed at Clifton Perkins and the Kirby Forensic Psychiatric Center in New York, the documentary purports to "uncover the facts and fictions of the criminally insane." In his introduction, Kurtis explains that the insanity defense is not an easy way of avoiding prison and that it succeeds only when a defendant is severely psychotic. In this sense, the documentary is enlightened and sympathetic, aiming to reduce the stigma of mental illness. At the same time, however, it panders to old clichés, alluding implicitly to violent men, ruined lives, the strange contortions of the sex drive. Viewers are lured with hints of the horror awaiting them "behind closed doors," where they'll come face-to-face with the "dangerously mentally ill" who have "committed brutal acts of unspeakable savagery."

In "Untying the Straitjacket," the Brian Bechtold of mid-1997, a twenty-nine-year-old psychiatric patient, has been caught and preserved in the amber of digital videotape. He's one of the first patients to appear in the documentary, and one of the most memorable. At this point, he's been at Perkins for just over five years, and he's still open, earnest, and upbeat about his treatment and prognosis. It's not surprising that he was chosen to appear on camera.

When we first meet him, he's sitting on a chair in his room. On a chest of drawers beside him are framed photographs of his dogs. Brian is good-looking, with pale skin and blue eyes whose color is brought out by his blue-and-white polo shirt. No longer the thin young man described by Officer Hightower in Port St. Joe, he now has the muscular chest and thick neck of an amateur weightlifter. His full black hair is cut into the hospital's standard bowl haircut, and he has a closely cropped beard somewhere between stubble and goatee. When he talks, he's earnest but also shy, and slightly wary. He speaks seriously, his voice slowed and a little blurred by the effects of medication. "Ten minutes before I shot my parents, I didn't know I was going to shoot my parents," he tells the interviewer. "I never thought it would happen to me. I never thought I'd be in this position. I never thought that this is going to be my lot in life, that I would kill my parents. . . . And I just have to live with it, from day to day."

The camera moves in on Brian's face, then cuts to a self-assured man in a beige suit and white tie, identified as Dr. Jonathan Briskin. "When Brian committed his crime, he was suffering from delusions," the psychiatrist explains. "He believed that he was in danger and that he had to do what he did in order to prevent something worse from happening."

Later in the documentary, Bill Kurtis, with stentorian solemnity, briefly describes Brian's crime in voiceover as the camera shows Brian walking down the hall of his ward, past a busy nurses' station and bustling dayroom. In this scene, he's wearing cargo pants and a beige polo shirt, and he holds a coffee cup from which, as he walks past the camera, he awkwardly sips. For some reason, the scene plays in slow motion, which makes it seem stilted and unnatural.

We encounter Brian again a little later in the documentary, performing a vigorous workout routine. Dressed in a T-shirt that depicts a Rottweiler eating a triple-decker club sandwich, he launches into an energetic set of push-ups, his feet raised on a tabletop, his fists clenched against the floor. "The process of moving off a locked ward is both slow and tedious," Bill Kurtis informs us. "Brian Bechtold has never acted out in the five years since he arrived at Perkins after murdering his parents, but because of his extremely violent crime, doctors are still reluctant to give him more degrees of freedom."

By the fall of that year, however, based on Brian's good behavior and his responsiveness to therapy, he'd been recommended for minimum security. In November, he was allowed to take a two-hour trip outside the hospital, accompanied by an aide. He chose to visit an upscale barbershop. It was an unforgettable experience.

That morning, he walked down the hallway of the hospital toward the exit, past the security doors, and into a lobby that contained storage lockers, a metal detector, and a waiting area. A television was playing at low volume. On a low table were a few copies of magazines: *Good Housekeeping, Parent and Child.* A vertical glass case displayed patients' artwork. Accompanied by a "psychiatric service technician," Brian walked out through the hospital's front doors. There was a chill in the air. The graded surface of the parking lot felt strange and precarious under his feet—for the last five years, he'd been walking on level ground. At the barber shop, his hair was washed, cut, and dried by a beautiful young woman—an experience that he found unpredictably and wonderfully sensual. Outside Perkins, he realized, no one knew he'd killed his parents or that he lived in a mental hospital. To them, he was just another young guy who needed a haircut.

All in all, Brian took fourteen supervised trips outside the hospital while he was on minimum security. Because he had no problem navigating the world outside the hospital fence, he assumed the success of these trips would strengthen his case for release. By now, he'd been at Perkins two years longer than the average stay. In that time, he'd seen plenty of patients come and go—including ones who'd committed crimes as serious as his and far worse. But whenever he asked his treatment team if it was time for him to apply for a discharge hearing, they always said he wasn't ready. Brian suspected this was due to his reluctance to take medication. Still, now that he was allowed out of the hospital on community visits, it was difficult to know what other privileges he could earn, short of a conditional release.

At Perkins, the granting and withdrawing of privileges was the chief way of building up (and breaking down) a patient's self-image—a system that functioned at an institutional as well as an individual level. Patients' behavior was constantly monitored, so no one could let their guard down. There were only two days a year when everyone could relax. On Family Day, in August, and at the annual Christmas party, in December, the ordinary routine of hospital life was set aside for a few hours. Patients were allowed to invite up to three friends or family members to share a buffet-style meal with staff, other patients, and their guests. At these parties, you could enjoy a feast of ribs and shrimp, take part in a prize raffle, have your photograph taken, sit outside in the summer, chat, mingle freely, and even dance.

In the weeks leading up to the Christmas party, a contest was held for the best-decorated ward. (Over time, this tradition became so fiercely competitive that it had to be discontinued.) In 1997, the prize was $150, a large sum compared to the patients' wages, but because it had to be split among everyone on the ward, each person's payout was relatively small. More important than the cash was the thrill of battling against other wards with equally aggressive teams. At Perkins, the patients didn't have much opportunity to distinguish themselves, and never got the chance to face off against their rivals, so the contest bore a heavy symbolic weight. Adding to its importance, its judges consisted of a panel of four "outsiders" (hospital trustees) who came into the hospital solely for this purpose.

That year, competition was feverish. On Brian's ward, the patients fashioned their own unique display of snowflakes, reindeer, candy canes, angels, and elves. The walls and windows were adorned with cotton ball snowflakes, the television set was disguised as a cozy fireplace, and the words "Happiness and Joy" were spelled out in letters taped to the back of each plastic chair. (The letters couldn't get jumbled up: the chairs were bolted to the floor.) The decorations were vivid, even flamboyant, but as he stood back to look at them, Brian couldn't help thinking that there was very little happiness or joy displayed by the men slumped in those chairs, most of them semiconscious, one with a set of reindeer antlers perched incongruously atop his head.

His ward didn't win the competition, but Brian remained grateful to be on minimum security. He was less excited about the ward psychiatrist, a Puerto Rican doctor named Paulo Negro, a short, middle-aged man with a pugnacious bearing and a heavy accent, and disappointed by his therapist Jason Farley, a young social worker who, despite his prematurely graying hair, appeared to be fresh out of college. At first, Brian hoped that because he was young, Mr. Farley would be willing to take risks and think outside the box, like Dr. Briskin. But while Dr. Briskin's youth had been an asset, Mr. Farley's was a liability. From Brian's perspective, he was like a big-headed frat boy—he recalls the social worker boasting that he played in a rock band and that he was the only one strong enough to lift the amplifier. Brian found this hard to believe, given that Farley was thin as a weasel. Brian also recalls that Farley bragged about his courage, telling Brian that if the two of them were in the army, he'd have made the better soldier. Brian concluded that Farley was embarrassed by his lack of experience, which he was obviously trying to disguise through bluffing, bragging, and refusing to bend the rules.

The worst display of his petty tyranny took place whenever Brian got a migraine. The nurses were under strict orders from Mr. Farley to give Brian nothing but two regular Tylenols. This might have been enough for an ordinary headache, but Brian's migraines were different. He'd suffered from them for as long as he could remember, and they were agonizing. The pounding pain would last all day. Every light, sound, and smell assaulted his senses. He'd curl up in the corner of the dayroom, rocking back and forth, vomiting repeatedly, begging for relief. He needed something heavy-duty. Tylenol would have been better than nothing—but only at a large dose and taken frequently. Yet no matter how he begged, the nurses wouldn't give him any more than the standard two pills. He pleaded with every on-call doctor and nursing supervisor, but nothing he said or did made a difference.

It wasn't much compensation, but once a migraine had faded, the feeling was exhilarating. He'd get a fantastic appetite, and everything he ate tasted delicious, especially the takeout food they were allowed to order from local restaurants on Sundays. He'd get Chinese food and make it last all week—chicken wings for breakfast and spare-ribs for lunch. The high-protein diet kept him strong enough for his workout routine, and he always watched his blood pressure, blood sugar, and cholesterol to be sure they were well within normal range. Apart from the migraines, Brian thought he was in good shape, both physically and mentally. He kept thinking about what Dr. Briskin had said: "A year on minimum, and you'll be ready to go home." But his progress was about to be undermined, and by a series of events over which he had no control.

Someone, he believed, was spreading lies about him. False rumors circulated all the time at Perkins, whispered by gossipy nurses' aides, bored security guards, and patients with nothing better to do, but this was the first time Brian had found himself on the receiving end.

One morning, in the dayroom, a friend of Brian's named Enzo Salgado sat down beside him and spoke to him in a low voice: "Don't tell anyone, but Dr. Bono left his attaché case on the porch," he said. "I've just been reading my case notes. He's got notes on you as well. Check it out."

Brian went out into the small courtyard adjacent to the ward. The brown leather briefcase was on a bench in the porch area just beside the door. It was unlocked and bulging with manila folders. One of them had his name on it. There were only a few documents in the folder— Brian had seen Dr. Bono only once or twice—and he didn't have time to read them thoroughly. Instead, he glanced through the case notes and then swiftly returned the documents to the folder. He recalled only a few phrases, but they were all baffling: "anti-Semitic," "racist," "possible ties to the Aryan Nation and similar neo-Nazi groups."

Brian was stunned. "That guy must be a nut," he told Enzo. "He says I'm a racist with ties to the Aryan Nation. That's crazy. I grew up with black kids. My best friend is Korean. My first girlfriend was Middle Eastern."

Enzo said, "Somebody must be out to get you."

"It's total bullshit," Brian repeated. "I still listen to black go-go music from DC."

"It doesn't matter," Enzo said. "They believe what they want to believe."

Later, when Brian thought about Dr. Bono's notes, things started to fall into place. He'd noticed the African American staff members would speak to him more harshly than they did to other patients, and they sometimes "forgot" to call him for the evening snack. Back then, there were no cameras on the wards, and while many of the guards were helpful and reasonable, others—especially those who came to Perkins after working in the prison system—could be cruel and unscrupulous.

Everybody knew the security guards were badly paid, bored, and resentful. Brian had seen them teasing, slapping, and pinching patients for no reason at all. In the evenings, if there was nothing to amuse them on television, the guards would turn to the patients to provide them with entertainment. They'd try to get a rise out of them, hitting them with pillows and calling them names. In the Perkins hierarchy, the guards were only one step above the patients; belittling the "crazies" helped to shore up their frail egos, emphasizing the difference between them and those "beneath" them. In this way, the guards took on the anger of the abused and frustrated patients, just as, among one another, patients would take on the bullying machismo of the guards.

"I've been told on more than one occasion, by the guards, that I'm going to be stuck here forever while they get to go home at night. They make it very petty," Cliff told me one day after a Focus on Fiction meeting. "This one nurse, he wouldn't give me my medication. He wouldn't give me food for my diabetes when my blood sugar got dangerously low. They want to pick on you and see if they can make you lose your temper. They push and push. I used to let it get to me. That's why I'm still on maximum security."

In a way, Brian understood the tension between the inmates and their attendants. After all, the guards came to know the patients better than anyone else. Unlike the doctors or nurses, they were with them eight hours a day or more. They were familiar with all their states of mind—they knew when individual patients were upset, when they were happy, when they were anxious, when they were about to panic. The guards bore the brunt of their unpredictable moods. But they weren't doctors; they weren't even medical professionals. In fact, most were ill-equipped to administer care to anyone.

It was never clear to me whether Brian was actually paranoid or whether the African American staff really were hostile toward him, but I knew from my own experience that Perkins could be a hothouse of suspicion and mistrust. It wouldn't have surprised me if, after six years of having his everyday words and actions scrutinized and analyzed for evidence to validate his diagnosis, Brian had grown suspicious, guarded, and tense. Staff were constantly watching, taking notes, and analyzing. What in anyone else would be an individual choice or personality traits—a preference for isolation, for example, or a love of cleanliness—becomes in a psychiatric patient a symptom of mental illness. Problems in the family, even before the patient was born, may be read as an early "taint" or a "sign." On the ward, ordinary behavior has pathological connotations; missing breakfast becomes "acting out."

Because patients are considered to have little insight into their illnesses, doctors will often gather "collateral" information about them from other sources—things they've said, for example, or books they've checked out from the library. Everything and anything can become a potential symptom of pathology, and there's something very unbalanced about this lack of reciprocity.

I was dubious, then, about the validity of the therapy notes in Brian's files that referred to his "unkempt appearance," "grievances," "nominal compliance," and "guardedness." To me, these seemed like natural reactions to being confined in a maximum-security hospital.

Brian's psychiatrists, however, considered them to be symptoms of his mental illness. Their reaction, in turn, made him even more fearful and guarded, and so the cycle continued, and he never knew if people were suspicious of him because they thought he was paranoid, or if he didn't trust people because they were suspicious of him.

Eventually, Brian came to the conclusion that it wasn't the guards, but another patient on the ward who'd been spreading stories about him. He never discovered who it was, but he had his suspicions. One contender was a dark, surly guy in his thirties named Jeff Padgett. Like Brian, Padgett was athletic and very strong. He had a hostile, defensive attitude that made Brian wonder what his problem was. Brian had heard that Padgett had attacked and beaten his abusive stepfather, a crime for which he'd served a prison sentence. When he got out of jail, he bombed a building. Sometimes, even at Perkins, Padgett seemed about to explode.

Another candidate was Mark Elliott, a healthy guy with a good sense of humor. Before coming to Perkins, Elliott had graduated from college and recently settled into a well-paying job when he suddenly snapped, quit his job, and killed his mother. At first, because he was intelligent and caused no trouble, he flew through the hospital system to minimum security, but when, like Brian, he refused to take medication, he was bounced straight back to maximum, where he was forcibly tranquilized. Now his mind was clouded by a high dose of antipsychotics. Brian wondered if Elliott might be unhinged enough to be confusing fantasy with reality.

Sometimes Brian wondered if his own thoughts weren't equally irrational, but he was pretty sure he knew the difference between reality and illusion. He knew that six years ago, he'd undergone a psychotic break that had caused him to experience terrible hallucinations. And while he knew that people with psychiatric illnesses don't always recognize that they're not "normal," he was sure that now, in contrast to six years ago, he was back to his old self again.

But despite Dr. Briskin's belief that he had "virtually no remaining symptoms of schizophrenia," Brian's "Axis I" diagnosis (a grouping of the *DSM*'s psychological diagnostic categories that comprises major clinical disorders) was still "paranoid schizophrenia." This, he realized, was because most of the time, when a new doctor picked up his last chart, they merely copied the original diagnosis from his previous evaluation or his commitment papers, rarely stopping to weigh the evidence for themselves (an opinion endorsed by psychiatrist and advocate Dr. Morton Birnbaum, who came to believe that "state doctors just copy over from year to year what is on one's commitment papers"). Psychiatrists, Brian had noticed, seemed to believe they were infallible, and their faith was contagious: nobody seemed to accept that a doctor could get something wrong. Brian was starting to realize that most people had only the vaguest idea what went on in the confines of a maximum-security psychiatric hospital. They had no idea that Perkins, like many other state-funded institutions, was struggling with budget cuts, excessive paperwork, and bureaucratic dysfunction. Most people preferred to imagine it as a dungeon full of madmen in straitjackets, like Hannibal Lecter.

The rumors were another stain on Brian's record, making it hard for him to enjoy the privileges he'd worked so hard for. What's more, they showed no sign of going away. After a disagreement with a kitchen worker about the best way to clean cookie sheets, he was written up for "acting bizarrely." As far as he could tell, his offense had been to let the sheets soak because they had cheese stuck on them. The kitchen worker had told him to scrub them to get the cheese off, but Brian had held dishwashing jobs in the past, and he'd learned that when a pan or cookie sheet got burned, no amount of scrubbing would do any good. You left it to soak. It wasn't complicated.

"Mr. Bechtold acknowledged having trouble with the African-American staff," read the next new note in Brian's file. "He believes that there is a concerted effort on the part of the African-American staff to make his life difficult. One incident he shared was that he was constantly getting into trouble for urinating in the shower/bathroom area. He emphatically maintains that it was not him but it was an African-American staff member who did it in order to get him into trouble." Reading this, Brian rolled his eyes in exasperation. What had happened was that one morning, when he had a cold, he went to get a can of Coke to soothe his throat. Only, the can was freezing, so he held it under a bathroom faucet to warm it up before drinking it. A janitor who'd been cleaning the bathroom floor at the time claimed that Brian had been "urinating in the sink."

To complain about this error in his file, Brian went to the clinical director's office. He knocked and waited, but no one came. Unaware that she was on vacation, Brian knocked a little more loudly. Someone accused him of "pounding on the door." Another black mark.

Brian felt as if he'd become the ward scapegoat overnight, and that everybody was taking out their frustrations on him. He started to grow vigilant, wary of rumors and false accusations, leery of other patients, especially well-known troublemakers like Bert Fenn, who'd sneak into Brian's room at night to dig around for loose change in his pants pockets. If Brian woke up and caught him in the act, Fenn would claim that Brian had a phone call and scuttle away like a rat. Another patient Brian tried to avoid was Leroy Jones, a rich kid who'd killed his mother with a hammer. Jones, who said he was heir to his family's "shampoo fortune," looked down on the other patients and called them "trash." No one lost any sleep when his petition for release was rejected and he had a breakdown. He started keeping his piss in a special cup and submerging batteries in the urine as part of a complicated experiment. He'd go to the gym and ride the exercise bike in super slow motion for hours. He once spent an entire afternoon instructing everyone on the ward how to tenderize meat with a mallet. If you were smart, you gave him a wide berth.

For Brian, the final kick in the teeth came during one of his therapy sessions with Jason Farley. The social worker said he wanted to try something new. He'd been taking lessons in hypnosis, he told Brian, and he thought Brian might benefit from being hypnotized.

"I want you to lie down," Farley said to Brian.

"Are you serious?" Brian said. "No way." Because Mr. Farley didn't seem to know what he was doing even in therapy sessions, which he was presumably trained to give, Brian certainly didn't trust him to mess around with hypnosis.

The note in his chart reported that Brian had "refused therapy," an infraction whose penalty was a mandatory transfer of ward. He was sent back to medium security. It was a blow, but at least he'd be getting away from all the lies and rumors and back to Dr. Briskin's ward.

10

"Hyper-religious"

Back on medium security, everything had changed. Dr. Briskin had left the hospital. His replacement was a psychiatrist named Stephen Stolzberg. Because Brian had consistently refused to take more than the minimum dose of Stelazine, a drug used to treat schizophrenia, Dr. Stolzberg thought he might benefit from shock treatment. Brian refused. Later that week, he asked to withdraw $150 from his account to buy two pairs of shoes. Now it was Dr. Stolzberg's turn to refuse. His reason, according to Brian? "You could hire a hitman with that kind of money."

What hitman, Brian wondered, *would work for the price of two pairs of shoes?*

To add insult to injury, at his next appointment, Dr. Stolzberg told Brian that his medication had to be increased.

It was true that he was taking only five milligrams of Stelazine (the recommended daily dose was twenty), but as before, Brian was under the impression that the low dose worked for him. His head was clear, and he had plenty of energy. He hadn't been in trouble, although for some reason, Dr. Stolzberg seemed suspicious. Brian wondered if he'd heard the rumors about him. If that was the reason for the medication increase, it hardly seemed fair to him. He'd seen other patients who were taking twenty milligrams, and it made them fat, slow, and miserable, not to mention increased the risk of diabetes and heart disease. Most of them felt the same way Brian did about taking meds. ("If I didn't have to interact with anybody, I'd be so much better without taking drugs," Cliff told me. "I take drugs so that other people can deal with me.") The prospect of being medicated into a daze again depressed Brian, and his anxiety dragged him down. When he heard there was a new maximum-security ward opening up in June 1998, he asked to be sent there instead. True, it would be more restrictive, but at least he'd get a different psychiatrist and, he hoped, avoid being drugged into oblivion.

Life on the new ward got off to a shaky start. The staff was a tight-knit group of nurses who all came from the same Baltimore suburb, Edmondson Village, and they reigned unchallenged. Their first mandate was to deny the patients their weekly takeout order. No reason was given; there was none to give. To Brian, it looked like a power play.

The new ward housed a lot of "IDD," or intellectually and developmentally disabled patients, many of whom were unable to follow an argument or express themselves clearly. Brian, more functional and articulate than the others, stepped up and took the lead. It didn't hurt that he was in fighting shape: muscular, tough, and angry. He no longer had any qualms about speaking aggressively to staff. At the next ward meeting, he stood up and told them they were out of line.

"We have rights," he said. "You can't take away our major privilege for no reason." When he threatened to file a grievance with the superintendent, the nurses backed down, and the weekly takeout was restored.

Round two came soon enough, and it was a dirty fight, literally. At the next meeting, one of the nurses announced that the patients were using too much soap and toilet paper and too many paper towels. "We're going to put a monthly limit on the bathroom supplies," she said. "If you use them up before the end of the month, too bad."

Things got nasty. Brian began to dread the end of each month. As supplies of toilet paper grew low, patients would start hoarding paper towels in their rooms. Some of them didn't have the best hygiene to begin with. The sedentary and wheelchair-bound patients frequently suffered from hemorrhoids, and with only rough paper towels to wipe themselves, they'd often bleed on the toilet seats. It was unsanitary, to say the least.

A group of the ward's more competent patients got together to talk over their options. Many were afraid of making waves. Those who were hoping to move to a less restrictive security level didn't want to jeopardize their status. Because Brian had made a good spokesman for the ward, successfully reversing the policy on takeout orders, they asked him to speak up again.

At the next community meeting, Brian raised his hand. He wasn't planning to be diplomatic. "We need more soap, toilet paper, and paper towels," he announced. "If you don't start treating us like human beings, there's going to be trouble."

The threat worked, and the bathroom supplies were restored, but from that day on, to the hospital nursing staff and security guards, Brian became Public Enemy Number One. They accused him of "hostile behavior" and expressed their resentment to his psychiatrist. (Ironically, this was still Dr. Stolzberg, who was covering the ward until a new doctor was hired.)

After learning that patients were by law allowed access to their hospital records, Brian had been checking his chart on a regular basis. After the incident with the bathroom supplies, a note was written in his file by one of the nurses describing him as "manipulative and intimidating, lacking insight into his past behavior, and the serious nature of his illness." Even more frustrating, after complaining to his treatment team that the ward staff were against him, Brian found another note in his chart, this time from Dr. Stolzberg, describing "continued paranoia," "hostile speech," "suspiciousness," "fearfulness," "uncooperativeness," and "poor problem solving."

Although HIPAA allowed patients to have access to their medical notes, most doctors (psychiatrists in particular) write notes intended for themselves or for other medical professionals rather than for the patient, who might find their language vague and confusing. At Perkins, phrases like "persevering" and "lacking in insight" meant something very specific, although it wasn't always clear to the patients what that was. Estrangement from language is a common feature of paranoid schizophrenia—in fact, the word *schizophrenia* means "split mind," in the sense not of a mind split in two, but of a splitting between concepts and their associations—and this psychiatric shorthand, to a suspicious patient, could easily seem like a code designed to trick them. This breach in language is part of the way selfhood and personal identity seem to break down in psychosis, and so, in the words of author and schizophrenic Elyn Saks, the "solid center from which one experiences reality" can become "fuzzy" and "wobbly" at times, "breaking up like a bad radio signal" or eroding "like a sand castle . . . sliding away in the receding surf." In another first-person account, a schizophrenic patient describes his paranoid delusions about language:

> Effectively, I became addicted to thinking about how words could
> be used to make coded references. I become obsessed with playing
> language games instead of using language primarily as it is normally
> used. As a result of this, my interpretation of what was really going
> on became more and more detached from reality and instead was
> directly derived from interpretations of the language games that I
> believed people were playing.

In this light, it's ironic that ordinary words, at Perkins, had unpredictable meanings. The word *escape*, for example, was never used; instead, it was replaced by *elope* (to mean exactly the same thing), a word that allegedly "minimizes the negative connotation of prison-like behavior" (although, surely, it's not the patient's behavior that's "prison-like," but their environment). Essentially, "escape" is avoided because it suggests forced confinement, whereas an "elopement" is usually temporary (and often for a pleasurable purpose) or, perhaps, accidental, like the wandering of an aged parent with Alzheimer's disease.

Words had enormous power at Perkins; it was hardly surprising, then, that people would fret about them, puzzle over them, pounce on them with feverish enthusiasm. Both doctors and patients would analyze each other's language endlessly and in detail. Doctors wanted to get beneath what they believed to be patients' defensive façades, and patients wanted to gauge what doctors really thought of them and whether they might be getting any closer to release.

Psychiatric terminology, in particular, would often be picked up and appropriated by nonmedical staff, including security guards and psychiatric service technicians. Everyday emotions were given clinical names. Unhappiness became "anhedonia." Thinking became "cognition." Facial expressions were "affect." Feelings about other people were "transferences." People didn't get to know each other or become friends; their "boundaries became confused." In this way, ordinary feelings and experiences were made distant and strange. This kind of language kept patients at arm's length—the same effect was achieved by addressing them (both in person and in their files) as "Mr." or "Ms." rather than by their first names—as if they didn't share the same emotions as everyone else. Brian had also noticed that doctors got annoyed when patients used the institution's terminology and would accuse the patients of "intellectualizing."

Discharge was a sacred word, the holy grail toward which everything reached. *Support* was another; it meant everything and nothing.

You could bring it up in any situation; it always fit. Having "insight into your illness" meant you accepted your psychiatrist's diagnosis, and "compliance" meant you took your medication without having to be forced. "Unsafe" was code for "suicidal." It was important to be "well adjusted," which meant you "complied" with your "support system"—in other words, you followed the rules. Compliance, in fact, was the way out of the hospital. If a patient was compliant enough, they were discharged—which didn't necessarily mean their symptoms had gone away, but that they'd learned to repeat the magic words that led the doors to open. Brian knew what he was supposed to say, but either he couldn't say it or he couldn't say it convincingly enough. Because the rules made no sense, he thought, resistance was a healthier response than "compliance."

In addition to paranoia, he was also accused of setting himself "unattainable treatment goals." This was especially depressing for him, as his only "treatment goal" was to one day leave Perkins and support himself in the outside world. Achieving this would be much easier, he thought, if the goalposts didn't keep moving. During his first years at the hospital, everyone had been concerned with how well he understood himself; now his "insight" seemed irrelevant. What mattered now was his "compliance" in taking medication and how much "support" he had.

Those patients lucky enough to get regular visits from friends and family, people on the outside who cared about their well-being, were considered "well supported," which (rather than self-reliance) seemed to be the new criterion for release. Like most patients, Brian, through no fault of his own, wasn't so fortunate. Over the last five years, his friends, relatives, and siblings, unable to contact him easily by phone or email, had gradually fallen out of touch. He'd seen it happen to other patients. Perkins is in the middle of nowhere, virtually inaccessible by public transport. Visiting hours are limited and inconvenient, the dress code is strict, and it's humiliating for visitors to be searched by security guards. If they have money, patients can use the phone, but only at certain times, and there's only one line for each ward. The family members who'd forgiven Brian for his crime lived far away: Marcia was in Atlanta, his uncle Walter was in Pittsburgh, and Cathy, who was Brian's main connection on the outside, had recently moved to Ohio. Kyu, his friend from the karate studio, still called and visited when he could, but he had problems of his own and wasn't always available.

Brian's greatest source of support, in fact, was his religion.

But he kept that to himself.

Religion was one of the subjects I hardly ever spoke about with Brian; I sensed we were both afraid it might expose a fault line in our friendship. I'd told Brian I didn't practice any particular religion, and he'd told me he believed in a kind of charismatic Christianity similar to Pentecostalism. He didn't like to discuss it at any length, he said, because when he'd done so in the past, his psychiatrists had always seen it as a symptom of mental illness. And much as I sympathized with Brian, I could see their point.

When he'd first arrived at Perkins, Brian had attended church regularly, but after a couple of years, he stopped going. Although it drew around thirty patients, the hospital's Sunday church service (a vague, insipid nondenominational get-together in a multipurpose room) was hardly inspiring. Still, even though he'd stopped going to church, Brian never stopped believing in the revelation he'd had in Port St. Joe. He was convinced that at the time of the murders, he'd been possessed by the devil. He spent three days in the campground reading the King James Bible, and he had a Bible in his room in the detention center where he was sent after turning himself in. He read it from cover to cover, both the Old and New Testaments. During his time at Perkins, he'd also read books on divine healing and studied different forms of Christianity, and from his reading and experiences, he had developed his own understanding of biblical doctrine.

He knew there were many people in the United States who

subscribed to the idea of an Islamic revolution, and he also knew that Islam was the only religion growing faster than the world's population. He saw how it could easily dominate the world in twenty years or less. He was familiar with chapter 8 of the Book of Daniel, which describes "the time of the end" in which "four kingdoms shall stand up out of the nation." Brian interpreted this as meaning that the Islamic forces would attack by arson to unbalance the country from within, while the Middle Eastern, Communist, and Oriental countries would attack from the outside. This would mark the beginning of the Tribulation, during which Christians would be tortured as penance for their sins. After a fierce battle, Islam would be defeated, and Jesus would return to earth.

When he first got to Perkins, he'd discussed his religious beliefs in group therapy and with his psychiatrists and was dismayed to find a note in his chart from Dr. Stolzberg that stated, "He is hyper-religious and has delusions about the nation of Islam." Brian's plan to donate money to charity was also pathologized. "He sees this in religious terms," the psychiatrist wrote, "but I believe that he wants to stop thinking about himself as a bad, violent criminal." A further twist of the knife: the doctor had suggested that increasing Brian's dose of Stelazine might help to "reduce his hyper-religiosity."

In Brian's experience, psychiatrists were generally uninformed about religion. "They're bullheaded," he told me. "Most of them don't know anything about the Bible, but they don't believe they could be ignorant about anything." Afraid to discuss his beliefs with anyone at Perkins, he began to spend more time talking on the phone with outreach representatives from various churches. Since he'd never had the chance to discover how different faiths interpreted the Bible, Brian didn't know if his own reading was way off base. He wanted to know if any other believers shared his conclusions.

He tried to solve this problem by calling the numbers of different churches he found in the telephone directory and asking if he could talk to a minister. After a lot of cold calls, he found two ministers who did share some of his Biblical interpretations—one Lutheran and the other Baptist—but they disagreed with him about the End Times. Both ministers believed NATO would conquer the earth, instituting a one-world government that would bring about the final days, and although interested, Brian was unconvinced. He believed this version of the apocalypse had originated with the Jehovah's Witnesses; other churches had adapted it to fit their own beliefs.

Unable to find a minister by phone, Brian tried the mail. He wrote a ten-page letter that he characterized as a "plea for help" and sent it to various church leaders whose addresses he found in the phone book. He wrote:

> Many years ago I lost my mind. After 5 years of torment I committed a very serious Crime for which I am truely sorry. . . . For the past 11 years I have been in an institution. I have not had access to any denominational doctrine. . . . Recently, however, my beliefs have come under serious scrutiny. I did not know that most Christians don't study prophesy. And as I had no teacher and pleanty of time I came up with my own interpretation. But when the administrators came across my letters to a friend they immeadiatly considered me dangerous as a result of religious delusions. It is protocol to have someone mediate who is an authority of the patients professed religion. The hospital staff did not believe this was necessary. I would like to know if your church <u>wholly or partially agrees</u> with my interpretation. Or it would really help me even if you disagree you could attest that under the circumstances I have made a <u>rational attempt</u> to construe the numerous prophetic books into a cohesive theme along a progressive timeline.

When he'd almost given up hope of hearing back, Brian received a letter from the leader of a church that called itself Watchman Ministries. "Dear Brian," it began:

I read your statement about your past and your new life in our Lord. You are right on, brother. God has rescued you from the clutches of Satan and his demonic hoards. Not only that but God has given you a great infilling of his Holy Spirit.... Your 10-page statement agrees with (for the most part) what the Holy Spirit has given to me. Subsequently the Holy Spirit has confirmed to us both with our agreement in the Scriptures (and through others) the events of these last days.... Do not think that I consider you any less of His servant because God makes the greatest saints out of the greatest sinners.

This minister sent material from his church that explained how "God's will is using Islam (ARABS) to purge America." Although there were a number of differences from his own interpretation of the Bible, there were enough connections for Brian to feel vindicated. Unfortunately, in terms of contact information, the minister provided only an email address and the website of his church, and patients at Perkins didn't have access to the internet. And Brian realized that even if his beliefs were endorsed by a minister, Dr. Stolzberg would probably see them as a symptom of schizophrenia.

Although it's true that religious delusions or preoccupations can be a feature of mental illness, they're not usually regarded as pathological unless they impair the patient's ability to function (and in Brian's case, it was his religious beliefs that had led him to turn himself in to the police). Perhaps it was the suddenness of his conversion that made his psychiatrists apprehensive, or perhaps they suspected it was easier for Brian to think of himself as possessed by the devil than to face the fact that he'd murdered his parents. Still, his beliefs weren't particularly bizarre. Many religions include beliefs or rituals that may seem delusional or unhealthy to outsiders (fasting, chanting, speaking in tongues, snake handling, animal sacrifice, self-flagellation). The difference between spiritual beliefs that are merely idiosyncratic and those that are pathological is especially hard to define at a place like Perkins,

where religion played a significant role in many of the patients' crimes. Among them: a pair of women who killed two children in an attempted exorcism, a man who killed his landlord because he thought the man was a warlock, and a patient who tried to subpoena fourteen resurrected Mormon prophets to testify for him in court.

Once he realized his religious beliefs were being classed as schizophrenic symptoms, Brian no longer brought them up—but this, too, backfired. Now, according to Dr. Stolzberg, Brian had "secretly decompensated" and learned to "hide his religious delusions." After that, Brian gave up trying to second-guess and just told the truth. While religion wasn't a subject he raised on his own, he didn't shy away from the topic if other people wanted to talk about it. He discussed his beliefs openly—although, to him, they were more than beliefs: they were facts. He was familiar enough with the New Testament to quote it verbatim, and when it was relevant, he did. This made him even less popular with the African American staff, many of whom were converts to the Nation of Islam. When his treatment team heard that Brian had been talking about the Bible, once again he was "lacking in compliance" and suffering from "delusions" and "inflexible thinking."

The *DSM-5* defines delusions as "fixed beliefs that are not amenable to change in the light of conflicting evidence." Yet, in matters like religious belief, we usually consider steadfastness of faith to be a virtue. Once we've made an emotional commitment to something meaningful, it's not easy for us to change our point of view; we cling to its truth, discrediting counterevidence. In the sense that we find reasons to go on believing what we want to believe, most of us experience "fixed beliefs" and "inflexible thinking." But we also tend to compartmentalize, restricting this kind of thinking to one part of our lives. In Brian's case, however, his life at Perkins was so limited—and his thoughts so carefully probed and analyzed—that it was difficult to keep anything separate or private.

Concerned about "hyper-religiosity," Dr. Stolzberg increased Brian's medication, raising his dose of Stelazine to twenty milligrams a

day—four times what he was currently taking. It was a standard daily dose, but to Brian, it seemed not only excessive but a form of punishment. He'd done perfectly well on the low dose and felt mentally stable. Now his future looked bleak.

He'd been sent to Perkins, Brian reasoned, to get help. Now he felt as if he were in court, being judged seven days a week. People watched him all the time, questioning the meaning of his every word. He was tired of having no control over his life, of having to do whatever staff told him to do—when to get up in the morning, when to eat, when to take a nap, when to go outside, when to watch television, when to go to sleep at night. He felt robbed of his identity. No longer a student, a karate teacher, a brother, or a boyfriend, he was now a mental patient, nothing more.

To make matters worse, there was no end in sight. His commitment was indefinite. As long as the doctors believed a patient could still be a danger to the community, they weren't released, and judging by his risk evaluations, Brian was still considered a threat. The only way this would change was for him to exhibit more "compliance," which meant accepting a higher dose of Stelazine. Once again, he had no choice.

He knew the high dose would obliterate him, and he was right. Before long, he was slurring his words when he spoke. He found it hard to carry on an ordinary conversation, and he had difficulty thinking and focusing. Walking across the dayroom became a major event. Eventually, he was unable even to stay awake. Slumped in front of the television, he'd sleep for sixteen hours a day, then go to bed and sleep all night. Once again, he was impotent and incontinent.

And once again, he fought back, pulling himself together with the help of contraband caffeine. On his current ward, coffee was banned, as were carbonated drinks that contained caffeine, but he managed to buy a jar of real coffee from a patient on minimum. It wasn't much, but it kept the fog from closing in. But while in possession of contraband, it was especially important for him not to let his guard down, and in August there was a series of back-to-back shakedowns. It made him nervous—something was going on, though he wasn't sure what. One day, before breakfast, every room was searched. The guards went through all Brian's possessions, but by a stroke of luck, they managed to miss the jar of instant coffee on the bedside table, hidden under his hat.

That year, Perkins was subject to budget cuts; as usual, the patients paid the price. After a lot of hand-wringing and paper shuffling, Dr. Fragala, the superintendent, announced he'd be closing down Hamilton House, a semi-restricted transitional community where patients could gradually prepare for release. For many years, between ten and twelve of them had been sent to Hamilton House every six months. After it closed, they no longer had a transitional place where they could get used to the prospect of life outside the hospital. With fewer patients leaving the hospital each year, a logjam built up of those waiting to move forward. To ease the gridlock, a number of patients had to be sent back through the system in the opposite direction.

Brian knew what this meant. It could be years before he left maximum security. He believed the guards were still spreading rumors about him to the doctors, because at his next clinical meeting, his treatment team began interrogating him about a series of mystifying violations he'd allegedly committed but that he had no recollection of, including "burning paper towels," "stealing the janitor's coffee cup," and "singing loudly in the courtyard." (Brian didn't sing.) He was also shown a strange letter he was supposed to have written, which, as he pointed out, wasn't even in his handwriting. It didn't matter how absurd the charges were to Brian, or how vigorously he refuted them—he knew the team would always give the staff more credit than they'd give a "mental patient." One day soon, he realized, they were going to medicate him even more. Paralyzed by inertia, he'd be an easy target for assaults. And he had plenty of enemies.

Not for the first time, he started to wonder how different life would be if he'd been found competent to stand trial. People on the outside often assume that if you were sent to a mental hospital, you managed to avoid a long prison sentence, but that isn't true. Defendants who are found not criminally responsible spend far more time in the hospital than they would have served in prison for the same crime. Plus, in prison, when you've done your time, you've done your time—but there's no minimum sentence for the criminally insane. If they'd given Brian thirty-five or forty years, it would have been tough, he thought, but at least he'd have had a release date to look forward to.

"For two first-degree murders, they would have given him life without parole," said Brian's attorney, Mark Van Bavel. But Brian was starting to realize he might never get out of Perkins, either, and if he was going to be incarcerated for life, he'd rather be in a prison, where he could lift weights and work out in the yard—and he wouldn't be forced to take medication that turned him into a vegetable. "A lot of people say the program in the prison is better than here," Louis, a patient in his early twenties, told me—although Jeremy, who'd been transferred to Perkins after six months in jail, disagreed:

> Being here is a little better than being in jail, because you're not locked in your room all day long. Here, you don't have to be in your room until naptime, or when the doors are opened after medication. In jail, if you're on general population, you get let out of your cell for an hour and a half two times a day. A couple of friends visited me here last week, and I was able to hug them, sit down at close range and talk to them. . . . Also, I have three opportunities to order food from certain restaurants outside if I want to. You can get that in a regional hospital, but you can't get that in a jail.

Even if a miracle happened and Brian was released from the hospital, he knew there was a high chance of his being sent back. He'd seen it happen. Patients who left Perkins had half the recidivism rate of prison inmates but were far more closely scrutinized. The slightest transgression, even a minor offense like petty theft, and they were back on the ward. Ex-inmates, on the other hand, could miss their parole meetings with little or no consequence, or even disappear into the community, escaping the justice system altogether.

Brian was sick of being medicated into a stupor, tired of making no progress toward release, and frustrated by the constant parade of patients who arrived at Perkins and got discharged while he stayed in the same place or went backward. Some of those patients had the advantage of wealthy and supportive families who could afford to hire private attorneys, or they were women, who seemed to move through the system more easily. As long as his doctors thought he was harboring secret reserves of hostility and paranoia, they wouldn't even consider him a candidate for release. To make any progress at all, he had to comply—and compliance meant medication. There was a strong possibility, he reasoned, that he was going to turn into one of those old men wearing diapers who'd spent the last forty years slumped in front of the television.

This, he told himself, was not a life worth living.

11

Breaking Point

Once he'd decided to escape, there was no going back. He lay awake at night working out the details of his plan. He'd enlist the help of an old friend of his named Richard Phillips, who lived in Pittsburgh. Richard was terminally ill, so he had little to lose. Brian remembered Richard telling him about the abandoned copper mines in the hills of Pennsylvania and Virginia, both within a day's drive of Perkins. He decided to write to Richard—it would be safer to avoid the phone, and mail wasn't read or censored—telling him to find one of the abandoned mines and fill it with the essentials necessary for a long time in hiding: around five years, he figured.

He made a list. He'd need a couch to sleep on, a system for purifying rainwater (ceramic would be best, but a Katadyn filtration system would also work), blankets, books, a five-year supply of survivalist food (which could be ordered and shipped from a company that advertised

its services in survivalist magazines), and, for protection and companionship, a puppy he could train. When everything had been set up,
he'd tell Richard to buy a used car, park it close to Perkins, hide three
or four five-gallon cans of gasoline under a blanket on the backseat,
and put the ignition key in an envelope and tape the envelope to the
car's undercarriage. If he got away at night, Brian figured, he could
drive to the mine without even stopping for gas. If the plan worked,
he could be in hiding before he'd even been missed. After five years
or so, he'd quietly leave the country.

If he succeeded, he'd be free; if he was killed in the attempt, he'd
be free in a different way. If he was caught and sent to prison, at least
he'd have a definite sentence. Even life without parole would be better
than this unbearable state of not knowing. At the very worst, he'd be
back at Perkins again. The way Brian saw it, he couldn't lose.

But before he had the chance to set things up, he got the news
that Richard Phillips had died. Now Brian's options were limited.
The second scheme he devised was less ambitious but more practical.
He'd acquire a weapon, take a hostage, and get shot by the police. If he
lived, he'd plead guilty and get sent to prison—the state of Maryland
couldn't force him to plead not criminally responsible, even if doctors
thought he was incompetent. If he got killed, so be it. He didn't want
to hurt anyone, but he'd reached the limit of what he could bear.

A couple of months later, finding himself alone in the laundry
room, he managed to break a support strut off an ironing board, a
piece of metal about fourteen inches long and a quarter of an inch in
diameter. Back in his room, he pried loose one of the ceiling tiles and
hid the strut inside. After that, whenever he had the chance, he'd take
it out and file it down by rubbing it against the grout in his shower.
He made a sling for the shank and started wearing it all the time
under his regular clothes, waiting for his chance.

It never came, so he made his own. The nurses' shift change took
place between 2:30 and 3 p.m. Brian had noticed that, at this time,
the guards would always hang out at the back of the ward to flirt

with the pretty nurse across the hall, leaving the dayroom unattended. On Sunday, December 5, 1999, at five past three, when both guards were safely distracted, Brian strapped his shank inside his shirtsleeve, tensed his muscles, and took up his position inside the door of the ward, waiting for the handle to move.

Brenda Williams was tired. This wasn't her usual shift; she was filling in for a colleague. She didn't like coming in to work on Sundays, but she'd been offered the 3–11 p.m. time slot on maximum security, and the overtime pay was too good to turn down. She walked down the hall with the charge nurse from another ward, wondering what time she'd get home that night. She climbed the stairs to the second floor and held up her pass to the automatic lock. The door opened. Brenda screamed.

Brian Bechtold was standing facing her with a something sharp in his hand. It was a long piece of metal with a spike on the end, and it was pointed at her.

"Back off, or I'll hurt you," he said in a low voice. "Turn around and take me through Eight South."

The nurse remained motionless. She could feel her heart beating in her chest.

"Turn around," Bechtold said.

Brenda turned, but she was too terrified to move. Impatiently, Bechtold grabbed her by the shoulder and pushed her back through the door ahead of him, poking the spike into her back. She walked back down the hallway, trying not to panic. Whatever happened, she didn't want to die. As she came to the stairwell, she saw the door at the bottom and realized that it would lock automatically behind her. Without further thought, she tried to run down the stairs.

Bechtold grabbed her by the shoulder and pulled her back. She realized he'd kill her if he had to.

"Don't try anything like that again," he said. Brenda could hear the anger in his voice. "Come on, lady. I'm serious. Let's go."

With the point of a metal spike to her back, Brenda walked on. There was nothing she could do. Bechtold marched her down the hall that led to 2 North, then gestured for her to open the door with her pass. As she did so, an announcement came over the intercom. "Bechtold is escaping through Two North!"

Brenda was relieved to know the alarm had been raised. At the same time, it crossed her mind that once they'd passed through the ward, they'd be in the minimum-security area. The door at the other end of the ward was unlocked. Once they got through that door, there was nothing to stop Bechtold from getting out of the hospital. What if he took her with him, using her as a hostage or a human shield? She didn't want to make him angry, but she knew this was her last chance.

She tried talking to him like a mom.

"Listen, honey, I don't know you, but I've got to tell you, this is a bad idea," she said. "Think about it for a second. You really don't want to do this."

"Keep moving," Bechtold said, urging her forward.

They continued walking across the ward. Brenda could see the nurses' station ahead. When she was close enough, she tried making eye contact with one of the other nurses. She could tell they knew what was happening. Their presence gave her another burst of courage. As they passed the nurses' station, she stopped moving.

"Why don't we stop here for a second, honey?" she said. "You can get some help from these ladies." Her voice was trembling.

"Keep moving," Bechtold repeated.

Brenda realized this was her final chance. "I think I'm just going to have a word with the ladies here," she said, and she slipped past the desk of the nurses' station and took refuge inside the office. She could tell Bechtold didn't care. He didn't need her anymore.

That afternoon, Sgt. Herbert McKethan was working in the control center at Perkins, sitting in front of a set of small television monitors that showed what was going on in different parts of the hospital. Like most Sundays, the day had been calm and quiet. But just after 3 p.m., the phone rang. It was the duty nurse on 2 North, and she sounded frantic. Brian Bechtold had just escaped through the ward, she said. McKethan ran out of the control center and, along with Officer Gary Adair, who'd been conducting bag checks in the lobby, he ran down the hall toward medium security. The two security guards turned a corner, and there was Brian Bechtold, walking toward them holding a long metal spike in his right hand and pointing it in front of him.

"What's going on, Mr. Bechtold?" McKethan asked. Even though the patient looked threatening, McKethan thought maybe he could talk some sense into him, get him to change his mind. "Is everything okay?"

"Back off, or I'll kill you," Bechtold said flatly.

Neither McKethan nor Adair wanted to put him to the test. Most of the patients at Perkins had committed violent crimes, and attacks on staff were commonplace. The guards didn't carry weapons, and Bechtold looked deadly serious. McKethan and Adair both raised their hands and let him go by, through the next set of sliding doors. *He might get into the lobby*, McKethan thought, *but someone will surely lock the doors before he gets outside.*

McKethan was wrong. Brian walked straight into the lobby, where a young woman with dark hair was retrieving her winter coat and keys from a locker. She saw the shank but played it cool, smiling nervously. Brian approached slowly. He didn't want to frighten her.

Too late. He'd been seen. Someone screamed. A heavily pregnant woman fell to her knees and began to pray. A guard ran into the lobby, lunged toward Brian, and tried to grab the shank. Brian switched the weapon to his other hand and turned to face his attacker, who immediately surrendered, assuming the fetal position at his feet. Brian felt strangely calm. He walked out of the hospital and into the parking lot. It was colder than he'd expected. He wished he'd worn long pants.

Psychiatric nurse Cassandra Mayfield had just finished work for the day and was sitting in her silver-gray Mercury Cougar in the parking lot of Clifton T. Perkins Hospital Center. She was looking down, checking that she had her lipstick in her purse, when someone banged hard on the driver-side window. Cassandra's heart leapt in shock. She turned and saw a crazy-looking man holding a huge metal spike. Again, he banged his fist against the car window. Terrified, Cassandra fumbled for her keys and, with shaking hands, managed to start the engine. She took off the hand brake and put her foot on the gas. The car hurtled forward, leaving the patient behind clutching his spike like a caveman.

Brian ran half a mile or so, heading east, and didn't leave the woods until he came to a path with no traffic. He followed the path, wandering through a no-man's-land of factories and loading docks, keeping out of sight behind buildings. He crossed a railroad track and continued on the other side until he came to a main road. He followed it for a time, but it had no sidewalk, and although he'd hidden the shank up his shirtsleeve, he felt vulnerable and conspicuous out in the open. A car passed, then two more.

At around 3:15 that afternoon, Toby Fulton, an officer with the Howard County Police Department, was driving south down New Ridge Road when he got a call on his car radio informing him that a patient had escaped from Clifton T. Perkins State Hospital. The radio operator added that the patient had been sent to Perkins for murdering his parents. Fulton checked his gun, then put his foot on the gas.

The patient was described as a white male of medium height and weight wearing red shorts and a dark blue or black pullover. While driving eastbound on Patuxent Range Road, about a mile from

Perkins, right by the Carvel Ice Cream Warehouse, Fulton saw ahead of him a man in red shorts and a blue pullover walking along the side of the road. At the same moment, a white van heading westbound pulled over, and a Perkins security guard jumped out. The guard saw Fulton and gestured toward the man in the red shorts, indicating that he was the escapee. Fulton took out his radio and called for backup, then pulled up alongside the patient and got out of his patrol car.

"Hey! Stop!" he yelled.

Brian turned to face him. "Fuck you!" he said.

Fulton reached for his holster, drew his nine-millimeter Sig Sauer, and shouted, "Get down on the ground!"

Brian stopped walking, turned toward Fulton, and opened his arms. "Come on, shoot me," he said. "You're going to have to shoot me. I'm not going back. You'd better shoot me in the head."

"Get down on the ground right now!" Fulton yelled again.

Brian, standing still in the middle of the road, ignored him. "Someone's going to die tonight," he said. His words raised the hairs on the back of the officer's neck.

Holding his gun in front of him, Fulton moved closer. He really didn't want to shoot anyone if he could avoid it, especially not if they were unarmed.

"Has he got a weapon?" Fulton shouted over to the Perkins guard.

The guard misheard him. "We don't carry weapons," he shouted back.

Fulton relaxed his stance, returned his gun to its holster, and took out his pepper spray. He shook the cylinder, unsnapped the top, and moved closer, so the patient could see he was going to get sprayed.

"You'd better draw your gun and shoot me," Brian repeated. He then reached into the sleeve of his sweater, pulled out the foot-long metal spike, and pointed it at Fulton. "Someone's going to die tonight," he said again. "And if it's not you"—he gestured toward the security guard—"it'll be him."

Fulton replaced the canister of pepper spray on his belt and took out his gun again. There was nothing wrong with shooting an armed man, especially when that man was threatening and mentally ill and had already committed a double homicide. Still, Fulton didn't want to shoot unless it was absolutely necessary. He gave the guy one last chance.

"Come on, man. Don't do this," he said. "You're going to get hurt."

Still holding the spike in front of him, Brian turned and walked toward Sherwick Court, a side street. At that moment, a second patrol car pulled up, and two cops got out. Fulton recognized them as Officer Jason Hall and Corporal Linda Freeman. The three of them, along with the Perkins security guard, began following Brian on foot, all yelling at him to stop. He ignored them but turned and shouted at Corporal Freeman, "I'm going to take one of you, so you'd better get your gun out, bitch!"

At that point, Officer Hall ran toward Brian, took out his pepper spray, aimed it in his direction, and released a jet of gas—but it was a windy day, and it blew straight back into Hall's face.

Brian stood and watched the scene for a moment. "Don't try spraying that shit at me," he told them.

Fulton moved closer—he wanted to try talking again—but Brian suddenly turned around and pointed the spike at him menacingly.

"You'd better shoot me in the head," he threatened. Then he turned, tucked the shank into his sleeve, and began to run. The officers ran after him. When he reached the end of the road, Brian turned right, went past the Aqua Cool warehouse, and headed toward a series of loading docks beneath a sign that read "Apollo Moving and Storage." A black pickup truck was parked in one of the docks. When they got closer, Fulton saw that there was an older man sitting in the truck's cab, engrossed in a book. Brian was about eight feet away.

"Don't get any closer!" Fulton yelled.

Brian turned to face him. "You're going to have to shoot me," he said again.

This guy really wants to die, Fulton thought. "Hey!" he shouted at the driver of the truck. "Get your truck out of here. This guy is dangerous! He's just escaped from a mental hospital!"

The old man looked up, unsure of what was happening. When he saw Brian, he panicked and started to climb out of the cab.

"Stay in the truck!" Freeman kicked the vehicle's tailgate to get the man's attention. "Stay in the truck and lock the door!"

Brian stood facing Fulton. "I'm not going back," he said. "Come on. What are you waiting for? Shoot me!"

Fulton hesitated. He wondered if he could tackle the patient and bring him down.

"I'm going to count to three," Brian said. "Then I'm going to stab this guy and take his truck, so you'd better get ready to shoot me. Okay?"

"Don't do this, buddy," Officer Hall said.

"Move back," Brian told Corporal Freeman. "You're in his crossfire. Move over there." He pointed over to the other side of the truck, and she did as he asked. Then he began to count.

"One," he said. "Two . . ."

"Don't do it," Fulton said, drawing his gun.

"Three." Brian lunged at the man in the truck.

Officer Fulton fired. A series of cracks ripped through the air.

Brian felt like someone had hit him in the middle of his body with a baseball bat. All the breath left him, and he went down. There was no pain, only a burning sensation in his stomach. He felt too weak to move. He was lying on his left side next to the pickup truck. A cop was standing with one foot on either side of his body. The officer told him to turn over, then reached down, roughly pulled his wrists behind his back, and snapped on a pair of handcuffs. After that, things were vague. Someone knelt beside him and applied pressure to his right forearm and right thigh. They loaded him onto a gurney. They lifted him into a medevac helicopter.

Not dead. Not yet.

12

Medicine Man

The helicopter flew Brian to the Cowley Shock Trauma Center in Baltimore, where he was taken directly into surgery. Hours later, he awoke to find bandages wrapped tightly around his stomach, a cast on his right arm, a catheter in his bladder, and a tube in one of his nostrils. The damage to his intestines had made it impossible for him to eat or swallow, so he went without food for almost three weeks, which caused him to lose fifty pounds. A doctor told Brian he'd been shot three times: once in his right elbow and twice in his abdomen. (The surgeon had removed a bullet fragment from his stomach.) When he was finally able to move, they took him to the University of Maryland Medical Center. He was there for three weeks, on a ward normally reserved for prisoners.

His stomach, held together with surgical staples, was pumped around the clock and was so sensitive that even the touch of a fingertip would cause him sharp pain. One day, a nurse cut open his surgical staples, packed gauze into his stomach wound, and then came back a couple of hours later and pulled it all out again—a process that was supposed to make the wound bleed so that the flesh would start to grow back. It was intensely unpleasant.

Being shot hadn't hurt much, but the recovery was slow and arduous—especially since, averse to all medications, Brian refused the opiate-based pain relievers he'd been prescribed. For three weeks, he was completely immobilized, attached to various drains and drips, and always desperately thirsty. He begged the doctor for water. The doctor said he could have a drink, but only after he'd urinated, which Brian knew wasn't going to happen; his whole body was bone-dry. Finally, the guard left him alone for a while. Brian managed to haul himself out of bed and, despite cast, drips, drains, and catheter, dragged himself across the room to the water cooler. He filled a big plastic cup with water, drank it, then drank a second. He was instantly revived. Not long after that, the doctor got what he wanted. Brian produced a waterfall.

Christmas 1999 came and went, followed by not just a new year, but a new century. Brian didn't leave his hospital bed until a cold morning in the middle of January, when two officers from the Howard County Police Department turned up to take him into custody for questioning. He was shackled, placed in the back of a police van, and driven down to headquarters. Here, still hoping to be sent to prison, Brian waived his Miranda rights—the officers refused to give him a pen to sign the form, afraid, in light of his history, that he might use it to stab one of them. They asked him a few basic questions about his name, age, and address, then said, "Do you know why you're here today?"

"Sure. I escaped from Perkins Hospital," Brian replied. "I took a hostage. I tried to steal a car. I threatened a citizen. I got shot by police."

"Okay. Now, will you answer a few questions about these events?"

"No," Brian said.

With that, he was charged with two counts of second-degree assault for his threats to the police officers, a third count of second-degree assault on the nurse, one count of false imprisonment for taking a hostage, and one count of first-degree assault for threatening the driver of the pickup truck. He was also charged with "carrying a weapon with the intent to injure" and "escaping from confinement." He was told he'd get a letter in the mail informing him of his trial date.

Not too many patients had actually managed to escape from Perkins, and those who did were usually sent to prison rather than back to the hospital, as if fighting back against the indignities and restrictions of the hospital were adequate proof of their sanity. But Brian was sent back to Perkins, where the public defender told him that it could be as long as two years before his case was heard—and not just because there was a backlog. Before he went to court, Brian was informed, they had to find him competent to stand trial.

If things had been bad for Brian before his escape attempt, they were now far worse. He was sent all the way back to Admissions, the ward he'd been in eight years ago, when he first arrived—the ward for patients who ran the gravest risk of suicide and attempted escape. Everybody seemed to think he'd try to "elope" again, and as a compromise, he was kept in restraints, which, while permitted at Perkins, were to be used only in emergency situations and when other forms of restriction had failed. "Once you get tied down in a restraint bed, your rights go out the window," Cliff told me. Jeremy said he'd been put in restraints for doing pirouettes on the ward. "I was joking around, acting like a ballerina," he said. "They gave me an intramuscular medication and put me in four-point restraints. I was, like, 'Are you guys serious? I was just kidding around.'"

Tied down to a bed, Brian was bullied and harassed without fear of reprisal. He says the nurses ignored his requests, paying cursory attention to his injuries. When he asked for the kind of bandages they'd used to wrap his stomach at UMMC, strong, flexible adhesive dressings that could be changed easily—later, he learned these were called Montgomery straps—they said they had no idea what he was talking about. He wondered if they were feigning ignorance just to anger him or get him in trouble. If so, it worked. "He got into power struggles with the staff about his dressing changes," Dr. Stolzberg wrote in Brian's chart.

For security staff, working at Perkins was no picnic. Patients could be eccentric, irritable, paranoid, and dangerous. They'd get restless, pace up and down the halls, howl, spit, and kick. The guards were supposed to "deescalate" troublesome situations without using physical force; they weren't even allowed to lose their temper. It was hardly surprising some of them grew to hate the patients, and expressed their resentment by refusing requests to use the phone, go outside, or get a snack. While the hospital rules looked good on paper, carrying them out on the ward was simply unfeasible. You can't calm a violent schizophrenic with gentle phrases. The guards sometimes had to use force just to save themselves from serious injury.

The patients' schedules, too, looked good on paper. There were lots of activities available, but the reality was rather different. "On our ward, there are supposed to be maybe fifty-two groups throughout the week," Cliff told me. "The last time I counted, there were twenty-six groups that didn't occur, on a weekly basis. We're supposed to go outside in the morning, but we never go outside in the morning. It just never happens. There's an exercise class that a doctor is supposed to run, but he never seems to have the time."

Some nurses and guards had been at Perkins for decades and truly cared about the patients. But there were also staff members who were hostile, fearful, or just incompetent. Cliff told me he'd been given the wrong medication on four or five occasions. "They don't know what they're doing," he said. "They're rushing. . . . Nobody wants to address it. Nobody wants to say, 'This is a problem.' No one gets penalized for it. Nothing gets done. I think that's absolutely atrocious."

While recovering from his gunshot wounds, Brian had to deal

with some of the most unpleasant of the nursing and security staff. Their mistreatment of him continued even after his restraints were finally removed. He was forced to double up with another patient in a small single room fitted with two beds. Everyone else got individual and group therapy; Brian got group only. He was put back on antipsychotic medication, though he rarely laid eyes on Dr. Stolzberg, who was still his psychiatrist. When the patients went outside for their "fresh air break," Brian wasn't allowed to wear a winter coat; it could be used to hide a weapon, the nurses said. Doctors at UMMC had given him a compression belt to support his abdomen; at Perkins, he wasn't allowed to wear it. He was also told that because he was now a high security risk, he couldn't take part in voluntary activities such as cooking and gardening. To Brian, this seemed counterproductive. These were things he enjoyed. They were therapeutic; they helped build social bonds and were looked on favorably by the treatment teams. Now, because they rarely saw him off the ward, and because he'd used a weapon to take a hostage, even veteran staff members started to grow afraid of him. To recent employees, he was dangerous and frightening. He felt that new staff had been indoctrinated into believing he was a terrible menace who was ready to attack anybody at any moment.

Beside himself with frustration, Brian made a vow. Instead of relying on Perkins staff, he was going to take charge of his own recovery. After eight years at the hospital, he'd come to realize that the majority of the Perkins staff didn't have his best interests at heart. Their first priority was not making waves. He certainly couldn't rely on the hospital food, which was scarcely edible. To rebuild his stamina, he depended on the weekly carryout meals and started to exercise as soon as he could. With his stomach tightly bandaged, he began with safe and gentle movements; then, as his vigor returned, he progressed to a more strenuous routine involving push-ups, squats, and curls. He was well on the way to recovering his former strength when, one day, a guard saw him doing pull-ups on a toilet door frame and filed a report. If anyone caught him exercising again, Brian was told, he'd be back in restraints. Period.

As usual, no reason was given for the sanction. He thought they must have been afraid of what he might do if he got strong again. Or maybe it was just an arbitrary punishment. Either way, the result was the same: he got sick. Exercise, as Brian knew from his martial arts training, promotes blood flow. When he stopped working out, the scar tissue in his arm hardened; his blood couldn't get to it, and the wound became infected. He awoke one morning shivering and feverish. At the Perkins medical clinic, the physician gave him some antibiotics and told him the infection would probably go away over the weekend. Brian refused to take the pills. He knew his condition was serious. He insisted on going to a "real" hospital. It took days for him to get the Perkins staff to take his situation seriously and make him an appointment with an outside doctor. By the time the appointment arrived, the infection had spread through his torso and into his right arm.

"You've got blood poisoning. We'll have to operate on you to open up the scar," the doctor at UMMC told him matter-of-factly.

By the time Brian reached the operating table, he was told that if the infection had reached the artery, they'd have to amputate.

As he slipped into unconsciousness, he wondered what it would be like to wake up and find himself with only one arm. He imagined filing suit against the hospital, using the payout to fund a private psychiatrist, hiring a dream team of top attorneys, getting released, and then going to live on a beach in Tahiti. You don't need two arms to lie in the sun.

When Brian woke up, his body was intact.

His first reaction was disappointment.

By March, he was well enough to hang out in the dayroom with the other patients and catch up on Perkins gossip. Most of the talk was about Hanif Gopalani, Brian's old psychiatrist from Ward 8. Rumor had it the doctor had been exhibiting some odd behavior. He'd turn up late to appointments and miss important meetings. He wrote strange notes in patients' files. He'd spend group therapy sessions boasting about his prowess at competitive Ping-Pong. He'd appear on the ward unexpectedly, red-eyed, with bad breath. He seemed to be smitten with Susan Steinberg, who, as the assistant attorney general for the Maryland Department of Health and Mental Hygiene, was the hospital's legal representative. Steinberg was in her midthirties and very attractive, with shoulder-length black hair and creamy white skin, but her demeanor was stern, even fierce. She wasn't the type to take pity on an infatuated doctor.

One day, Brian was pacing up and down the hall where a lot of psychiatrists had their offices; he was waiting to see Dr. Stolzberg. Each office door contained a small glass window. As Brian walked past Dr. Gopalani's office, he couldn't help noticing that the doctor had a paper target from a shooting range pinned to the wall. It was studded with bullet holes. Brian knew there was a shooting range not far from Perkins. He thought that perhaps the doctor went target shooting on his lunch break.

A couple of days later, Brian ran into Dr. Gopalani in the Silver Wing.

"I noticed you have a target in your office, Doctor," Brian said to him. "What kind of gun do you use?"

The psychiatrist had a strong Indian accent and a flat, monotonous voice. "I beg your pardon?" he replied.

"The target in your office," Brian said. "Looks like you're a pretty good shot."

"I'm sorry," Dr. Gopalani said, "I have no idea what you're talking about." He walked away shaking his head, as if tired of dealing with lunatics.

This wasn't the first time Dr. Gopalani had exhibited bizarre behavior. His nickname among patients was "Medicine Man," derived from a period a few years earlier, when it was rumored that everyone on Dr. Gopalani's ward had started twitching and jerking, as if they'd been struck by some kind of epidemic. Others would drool, stare, gesticulate, or fidget. Some started to twitch and grimace, and some would stand motionless all day, their bodies frozen in curious poses. Brian's friend Alvin Ledger had been on Medicine Man's ward at the time. His conclusion at the time was that Dr. Gopalani had to be conducting some kind of experiment.

Alvin told Brian that Medicine Man had ordered all his patients to be taken off the drugs they'd been prescribed to counteract the side effects of their antipsychotics. While it wasn't uncommon for psychiatrists at Perkins to "deprescribe" medications they felt were no longer useful, they generally did so slowly and selectively, to avoid the difficulties of withdrawal. No one had ever known a psychiatrist to stop everyone's medication completely and unilaterally, the way Medicine Man had done. Patients on the ward kept wondering what he was thinking. They speculated, like Alvin, that he was carrying out some kind of bizarre private experiment—and using the patients as his guinea pigs.

Brian thought Medicine Man had to be very disturbed, even dangerous, given that he might have been keeping a loaded gun in his office. He didn't understand why the doctor's colleagues weren't alarmed. Every time Brian saw Medicine Man walking down the hall chatting casually with his colleagues, he always wondered why nobody seemed concerned that this doctor, who was clearly unhinged, was still allowed to practice medicine. If the psychiatrists at Perkins were so skilled at recognizing mental illness, why, Brian wondered, couldn't they see it in Medicine Man? Or did they know he was nuts and just not care?

Ironically, as Dr. Gopalani was taking his patients off their medications, Dr. Stolzberg wanted Brian to take more. When he refused, Brian, for the first time, was "paneled," which meant that his case was assessed by the hospital's Clinical Forensic Review Board. The board ruled that Brian could be medicated against his will. Brian was hardly surprised, but he wasn't going to submit without a fight. He filed an appeal of the decision with the Howard County Circuit Court.

His resistance to medication wasn't arbitrary. No matter how many different antipsychotics they put him on, Brian never felt the medications helped him at all; they only seemed to cloud his brain and knock him out. His psychiatrists disagreed, arguing that the medications helped to calm his symptoms, although it was never clear to Brian what those symptoms were supposed to be.

Antipsychotics are invariably prescribed (often for a lifetime) to anyone with a diagnosis of schizophrenia—even if their illness took the form of a "single episode," like Brian's, but was now "in remission"—but not all psychiatrists agree that antipsychotics are useful, even for those showing signs of psychosis. Dr. Thomas Insel, former director of the National Institute of Mental Health, has publicly stated that in his experience, some individuals with schizophrenia do better with less medication over the long run; and schizophrenia researcher Dr. Nancy Andreasen has claimed that antipsychotic medication does little to help psychosis and may even cause brain atrophy. The psychiatric researchers Germán E. Berríos, Rogelio Luque, and José M. Villagrán, in their 2003 paper "Schizophrenia: A Conceptual History," point out that when it comes to schizophrenia, the latest form of treatment is always assumed to be the most appropriate, but there's no reason for this to be the case. They remind us that "no crucial experiment has ever been carried out to demonstrate that 'latest means truest' or that 'high usage' constitutes adequate evidence for validity."

Brian realized that, for many patients at Perkins, antipsychotics were vital. He'd talked to patients there who said that medication had definitely helped them get better, but for most, what really helped them was simply being around other people.

"For most of the day, you can be let in and out of your room, but you can't stay in there," Jeremy told me. "It gets you used to being around other people and interacting with them on a long-term basis."

The company of others is usually a grounding influence, helping us keep up a relationship with the objective, external world. Too much isolation can be self-destructive. If we're always alone, even if we like it that way, we can start to lose perspective. Being around other people is a constant reminder that we're human beings just like everybody else, neither irrelevant nor exceptional, and that we're all in it together.

Many patients, before coming to Perkins, had isolated themselves in one way or another. Even if they lived in the family home or in a college dorm, they usually had the opportunity to retreat into a private world, at least from time to time. At Perkins, however, patients were closely monitored not just by hospital staff and clinicians, but also by other patients. They couldn't retreat into delusions—at least, not for long. While they were given a certain amount of privacy, they were also forced, often reluctantly, to develop social habits and routines. Simply being around other people, according to many patients, helped them far more than any therapy or drugs.

As punishment—he believed, for refusing medication—Brian was moved back to maximum security. He was angered by the "transfer note" Dr. Stolzberg had written in his file to justify the move. He considered it unwarranted and prejudicial. In the note, Stolzberg gave Brian's diagnosis as "paranoid schizophrenia, polysubstance abuse." (In fact, apart from the medications his doctors insisted he take, he hadn't used drugs in thirteen years, but he knew his past history would always be a part of his diagnosis.) He was said to exhibit "hostile speech, suspiciousness, hyper-religiosity, fearfulness, uncooperativeness," and "poor problem-solving." "He has delusions about the nation of islam," the doctor added. Part of Brian's diagnosis was "suicidality," but Dr. Stolzberg seemed skeptical. "He admits that he did ask the police to kill him after his escape," the psychiatrist wrote. "However, he had not done anything to seriously threaten his recovery when he had a huge open abdominal wound."

The "huge open abdominal wound" had healed, however, and

Brian had now recovered from his injuries. As Dr. Stolzberg noted, "he has had some loss of mobility of his right elbow, but appears to have no other permanent impairment." The doctor also added—without referring to evidence—that "I have no reason to doubt that he has the most violent fantasies of homicide and suicide but he is unable to discuss them." Perhaps the deepest cut was the final sentence: "He has had one 'migraine' that responded after several hours to 4 tylenol tabs."

Those quotation marks around the word *migraine* made Brian feel that Dr. Stolzberg was belittling his condition, making it seem like merely griping or whining, possibly even malingering. Putting those quotes around something he'd said was a kind of implicit judgment, an example of the word juggling that went on all the time at Perkins. What irritated Brian the most about Dr. Stolzberg's report, however, was its patronizing tone, as if the doctor understood Brian's motives and desires much better than he understood them himself. From Dr. Stolzberg's perspective, "suspiciousness" and "fearfulness" weren't natural reactions to being locked on a psych ward for eight years, but symptoms of a mental illness. And Brian knew that once something had been noted in his file, it was permanently on the record. There was no arguing with it. Moreover, he had no control over who got to look at his chart, as the HIPAA laws allowed doctors to share patient information and records with other doctors. As a result, Brian had no idea what kind of "symptomatic" language and behavior people involved in his case might be looking out for.

In addition, those who made the most crucial judgments and had the most power at Perkins, the psychiatrists, were those who spent the least amount of time with patients. For patients, your importance in the hierarchy could be determined by the length of time you had to wait to see your doctor compared to the duration of time you were seen. The longest waits were for the ten-minute visits with the psychiatrists, each of whom had around thirty patients on their ward. For many of the doctors, hospital work was only one part of their job, and meeting each one of their Perkins patients every week for an hour would have been completely inefficient, dragging them into a mass of circumstantial detail. Instead, they'd quickly glance at the patient's chart in a ten-minute meeting, or perhaps they'd get a quick debriefing from a nurse, therapist, or social worker. At Perkins, patient contact was not a significant priority.

Over the eight years he'd been at the hospital, Brian had learned that the insights contained in medical notes, psychiatric evaluations, and risk assessments were limited and could be skewed in the direction of whatever the doctors wanted to prove. True, interviews and tests could give the psychiatrist a sense of someone's mental capabilities, an idea of how clear their thoughts were and even how they were feeling—whether they were angry, depressed, irrational, obsessed, or resentful. What tests couldn't show was why someone was feeling that way, whether they'd felt the same yesterday, or whether they'd feel the same way tomorrow. They were a snapshot in time, a picture of a patient at the moment they talked to the doctor or took the test.

If a patient was taking a new medication, an assessment might show how it was affecting their mood and thinking. It might show whether they had the capacity for violence, but not whether they'd act on that capacity or, if they did, whether the violence would be directed toward other people or themselves. Plus, for the assessment to be effective, patients had to be open and honest—and at Perkins, as Brian had discovered, honesty was in short supply given that anything you said could (and usually would) be used against you.

After reading Dr. Stolzberg's report, Brian realized that the possibility of his being released was growing increasingly distant. If he was becoming guarded and hostile, he thought, who could blame him? He felt bullied by the hospital staff, and his "treatment conversations" were worse than useless. To add insult to injury, his attempt to commit suicide by cop (or, if that failed, to be sent to prison) was consistently misinterpreted by his doctors, who connected his "elopement" with his religious beliefs, concluding that he'd tried to "elope" from Perkins because he thought the end of the world was coming. A psychology risk assessment written in 2002 by a psychiatrist named Michael Sweda noted that Brian "believed the world would end in 2000 and that it was his responsibility to lead his people to the Amazon where they would be safe" because he "believed that he was one of two prophets destined to lead the Israelites through 'The Great Tribulation.'" This information, Dr. Sweda added, had been obtained from "a peer," meaning another patient on Brian's ward, whose secondhand account of hearsay was apparently deemed reliable evidence.

Yet the psychiatrist's confusion was not completely ungrounded. Brian did believe in the End Time; he had made predictions about Christians being attacked by the Nation of Islam; and at other times, he'd talked about moving to some distant, isolated place like Alaska (or a jungle) if he were ever released. And his reluctance to talk openly about his religious beliefs may also have fueled speculation.

Because religious faith exists outside the scientific domain, psychiatrists at Perkins generally regarded it as pathological unless it was shared by others. Religious experiences that were widely recognized—be they Christianity, Islam, Rastafarianism, Scientology, or voodoo—were classed as "genuine" and supportive of recovery, unlike idiosyncratic spiritual experiences, which were "delusions." Because very few of the psychiatrists at Perkins were familiar with the details of different religious doctrines, patients could, if necessary, request the presence of a spiritual mediator (usually a minister, priest, or traditional healer) when questions about their beliefs arose. But Brian had developed his interpretation of the Bible inside the hospital, with little outside advice or support, which meant his religious beliefs fell into the category of "delusions" (even though they'd been endorsed by the pastor from Watchman Ministries).

These "delusions" were held against him during his appearance before the CRFB on May 9, 2000. During these proceedings, Assistant State's Attorney Susan Steinberg, testifying on behalf of the Maryland Department of Mental Health and Hygiene, told the court that Brian "held false beliefs. . . . He's paranoid about staff. . . . He has also been paranoid about the end of the world." She argued that "the hospital believes he needs this amount of medication, and with the medication, he has improved. . . . There is no indication in the medication record of him suffering any side effects."

This statement was true. Perhaps there was nothing in Brian's file about the medication's side effects because they weren't unusual or unexpected—all patients taking antipsychotics were lethargic, flat, and numb—but they were still intensely uncomfortable. Nonetheless, the judge upheld the hospital's decision to continue requiring Brian to take drugs against his will. Discouraged and frustrated, he started doing something he'd never done before, although he'd often been tempted. He started "cheeking" his meds, pretending to take the pills but slipping them into his cheek as he swallowed, and then spitting them out afterward, into the toilet. A lot of patients did it. There was a knack to it. Once you learned how, it was simple.

Cheeking his meds restored some of Brian's self-esteem, and his spirits were lifted further when he learned that the hospital's clinical director was going to come to the ward to explain what had happened to Dr. Gopalani, who'd been conspicuously absent from the hospital for almost two months now. The clinical director at the time was Alice Shannon-Stolzberg, wife of Brian's current psychiatrist and nemesis, Stephen Stolzberg, and when she appeared on Brian's ward, she managed to look simultaneously dignified and sheepish.

Using a mash-up of corporate euphemisms and psychiatric jargon, Dr. Shannon-Stolzberg announced that "Dr. Gopalani would be taking a temporary leave of absence from the hospital" due to a "nervous breakdown."

A handful of patients, including Brian, had trouble keeping a straight face. They already knew what had happened to Dr. Gopalani; they'd been following the story in the *Baltimore Sun* and making small cash bets on what the "official" explanation would be.

"That's the first time I'd ever heard anybody at Perkins use the term *nervous breakdown*," Brian told me with a grin. "Normally, they're really careful to make a detailed diagnosis from the *DSM*, but nobody was going to stand up and admit the guy was a paranoid schizophrenic."

In mid-January 2001, the *Baltimore Sun* reported that Assistant State's Attorney Susan Steinberg had been granted a restraining order against the forty-eight-year-old Hanif Gopalani, who'd been stalking her for at least six months after she refused to go on a date with him. The psychiatrist had repeatedly turned up at Ms. Steinberg's home to tell her that he loved her. When the restraining order was filed, Dr. Gopalani had already been suspended twice by Perkins for lateness, absenteeism, lack of attention, and unprofessional conduct, as well as for his harassment of Steinberg. Despite the restraining order, the doctor's pursuit of Steinberg continued, and she filed for a second order ten days later.

According to the *Sun*, between the date the second restraining order was filed and the date on which Dr. Gopalani was finally arrested, he contacted Steinberg at least twenty-two times. On February 9, 2001, he was charged with stalking, harassment, and the violation of a protective order. And still he didn't stop. Between his release on bail and his next arrest on March 19, he tried to contact Ms. Steinberg an additional thirty-one times. He was finally arrested when Steinberg's mother called the police to complain about Dr. Gopalani constantly ringing the doorbell of the home where she lived with her husband, the former lieutenant governor of Maryland. When officers got to the scene, they discovered the psychiatrist hiding in Mrs. Steinberg's shrubbery; he was held on $100,000 bail and charged with harassment, violating a protective order, and trespassing.

The *Baltimore Sun* also revealed that, according to court records, Hanif Gopalani had a history of mental illness long before he began working at Clifton T. Perkins Hospital. In 1995, psychiatrist Larry B. Silver testified that Gopalani suffered from a "serious psychiatric disorder." In 1997, he was described as "delusional." In September

1998, he was reported to be "paranoid in his thinking," and by October, according to Gopalani's own psychiatrist, he had begun to experience "loss of reality" in his personal life. Brian's suspicions were confirmed: the doctor had been dangerous and unhinged.

After his 2001 arrest, Gopalani was examined by a psychiatrist who found that he had a serious mental disorder, was incompetent to practice medicine, and needed around-the-clock supervision and long-term psychiatric treatment. "His impaired cognition raised serious questions about his accumulated knowledge and skills in psychiatry," the evaluator's report concluded. "He needs to be incarcerated and kept away from the public." As for the stalking charges, Gopalani was found "not criminally responsible."

"The psychiatrists at Perkins are supposed to be these great experts in recognizing and understanding mental illness," Brian said, "and they couldn't even tell that one of their own doctors was a paranoid schizophrenic. He was working here for years, and he was clinically insane. If he hadn't been a Perkins psychiatrist, he'd have been sent to the Admissions Ward—his own ward—that's where they should have sent him. But they sent him to a regional hospital instead."

Still, as Brian observed, even at the regional hospital, Dr. Gopalani would surely run into patients he himself had originally declared mentally incompetent. It was satisfying for Brian to think that the doctor would be getting a taste of his own medicine.

That, at least, was a small dose of justice.

13

Shadow of a Doubt

Brian's next psych evaluation was conducted by a doctor named Timothy Wisniewski. Brian had never met him before, but that was normal for evaluations of this kind, which, to be completely objective, were often administered by a doctor brought in from outside the hospital. Again, Brian was put through a set of structured interviews and a battery of tests to "determine his level of intellectual functioning and the degree to which he is currently experiencing active psychoses," and to determine "whether there was any evidence of the presence of a personality disorder." Because Brian had been cheeking his meds for the last six months, he was especially curious to see his test results.

The evaluation consisted of an interview followed by a series of tests: the Minnesota Multiphasic Personality Inventory, the Wechsler Adult Intelligence Scale, the Wide Range Achievement Test, the Bender Visual-Motor Gestalt Test, and the Rorschach ink blot test. The ordeal took all day. Brian felt relieved when it was over. He was exhausted, but the evaluation had gone well, he thought—and to an extent, Dr. Wisniewski agreed. In his report, the psychiatrist described Brian as "always very cooperative with the examiner," adding that he "displayed high levels of motivation towards the completion of tests administered." The doctor also noted appreciatively that Brian "maintained a sense of humor" but "always took the assessment tasks, per se, very seriously."

The final score on Brian's IQ test was 113, which was considered "high average," and higher than 81 percent of test takers. He had a significant strength in "long-term memory" (which was something I had noticed on many occasions). On the IQ test he'd taken seven years earlier, when he first arrived at Perkins, he'd scored a 94. His new score was a significant improvement. In his report, Dr. Wisniewski attributed this change to the "cognitive restoration" that had occurred during Brian's "treatment regime," returning him to his former level of functioning. His Rorschach ink blot test profile was also positive; in fact, according to Dr. Wisniewski, it contained nothing other than "what one might expect to find in the RIT profiles of most people."

All this looked hopeful for Brian, but the good news ended there. Dr. Wisniewski described Brian as paranoid ("he believes there is a concerted effort on the part of the African American staff to make his life difficult") and even dangerous ("he says that he may be forced to do something very drastic to get out of [Perkins] . . . specifically, he mentioned that he might need to seriously hurt a staff member in order for [Perkins] to send him to prison"). He was concerned Brian was hiding things from him, lying, or cheating. He found the results of Brian's vocabulary test "suspicious" because "his answers demonstrated a relatively high concordance to the suggested answers in the manual"—in other words, because Brian knew what they meant. As a result, "in an attempt to test for the presence of coaching," the doctor had decided to examine Brian further by "administering" to him "three additional words judged to be in the moderate-to-difficult range": *grandeur, epitaph*, and *efficacious*. (Brian knew the first two but not the third.) "It was concluded from this informal test that it was possible for Mr. Bech-told to be defining the words based on a real verbal fluency instead of an inflated fluency obtained through coaching," Wisniewski admitted begrudgingly.

Overall, he noted, Brian's test results "presented little psychomet-ric evidence for the existence of psychotic processes." Despite this, his original diagnosis of paranoid schizophrenia remained unchanged precisely *because* Brian's results showed he had no mental illness. This was regarded as proof that the patient was hiding his psychosis. From talking to staff members and other patients about Brian, Dr. Wisniewski had found it reasonable to conclude that "Mr. Bechtold was sufficiently defended and practiced during the testing to pro-duce the observed muted responses." He admitted that he gave more weight to what other patients had said privately about Brian (which he called "clinical evidence") than to Brian's own answers and test results. ("Additional validity is given to the clinical evidence because it was garnered in a surreptitious manner.")

Based on the history described in Brian's assessment from six years earlier, Dr. Wisniewski gave him an Axis II diagnosis of "antisocial personality disorder." Rather than mental illnesses like schizophrenia, which can be regulated with medication, personal-ity disorders are believed to be innate, present from birth or a very young age, and therefore incurable. But Brian's evaluation from 1994 hadn't contained an Axis II diagnosis. If he had antisocial personality disorder—which meant, essentially, that he was a psychopath—why had no one noticed it seven years earlier or when he was sent to the psych hospital as a teenager? Was his diagnosis based on the fact that he sometimes questioned the ward rules and because of his reluctance to take medication?

Brian suspected that Dr. Wisniewski's idea that he was antisocial was somehow related to his religious convictions. "The motivation for his escape attempt," Dr. Wisniewski wrote in his final report, "was purported to be connected to his delusionary beliefs about the end of the earth and God's desire for him to flee to some wilderness area to live off the land until the judgement period has ended."This must have been some of the "evidence" the doctor had gathered "surreptitiously" (presumably by asking other patients about him), Brian realized, as he no longer discussed his religious beliefs with psychiatrists for fear of being considered "hyper-religious." He'd been especially careful not to mention religion to Dr. Wisniewski, who admitted as much in his report:

> Mr. Bechtold is extremely well-defended so it is not known for certain whether he still entertains these delusionary beliefs. He will go so far as to admit that he is both deeply religious and that his religious beliefs are not widely held by most people, but he will not elaborate further in these areas.

It could have been the books he liked to read, Brian thought, that had given Dr. Wisniewski the idea that he'd wanted to escape from Perkins to "flee to the wilderness." "When asked what specific book titles he would be interested in reading," the doctor noted, "he specifically mentioned titles that involved the topics of 'The Great Tribulation' and 'homesteading.' These two subject areas deal with the end of the earth and how to live off the land. This information is consistent with the content of his aforementioned delusionary beliefs, and might be an indicator these delusions remain prominent." Brian's "current book selection interests," Dr. Wisniewski concluded, were in fact "sub-clinical manifestations of his previously florid psychotic symptoms."

This seemed a stretch. Plenty of people were "deeply religious" and interested in living off the land, Brian thought. He wondered, *Would Dr. Wisniewski have regarded all them as delusional?*

On the bright side, Brian finally got a new doctor that year. She came from Calcutta, and her name was Srirupa Ghoshtagore. While she had her drawbacks, Dr. Ghoshtagore was a vast improvement over Dr. Stolzberg. Brian was still on maximum security. Nonetheless, Dr. Ghoshtagore allowed him to taper down his antipsychotic medication. Although he hadn't been swallowing his pills for some time, it made him feel a little better to realize he was no longer considered psychotic. By August 2002, he didn't even have to cheek his meds anymore: he was officially no longer required to take them.

That same month, Brian left Perkins for the first time since his escape attempt. He was taken to Howard County Circuit Court in the suburb of Ellicott City, about half an hour's drive from the hospital, to stand trial for his escape attempt. The case was covered by Lisa Goldberg in the *Baltimore Sun*. Brian told Judge Diane Leasure that "he'd tried to escape because he wanted to force the hospital authorities to send him to prison," Goldberg wrote. "He compared his situation to the mental patients in Ken Kesey's *One Flew Over the Cuckoo's Nest*." She described Brian as "subdued" and "matter-of-fact," although she noted that he also "issued threats," telling the judge that "doctors at the institution do not treat his migraine headaches and that he may one day 'become irrational' as a result of the 'suffering.'"

Perkins staff and security guards who were called to testify at the hearing also described Brian as quiet and subdued. They called him "taciturn" and "introverted," adding that he'd shown no signs of violence during the seven years leading up to the escape, although the hospital's clinical director, Alice Shannon-Stolzberg, saw this as evidence of Brian's latent dangerousness. "This man obviously has a desperation going on that he kept from us," she said. After hearing all the evidence, Judge Leasure found Brian guilty of second-degree assault and a weapons violation. She did not, however, send him to prison. "In this particular case," she said, "I fear that by imposing a prison sentence, I am rewarding Mr. Bechtold." Instead, she sentenced him to thirteen years' probation and sent him back to Perkins.

Brian was disappointed but resigned. He'd been at Perkins for over ten years now. He assumed things couldn't possibly get worse.

He was wrong.

Nothing changed; that was the problem. The stasis became unbearable. Every day was the same. It finally started to grind him down. Every day, he woke up to the same cinder block walls, institutional gray paint, fluorescent lights, and stackable plastic chairs. He could no longer stand breathing stale air, facing deliberate unkindness. He lost interest in going outside. Everything had become endless and pointless.

Being on maximum security at that time was, Brian told me, like being in hell, not in the noble sense, as in war, but an insidious, monotonous hell where the battles were fought with words: stalling tactics in the form of court proceedings, psychiatric reports, and risk assessments. When, in 2002, Brian asked to be moved onto medium security again, another assessment was filed, this time by a doctor named Marc J. Tabackman, who gave Brian the worst report he'd had since coming to Perkins thirteen years earlier. Dr. Tabackman concluded his findings with a list of all the ways Brian had "exhibited poor clinical functioning." These included:

> Anti-authority attitude (derision of hospital staff and psychiatry); poor social skills and psychosocial adjustment (disruptive in groups); lack of insight into illness (denies mental illness, projects blame for his lengthy hospital stay onto others); poor institutional adjustment (maladaptive, rule-breaking, testing limits); guardedness (with treatment team); poor treatment compliance (refuses psychiatric and somatic medications); poor response to stress (copes by maladaptive plan to live in isolation); impulsivity (poor planning for future); poor symptomatic remission of major psychiatric disorder (schizophrenia); threat control override symptoms (delusional perception that staff "provoke" him); pathologically deviant thoughts

and fantasies (homicidal, suicidal, hyper-religious; staff is "afraid of me," games have element of "magic"); escape/elopement risk (attempted escape, preoccupation with leaving hospital).

Reading over this list, Brian was baffled. To him, it didn't seem unreasonable that after spending over a decade on a psychiatric ward, he "planned to live in isolation" when, if ever, he was released. And because it had been almost ten years since he'd exhibited any signs of schizophrenia, he saw no reason to accept that he displayed "major psychosis" when there was no evidence for it, especially when he was totally functional without medication. It also seemed natural that he "blamed others" for his "continued incarceration." After all, it wasn't his choice to be a patient at Perkins.

He'd never been one to give up a fight, but now Brian found himself thinking seriously about suicide. It seemed to be the only way out. And while he didn't want to die in Perkins, what was death but a form of escape?

Adding to his misery, he was afflicted by an unexplained physical malady. He got tired easily. He lost his appetite. His vision was blurred, and his eyes itched. In April 2005, he was taken to the University of Maryland Medical Center where he was diagnosed with a type of persistent eye inflammation called granulomatous uveitis. While he was at the hospital, he also had a routine chest X-ray, and the results, which came a few days later, showed something unexpected: what appeared to Brian to be a tiny smudge on the X-ray film was, according to the doctor, a shadow on his lung. It could be cancer, they told him.

Brian hoped they were right.

It wouldn't be an easy death, he realized, but he couldn't see any other way out. After being returned to Perkins following his escape attempt, he'd lost hope of ever being released. Even a painful death from lung cancer would be better than the slow death he was currently going through. If he had cancer, he decided, he'd refuse treatment.

He was scheduled for an MRI, but he told Dr. Ghoshtagore he wasn't going. He had cancer or he didn't. Either way, he'd know soon enough.

But it wasn't that simple. They weren't going to let him die.

According to his psychiatrists, Brian wasn't mentally competent to make his own decision in a matter of such grave importance. They said that by virtue of his mental illness, he was innately incapable of choice. Brian found this proposition ridiculous. Like anyone else suffering from a physical illness, surely he had the right to refuse treatment. He knew the implications of such a refusal, but he also believed he should have the ultimate decision about what happened to his body.

No one could make him change his mind, so the matter went to court—and as one of the patients told me, "the court listens to the hospital, for the most part." The Department of Mental Health and Hygiene filed a petition arguing that Brian Bechtold "lacked the understanding or capacity to make responsible decisions about health care because of a mental disability," and given that he had "no family or friends willing or able to act as a surrogate decision-maker," the State of Maryland should allow Clifton T. Perkins Hospital Center to have guardianship "for the purposes of giving or withholding consent for health care, including the administration of medications."

Brian demanded a trial. He thought he could convince a jury that he was in his right mind, that his desire not to be treated was rational and justified. The trial was scheduled for December 5, 2005, six years to the day after his escape attempt.

Meanwhile, on maximum security, things went on as before. Brian, as usual, was the subject of rumors. First, he was accused of being a stalker. A security guard told Brian's treatment team that he'd been "lingering in the area after attending groups that were run by a specific staff person." Brian knew the guard was referring to Kim Roberts, the volunteer coordinator, but he hadn't been stalking her; he'd just been waiting to speak to her. He liked Kim; they had a lot in common. True, he found her attractive—good-looking women were a rare sight at Perkins—but mostly she was easy to get along with. He insisted he'd never stalk Kim—or any other woman, for that matter. As usual, his attempts to set the record straight were ignored, and "suspicious lingering" went down in his file.

He wanted to show his treatment team he wasn't threatening or dangerous, so the next time they met, he asked for advice. It would help, his therapist told him, if he stopped being "isolated and with-drawn" and involved himself in more "pro-social activities." Taking his therapist's advice, he joined the annual Christmas decoration competition, volunteering to brighten the ward by drawing a Nativity scene on the windows in crayon. This, too, was held against him. A note appeared in his file describing his Virgin Mary as "distorted," with "piercing eyes and huge pointed breasts."

No one else had said anything about the picture; when Brian asked a few of the other patients if they thought his Madonna was "distorted," they all said she looked like any other woman. Again, Brian's attempts to accommodate his treatment team had backfired. He just couldn't win.

14

Thought Crimes

One of Brian's closest friends at Perkins was a patient named Leonard Dunmore, whose father had worked at Harry Diamond Laboratories, an army research, development, and test facility in Adelphi, Maryland, where Brian's father had also briefly worked. Leonard had inherited his father's interest in military weapons, particularly explosives, and before being sent to Perkins, he used to like experimenting with homemade bombs. He was committed to the hospital in 1983, at the age of twenty-one, after breaking into the Maryland Vocational Rehabilitation Center carrying five homemade pipe bombs. He took twelve hostages and called a local radio station demanding they play his favorite hits. The bombs were defused safely by police, and no one was hurt.

When the pair first met, Dunmore had already been in Perkins for almost twenty years, and Brian could tell he was very smart.

A night owl like Brian, Leonard slept by day and stayed up in the evening reading books on calculus and electronics. During the two decades he'd spent at Perkins, he had filed many grievances, both internally and in the courts. He complained about the hospital's lack of vocational, recreational, educational, and therapeutic services; he complained that he wasn't allowed to read textbooks, use a calculator, receive catalogues, or take part in correspondence courses. He lodged a complaint about suffering from muscular paralysis as a result of overmedication. He complained that he had been made to stand on a scalding-hot floor for almost fifteen minutes, which had caused serious burns to his feet—wounds that then became infected because it was a month before he was allowed to be treated at an outside medical facility. (He was diagnosed with PTSD from the incident.) He filed complaints about being injected with antipsychotic medications and being put in five-point restraints as punishment for suggesting that his treating psychiatrist speak English more clearly. He also complained about being assaulted by other patients.

In April 2004, after he'd spent twenty-two years at Perkins, Dunmore's case for release was presented to a jury, who decided that, because he didn't pose a danger to himself or others, he was ready to return to the community. As soon as social services had arranged a place for him to live, a discharge plan, and Social Security benefits, a judge ordered his release from Perkins. But he wasn't released from Perkins; in fact, he remained on maximum security. When he asked his treatment team why they weren't obeying the judge's order, he was told that the major barriers preventing his release, according to their "clinical judgement," were his paranoid delusions that he was being treated unfairly and being unlawfully kept at the hospital; his depressed mood; his unauthorized, angry letters to authority figures; and his anxiety.

Dunmore complained to the Maryland Disability Law Center, and a representative from the center asked Dennis Barton, the clinical director of Perkins, why Dunmore was still being restrained. Dr.

Barton replied, "If the hospital maintains that Mr. Dunmore's clinical condition is of such severity to require treatment on the maximum-security ward, it has the duty to treat him at that level of care, regardless of any order regarding conditional release." This, Dr. Barton claimed, was "a clinical decision that is not subject to review by the judiciary."

In their habeas corpus petition demanding Leonard Dunmore's release, lawyers from the Maryland Disability Law Center were suitably outraged. "That a psychiatrist views it as his ethical duty to incarcerate a man in a maximum-security unit of a hospital is terrifying and reminiscent of the views of those powerful doctors in Nazi Germany," they argued, adding:

> Consider the situation in which the police and prosecutor are convinced with certainty that a particular person committed heinous crimes. If the jury decides that the person is "Not Guilty," the person goes free. The fact that the prosecutor and the police department believe the jury's decision to be erroneous does not give them license to detain the person further.

Leonard Dunmore was finally released from Perkins in 2006, almost two years after a jury had decided he was no danger to himself or the public. Brian, witnessing his friend's ordeal, realized the same thing could happen to him.

When he started growing weak and short of breath, he felt relieved; he thought it was a sign he had lung cancer. He was still determined to refuse treatment, and in December 2005, he returned to Howard County Circuit Court in Ellicott City to argue his case. At the hearing, Brian told the judge, Dennis Sweeney, that he wanted to represent himself, and the judge acknowledged that he had the right to do so. His shackles and handcuffs were removed for the course of the trial, but he was closely watched by a sheriff and two guards from Perkins.

Alice Ike, state's attorney for the Maryland Department of Mental Health and Hygiene, wasn't happy that the judge had allowed Brian to represent himself. Throughout the trial, she muttered to herself impatiently, sighed deeply, rolled her eyes, and objected to almost everything he said. In her opening statement, she told the jury that while Brian was certainly an intelligent person, while he might even present a reasonable defense, they shouldn't be fooled by appearances. Mental illness, she informed them, manifests itself differently in different people. Brian might "look just fine," but he'd committed a terrible crime and was suffering from a serious disease. His particular form of schizophrenia wasn't obvious to ordinary people, Ike said, but qualified and experienced psychiatrists could recognize the signs. The issue of mental capacity, she said, should be left to "the experts."

Brian didn't want the jury to get hung up on the question of mental illness. His opening statement focused, instead, on his civil rights and his intellectual capacities. He pointed out that according to the psychiatrists, he had an above-average IQ, and he promised he'd answer every question "clearly, logically, rationally, and thoroughly." He reminded them that "this country was founded on religious freedom, and freedom of self-expression," and that people who don't believe in medication for personal reasons have every right to refuse it. "If a doctor says he wants to perform a biopsy, you have every right to say, 'No, thank you,' and go on your way," Brian said. "Individuals have autonomy, and things can't be done to them without their consent."

The clarity of his case made the state's arguments seem circuitous and often tautological. The state's main witness was Angela Kim-Lee, a poised and assertive psychiatrist with a fondness for the phrase "if you will." Although she'd been treating Brian for only a month—Dr. Ghoshtagore had resigned after being assaulted by a patient—Dr. Kim-Lee said that, in her opinion, he was suffering from paranoid schizophrenia, which she defined as "impaired reality testing" and "fixed false beliefs." She described schizophrenia as "a chronic illness that has a waxing and waning course in most individuals" and said that in Brian's case, it had first appeared when he was in his late teens. She recounted some of the things Brian had said to the police after turning himself in—that he was being "followed by agents of the devil," that he "kept his urine in jars to ward away evil"—and told the jury that he'd tried to escape from Perkins because "he believed the world would end in 2000 and it was his responsibility to lead his people out of the hospital into the Amazon." Currently, he held a number of "paranoid delusional beliefs," she said, which included the following: "that the staff are harassing him, targeting him, dominate him, that no matter how well he does, staff will continue to illegally hold him in the hospital for ever, that he does not have a mental illness and does not need medication." She also described him as suffering from "chronic denial" about his diagnosis, and said he was "non-compliant, and will only accept medication in limited doses." She characterized Brian as "guarded, paranoid, and not forthcoming," adding that "he has periods where he is extremely irritable, rambles in a disorganized fashion when under stress, and once stuffed his ears with toilet paper for an unknown reason."

Brian was indignant. As usual, the source of his behavior was his "mental illness" and not the environment around him. He'd stuffed his ears with toilet paper because he couldn't sleep—two patients at the other end of the hall wouldn't stop talking, laughing, and slamming doors—and he wasn't allowed to have earplugs or cotton balls. Asking the other patients to be quiet had made no difference. In Brian's view, cramming his ears with paper had been a desperate measure—the toilet paper at Perkins wasn't exactly soft—and in his frustration, he'd pushed it so far into his ears that it had become impacted. He had to be taken to an outside hospital to have it removed.

In his cross-examination of Dr. Kim-Lee, Brian questioned her statement that paranoid schizophrenics "wax and wane" in their illness. Privately, he was shocked that a psychiatrist could look at him and see simply another schizophrenic, no different from others at Perkins. In Brian's experience, the other schizophrenic patients at Perkins were, for the most part, seriously ill. Some were catatonic, others incoherent and delusional, unable to take part in the ordinary back-and-forth of rational conversation. But Dr. Kim-Lee insisted that a patient could have a very severe case of schizophrenia while appearing unimpaired "to the average person." She continued:

> There are some schizophrenics who appear very disorganized, very disheveled, and behave inappropriately outwardly. They may be laughing. They may be talking to themselves or acting in a bizarre manner. . . . I think the key issue for understanding schizophrenia in an individual is in understanding what their thought content is, and Mr. Bechtold's thought content, if you spend time talking to him about issues related to his delusions, it becomes evident that his thought content is delusional, that he has paranoid persecutory beliefs that infiltrate his thoughts.

Brian grilled the doctor on her claim that what made someone mentally ill was their "thought content," even if it had no effect on their behavior. He asked how she knew that a person had "inappropriate thought content," and Dr. Kim-Lee replied that this would be obvious from their words and behavior.

Brian: Would you say, then, that the only way to confirm somebody has schizophrenia is by their actions and communications?

Dr. Kim-Lee: No.

Brian: How would you test somebody outside of their actions and communications to determine if they had schizophrenia?

Dr. Kim-Lee: As I mentioned, there are a number of things that go into diagnosing a patient or an individual with schizophrenia. In addition to observing their actions and speaking to the

individual about their thought content, also, a prudent psychiatric physician would also refer to or utilize collateral sources
of information—family members, friends, prior records, and
so forth.

Brian: So, Dr. Lee, when you refer to interviewing family members, friends, and people that know this alleged schizophrenic,
they would also be basing their assessment on how they act and
how they're communicating. There's no other test, other than
the person's actions and communication?

Dr. Kim-Lee: It's true that family members often rely on their
interactions with the individual, yes.

Brian: That would be the only way to determine if someone had
paranoid schizophrenia, is that correct?

Dr. Kim-Lee: I'm sorry, what would be the only way?

Brian: Based on a person's actions or communications.

Dr. Kim-Lee: It's not just based on their actions and communications.

Brian: What else is there?

Dr. Kim-Lee: It's based on . . . a number of . . . other sources of
information which I guess you could, you could say . . . I see
your point, that it's based on other collateral forms of observation, other actions and behavior.

Brian: Actions and behavior. There's no other way to prove somebody has paranoid schizophrenia.

Ms. Ike: Objection, your honor. This has been asked and answered
and asked and answered, like, three times.

Judge: Well, I'll let the doctor finish up her answer.

Dr. Kim-Lee: There is no test, if you will, for paranoid schizophrenia.

Brian then asked what evidence Dr. Kim-Lee could provide to
demonstrate that he wasn't mentally competent to refuse medical treatment. Evidence of his mental illness, she suggested, was his refusal of
treatment:

In terms of actions, his beliefs, or his paranoid thinking, has manifested behaviorally in his refusal to accept antipsychotic medication, his lack of co-operation with the treatment team in discussing his thought-content, the fact that he's guarded, suspicious. As I mentioned before, one of the hallmarks of schizophrenia, the paranoid type, is a tendency to misinterpret the motives of others. He has chronically misinter-preted the intentions of the staff at the hospital. He has repeatedly refused to go to somatic clinics . . . he's refused to accept treatment for evaluation of his medical issues. Again, he regards it as just another way for the staff to dominate and control him.

The second witness for the state was Ms. Cynthia Shinaberry, a Perkins social worker. When she was asked for evidence of Brian's mental illness, Shinaberry gave examples: he claimed "the hospital staff were mentally ill," and he "stuffed paper in his ears to the point where he had to be sent out to University Hospital because I believe the paper was impacted down in his ears." During cross-examination, Brian questioned her about this incident:

Brian: And did you have a conversation with Brian Bechtold about why he did that?

Ms. Shinaberry: Yes, I did.

Brian: And did Brian Bechtold state that there are a number of patients that keep him awake at night by making noises and slamming doors?

Ms. Shinaberry: What I recall from the conversation was that at nighttime, you could hear the nursing staff talking at the nurses' station, which was at the other end of the ward from your room, and that it was hard for you to sleep at night, hearing the nursing staff talk.

Brian: Would it be unusual for somebody to plug their ears at night in order to drown out noise?

Ms. Ike: Objection.

Judge: Sustained. Next question.

Brian: You said that Brian Bechtold claimed that some of the staff are mentally ill?

Ms. Shinaberry: Yes, I did.

Brian: Have you heard of Dr. Hanif Gopalani?

Alice Ike: Objection.

. . .

Brian: There've been statements made about Brian Bechtold having religious delusions. Can you give the jury some information about that? Does Brian Bechtold preach, or make loud statements about religion to other patients?

Ms. Shinaberry: I have never heard Mr. Bechtold preaching about religion. But Mr. Bechtold continues to do a journal for the treatment team, when we meet with him, and inside the journal, there is a lot of writing about religion, about Mohammed and Islam coming in and destroying the world, and a lot of the religious delusions come out in his writing, versus in what he says to other people.

Brian: Did the treatment team request that Brian Bechtold keep a journal?

Ms. Shinaberry: The initial request was that Mr. Bechtold write in the journal. . . . What in turn we got was the writings on the religious information and delusions that are going on in his belief system.

Brian: So, you're asking Brian Bechtold to write about his religious delusions, he's compliant with the writing, and now you're saying that this is the evidence that he's having religious delusions?

Ms. Shinaberry: What I'm saying is . . . that his thinking is more fixed, at least in his writing for the treatment team in the journal, on the religious nature of things.

The state's third witness was psychiatrist Marc J. Tabackman, who'd been on staff at Perkins for more than twenty years. Dr. Tabackman recalled Brian's admission to Perkins in 1992. He said he'd attended yearly Clinical Forensic Review Board meetings at which Brian's case had been reviewed, he'd been the treating psychologist on Brian's ward for a couple of years, and he'd performed Brian's most recent risk assessment. In Dr. Tabackman's opinion, Brian was a paranoid schizophrenic; his illness was "currently active and not in remission," and his diagnosis impeded his ability to make decisions for himself.

Finally, Brian took the stand in his own defense. The state's attorney questioned him about his diagnosis, suggesting that the fact he denied having a mental illness was itself evidence that he was mentally ill.

Ms. Ike: Do you believe you have a mental illness, Mr. Bechtold?

Brian: I don't believe I currently have a mental illness. I know that from the age of about eighteen till twenty-three I had a severe mental illness.

Ms. Ike: But you don't know if you have one now?

Brian: I'm not experiencing any kinds of symptoms. I'm not experiencing any type of thought disorder . . . I was run through the mill to find evidence of a mental illness, and when that didn't work, they said, well, we need to push and prod a little bit to make the illness come out. That's basically protocol—that if somebody's not on medication, they put them through some difficult stuff, because if you put somebody through stress, they will develop the signs and symptoms of mental illness. That's one of the things that led to a lot of the . . .

Ms. Ike: Excuse me, Mr. Bechtold. The question was whether you think you have a mental illness. Do you have a mental illness now?

Brian: No. No, I'm not having any problems today. I understand what's going on around me. I understand that I have a nodule on my lung. I understand all the questions put before me today.

Ms. Ike: Do you understand that you've been diagnosed as having schizophrenia?

Brian: Yes, I do.

Ms. Ike: Okay. And you disagree with that diagnosis . . . The diagnosis that Dr. Lee testified to, the diagnosis that Ms. Shinaberry testified to, the diagnosis that Dr. Tabackman testified to. Do you have schizophrenia, paranoid type?

Brian: No, I do not.

Ms. Ike: Did you ever have that?

Brian: I had an illness. What it was, what caused it, what made it go away, all those things are beyond anybody's comprehension. Nobody can say what was wrong with me, and why it's not wrong with me now.

Ms. Ike: And you were in the courtroom the whole time of this trial, correct?

Brian: Yes.

Ms. Ike: And you heard Dr. Lee testify?

Brian: Yes.

Ms. Ike: And you heard Ms. Shinaberry testify?

Brian: Yes.

Ms. Ike: And you heard Dr. Tabackman testify?

Brian: Yes.

Ms. Ike: But you do not believe you have schizophrenia, paranoid type, today, correct?

Brian: No. I'm not out of touch with reality today. I understand what's going on around me.

Ms. Ike: So, you don't believe you have that illness?

Brian: No, definitely not.

Finally, the judge announced it was time for Brian to present his closing arguments (at which point Alice Ike, loudly enough for it to be picked up by the court audio recording, muttered, "Man, this is going to take all day").

Addressing himself to the jury, Brian once again explained that while he'd had a mental illness when he was younger, he'd recovered many years ago, and since then, he'd been sane and rational. He expressed his frustration at his doctors' refusal to accept this fact and clarified that he tried to escape from Perkins not to "lead his people into the Amazon," but because he wanted to get shot by the police and either killed or sent to prison. His speech was straightforward and heartfelt:

> I think it's clear that I do understand these medical problems. I understand what a nodule on my lung may or may not be, and the various diseases associated with it. . . . We don't appoint guardians to everybody that's a habitual drunk or drug addict. We don't raid a crack house and say, "All you crackheads need guardians." . . . If you choose to be a drunk, you take that blame upon yourself. If you choose to be a drunk, this society says, "We don't like it, we don't agree with it, but you're only hurting yourself." And in this context, I am only hurting myself. If something goes wrong, I suffer the consequences—not the state of Maryland, not the hospital, not the jury. If I die of cancer, I'm the one that pays the price. . . . We have a different standard for a child or an elderly person with Alzheimer's disease. If someone with dementia gives away their savings to somebody they don't know because they're out of touch with reality, it affects other people. If I have cancer, it only affects me. . . . If you listened to the state's witnesses, they were very hesitant to answer basic questions about mental illness. . . . They've given you an inaccurate assessment of what paranoid schizophrenia is and what's wrong with me. Anybody could put earplugs in their ears just to get a good night's sleep. If your spouse snores, if your neighbor's dog barks, you might put earplugs in your ears. If I do the

same thing in a mental hospital, where it's very loud, where there are patients that don't sleep at night, it's evidence of schizophrenia. That's not "evidence of schizophrenia." If I disagree with them, then I'm "paranoid or delusional about the hospital staff." If I disagree with someone, that's not "evidence of schizophrenia."

In the state's closing arguments, Alice Ike warned the jury not to judge by appearances. She admitted that Brian was "a good-looking guy." She agreed he was intelligent. She affirmed that he didn't appear to show any signs of mental illness, but she reminded them of Dr. Kim-Lee's point, that not all mental illnesses are obvious to "ordinary people." In fact, she said, many aspects of Brian's behavior were indicative of mental illness, including his reluctance to admit there was anything wrong with him, his mistrust of his treatment team, his refusal to take medication, and his attempt to escape. Refusing to have his lungs examined wasn't a reasonable decision, she argued. Finally, she reminded the jury that some years earlier, "Brian took a shotgun and murdered his parents," and "the mental health professionals who testified all agree that he suffers from paranoid schizophrenia," and they couldn't all be wrong.

The jury then retired to decide, first, whether Brian suffered from a mental disability; second, if so, whether he lacked the understanding or capacity to make responsible decisions about his health care because of his mental disability; and, if so, whether appointing Perkins Hospital as his guardian was "less restrictive than any other form of intervention" that would be consistent with his welfare and safety.

The last part of the question was very confusing. After deliberating for an hour, the jury foreman handed a question to the judge: "We don't understand 'a lesser form of intervention,'" it read. "What are the other forms of intervention?"

"Well, I guess that's the question," said Judge Sweeney, who didn't seem to know any more than the jury did. "I'm happy to hear both parties on this. Does anybody have a suggestion?"

"There aren't many other alternatives," said Alice Ike. "I don't think they understand it because no one's explained it to them."

In fact, "lesser forms of intervention" could easily have been used in Brian's case—they included things like asking the patient in detail to explain his own plan of action, asking family members to get involved, assigning a court-appointed guardian *ad litem*, or referring the case to a state ethics committee. But it had been a long day, and no one wanted to bring up another complicated issue that might keep them in the courtroom longer. The jury was getting restless. The hearing had gone on all afternoon, and a big winter storm was coming in. There was talk about driving conditions and the possibility of heavy traffic. Alice Ike excused herself due to "child care obligations." Nobody wanted to hang around puzzling out the meaning of an ambiguous clause in state law.

"Maybe it's a matter for summary judgment," Judge Sweeney resolved. "The evidence is extraordinarily sketchy in this case."

It wasn't clear what he meant by this—whether the evidence of Brian's mental capacity was "sketchy" or that there was only "sketchy" evidence of mental illness. There were further mutterings about the weather. Then Judge Sweeney made a decision.

"With this snowstorm coming in," he said, "I'm not inclined to keep this jury much longer."

The jury was recalled.

"All right," the judge said. "Ladies and gentlemen, your question to me was that you don't understand 'less restrictive than any other form of intervention.' Your focus on that question, after my discussions, led me to conclude that I thought the record on the case on that issue is sufficiently undeveloped that it's not really fair to ask you to make that decision on that based on the information presented at this trial."

On that note, a mistrial was announced.

"It's starting to snow," the judge concluded, "but the roads are still very good, so you don't have to worry about getting home."

There was nothing for Brian to do except let the guards drive him back to Perkins and wait for the paperwork to be processed and a new trial date set. Meanwhile, the court granted the hospital temporary authority to make medical decisions on his behalf.

Ever since he'd been judged not criminally responsible, Brian felt as though he'd been treated like a child who didn't understand the implications of his actions. If he'd been sent to the Department of Corrections rather than the Department of Mental Health, although he'd be serving a long prison sentence, at least he'd be treated like an adult, his choices and rights taken seriously.

Now he'd tried taking his case to court, and the court, essentially, had deferred to the doctors, handing over authority to the hospital rather than thinking things through for themselves. Maybe the jury felt he couldn't have it both ways—he couldn't claim that he wasn't responsible for the murder of his parents and then claim to be responsible enough to make his own decisions when it came to his health. Maybe they felt a person was either mentally ill or sane and that they couldn't go from one to the other when it happened to suit them. Still, people recovered from physical illness, so why shouldn't they recover from mental illnesses, too?

The problem, Brian realized, was that nobody was prepared to challenge the opinions of the psychiatrists, who kept emphasizing the point that mental illness wasn't always visible—and after all, Brian *had* killed his parents. And if his doctors, who were supposed to know him inside and out, said he was still sick and dangerous, then nobody was prepared to disagree. Rather than weighing the evidence for themselves, when so much was at stake it was much easier for people to play it safe and accept what the "experts" told them.

This was true even of the judge. As Brian was beginning to learn, the courts rarely gave serious consideration to the requests of a petitioner who was an inmate in a mental institution. The issues these hearings usually brought up—questions about the limits of personal responsibility—were ethically and morally complex, but instead of taking them seriously and looking objectively at the evidence for themselves, judges and juries preferred to submit to the authority of psychiatrists, whose diagnoses and prognoses provided the illusion that they were standing on solid ground. In other words, the courts regarded these questions not as human dilemmas, but as medical questions, regarding legal interventions as an impediment to effective care.

In his 1976 book *Insanity Inside Out*, Kenneth Donaldson, a psychiatric patient who was kept in Florida State Hospital for fifteen years without treatment and with no evidence of mental illness, recalled that whenever he went to court to fight for release, his current doctors would simply point to the "preconceived notions" of his original doctors, "which were accepted by the courts as fact without weighing evidence in open court, as both defense of themselves and proof of my illness." Thirty years later, it appears, things have changed very little.

Throughout the following year, a further series of temporary guardianship orders was signed, and Brian was sent for an X-ray of his lung.

And there it was: no longer a shadow, but a solid mass the size of an apple.

15

Rage and Restraint

Brian stared at the X-ray. The mass was huge, around thirteen centimeters in diameter.

"Is it cancer?" he asked the doctor. By this time, he knew something was seriously wrong with his health. He was starting to tire easily, had trouble breathing, and was losing his appetite.

"I'm not sure," the doctor said. "We'll need to take a closer look."

"Could it be a tumor?"

"I suppose it's possible," the doctor replied. "Have you ever been exposed to asbestos?"

"Not that I know of."

"If it's lung cancer, your chances of living for another three years are around twenty percent. I'd say it's pretty likely. That's one hell of a shadow."

Brian's heart lifted. He might get out of Perkins after all.

There was a biopsy, but the results were inconclusive. The doctors seemed baffled. They couldn't figure out what was going on. They asked Brian all kinds of questions. They did another biopsy. There were more X-rays. PET scans and CT scans were ordered. Cancer experts from Johns Hopkins were called in to examine the slides. It went on and on—testing, screening, questioning.

And then . . . it vanished. The mass in his lung was there in one X-ray and gone in the next, like a cloud disappearing from a summer sky.

The doctors were left scratching their heads. They didn't understand what was going on.

Eventually, they concluded that it was "spontaneous regression."

"It happens sometimes," the doctor said. "There are lots of case studies on tumors that vanish overnight. Nobody seemed to know why it happens. Count yourself lucky."

Brian felt the opposite. He'd wanted to die. Now it appeared he was no longer even sick. And even if he got sick again, Perkins had guardianship, which meant he had to accept treatment whether he wanted it or not. There was absolutely no way out. Each time he dedicated himself to working his way out of Perkins by following all the rules, something happened to send him back to maximum security. He'd tried escaping. He'd tried to get shot. He'd tried to get transferred to prison. He'd often thought about suicide, but even suicide was impossible at Perkins—razor blades were inaccessible, mirrors unbreakable, sheets and blankets unknottable, light switches and plumbing fixtures recessed so they couldn't be used to support ligatures. Even the wall phones had stiff, inflexible handset cords.

When he looked back over his time at the hospital, Brian saw a clear distinction between the first six years and the time after that. For those first six years, he felt, Perkins had actually been a place of treatment, where patients were seen as people who needed help, not violent criminals unfit to walk the streets. While there'd still been problems, there were enough staff members like Dr. Briskin, who treated patients as equals, to make being at Perkins tolerable. But after his escape attempt, Brian realized, things had changed—not just for him, but all around. There were more rules, fewer privileges, and less kindness. Security was beefed up and opportunities restricted. Of course, his escape attempt made things worse. Since then, the staff held a lasting grudge against him, and doctors were more adamant that their diagnosis was correct and that Brian was a dangerous paranoid schizophrenic—either that, or a psychopath.

Now that his battle for guardianship had failed, Brian had no chance of getting out and nothing to lose. He wanted revenge. They said he was dangerous. Okay, he thought. He'd prove them right.

He turned his anger against his new enemies: those who'd testified against him in court.

It wasn't the judge's lack of sympathy or the state's attorney's stubbornness that had bothered him most about the trial—after all, they'd never met him before and were only doing their jobs. It was what Brian saw as the blind, self-satisfied superiority of Dr. Kim-Lee, Ms. Shinaberry, and Dr. Tabackman.

Brian couldn't help but take the doctors' testimony personally. He decided that, given that Dr. Tabackman considered him to be a maladaptive, deviant rule-breaker, he'd take him at his word. They couldn't do any more to him than they'd already done. If he caused enough trouble, Perkins authorities would get tired of dealing with him and turn him over to the prison system. He'd seen this happen before, in the case of patients who'd caused so much trouble for the hospital that they were "found competent" to stand trial.

It wasn't hard for Brian to behave badly. He refused to socialize or join the ward groups, and whenever he was reprimanded for his sullenness or his refusal to be "redirected," he made threats of violence. He told his treatment team that he planned to get more and more aggressive until he was sent to prison. "In discussions with his treatment team, Mr. Bechtold boasted about his past violence and appeared intimidating and threatening," his doctor wrote. "He could not assure them that he would not become violent."

On maximum security, Brian had a bedroom to himself and a lot of time to spend there. (There were no cameras in patients' bedrooms.) He'd already discovered that by standing on his chest of drawers, he could raise the steel vent in his bedroom ceiling. Now, using the upper arm strength he'd developed from years of push-ups, he managed to lift the vent and pull himself up into the crawl space. In the process, he tore his left biceps, causing dreadful pain. Unable to ask for help from hospital staff (who'd want to know how he'd obtained the injury), he wore a knee brace around his elbow to keep the muscle stable. He thought there might be a way out up there, but the space was blocked off at each end by brick walls. Still, he'd climb up there at night, after the lights were out, to explore the dark cavity on his hands and knees. One night he found five aluminum rods, each about as thick as a pencil and two feet long. He brought them down into his room and filed them down into points by rubbing them against the grout in his shower, as he'd learned to do with the strut from the ironing board he'd used as a shank in his escape attempt. This time, he wasn't trying to escape, just to make a point. Still, if he was sent to prison for the assault, he wouldn't complain.

On February 3, 2006, at around 4:45 p.m., Lee Murphy, an information technology consultant who'd been contracted to update the computers at Perkins, was leaving for the day. He'd been working in one of the offices on the south side and was heading back toward the sally port. As he walked past the maximum-security area, Cynthia Shinaberry emerged from one of the wards. Brian stepped forward with one leg, swinging the shank behind him, Korean-style, then stepped forward again. He was now about eight feet from Murphy. Ms. Shinaberry, meanwhile, had escaped into a stairway and was pulling the fire alarm.

Brian was a big man—not tall, but stocky. By coming between the woman and her pursuer, Murphy had made himself the target of the attack. The shank struck him in the chest. Brian stepped back and was about to repeat the martial arts maneuver when he saw two security guards running down the hall holding cans of mace. He dropped his weapon and lifted his hands in the air.

He had been planning the assault for some time. He knew his victim would be either Dr. Kim-Lee or Ms. Shinaberry, as Dr. Tabackman was on a different ward. Eventually, he decided the social worker would probably be the easiest target, given that Dr. Kim-Lee could lock herself in her office, but he decided to play it by ear. Ms. Shinaberry was on the ward until 5 p.m. The day of the attack, Brian brought the shanks into the day room wrapped in a towel. He went to his regular meeting with Dr. Kim-Lee with one of the pointed rods up his sleeve, just in case the opportunity arose to use it. After the meeting, he returned to the chair where he'd left his weapons. When he saw Ms. Shinaberry getting ready to leave he took one of the shanks from the towel, walked decisively over to the social worker, and followed as she left the ward.

After the assault was interrupted, Brian was handcuffed, placed in an isolation cell, and tied down to a stretcher by five-point restraints, a type of body harness resembling a seat belt crossed with a corset. A leather strap six inches wide ran across his stomach. At each side of his body, this strap was attached to two thick, padded wrist cuffs, which were themselves strapped to the stretcher. His legs were spread, and similar cuffs were attached to his ankles. The strap around his stomach was connected to two shoulder straps and a neck brace, to keep his head in place. The cuffs weren't tight, and the restraints weren't uncomfortable in themselves, but it was painful to stay in the same position for so long, and the discomfort made it impossible for him to sleep. Most of the time, patients about to be placed in restraints were given a sedative beforehand, to help them relax. Brian wasn't afforded this privilege.

His isolation—or, as he saw it, punishment—went on for the next five months. When he wasn't in restraints, he was on "one-on-one" (accompanied by a personal guard at all times); his exercise privileges were withdrawn, and he was put back on medication: this time, thirty milligrams of Zyprexa and thirty milligrams of Abilify, both antipsychotics. As a result, he put on weight, his cholesterol shot up, and he fell into a groggy stupor.

His attempted assault had been a failure. He'd successfully expressed his anger at Ms. Shinaberry, but that was all. Lee Murphy, the IT consultant, had only been scratched. Perkins tried filing a charge of first-degree assault against Brian, but the charge was dropped; the injuries he'd inflicted hadn't been serious enough.

For Brian, the only memorable part of those five months in restraints was the day he got word of another patient-on-staff assault. While he didn't condone unprovoked violence, Brian knew firsthand how life at Perkins sometimes pushed people beyond endurance, and in these situations, lashing out was simply a protest against being treated as less than human. And while he wasn't surprised to learn that the victim was the most hated nurse in the hospital, he didn't expect the person to finally take her down would be the polite, mild-mannered Mr. King.

Robert King, fifty-two, usually fought his battles in a more civilized way: by taking them into court. He'd come to Perkins seven years earlier, in May 1999, after being found not criminally responsible on charges of second-degree assault for bringing a concealed weapon into a courthouse. During his stay at the hospital, King had become a prolific litigant, filing numerous lawsuits against Perkins, the clinical director, the CEO, and many of the doctors. His suits were taken seriously by the courts, and some were even successful—a significant achievement given that filing a legal motion from Perkins was no easy matter. There's only one public defender for the entire hospital, and most patients are indigent, so "nonessential" cases like King's have to be filed pro se—that is, on his own behalf. Patients have no internet access, no law library, no typewriters, no computers, and no photocopier, which means all motions are written out by hand. Because the court usually requires multiple copies of each document to be filed—sometimes as many as eight—the work required can be overwhelming.

While the hospital had plenty of hardworking and compassionate nurses, budget cuts and chronic understaffing meant that even the most dedicated were exhausted and miserable much of the time, and bureaucratic demands meant that administrative tasks such as the filling out of forms were put before the needs of patients. Undervalued and often underpaid, nursing staff were ordered to monitor patients in highly structured, quantifiable ways that could be easily charted and that didn't allow for any deviation from "the treatment plan." The trend in mental health was to measure illnesses with checkboxes and scales rather than actually sitting down and listening to people's stories (which would have taken too much time). In addition, the pressure to "maintain appropriate boundaries" meant that nursing staff were discouraged from getting to know patients on a human level.

In places like Perkins, nurses who care too much are quickly broken down; they become emotionally, spiritually, and physically fatigued from the human suffering they witness every day. They developed different ways of coping. Some became distanced and robotic; some learned to compartmentalize; others turned into slackers. Some, especially the senior nurses, developed a sense of entitlement, and this was the case with Nurse Gloria Holt, or, as the patients knew her, "the worst nurse." Holt, who'd been at Perkins for over twenty years, was seen by many patients as arrogant, rude, and condescending, treating patients as underlings, even appearing to take pleasure in making them suffer. And in May 2006, her chosen victim was Robert King.

Over time, partly due to all the legal cases he was involved in,

King had accumulated a lot of paperwork, and Nurse Holt was a neat freak. His room was a fire hazard, she told him. In his file, she described him as "a serious hoarder." After weeks of asking him to clean his room, she said if he didn't tidy up his piles of paperwork, she'd take everything out and dump it in the trash.

King was furious that the nurse saw his writing as just another example of pathological behavior. What to her might have looked like random piles was, to him, a carefully organized filing system. He knew exactly where everything was. His paperwork was divided into separate categories: legal, religious, business, education, and foreign languages. His legal pile was particularly substantial because he happened to be composing a brief for the Court of Special Appeals asking for a writ of habeas corpus in a request for judicial release. This long and complicated document had originally been due in the middle of January, but because he had to write all three copies out by hand, King had asked for an extension. He finally submitted the brief in late February 2006, but the clerk had written to tell him that it didn't comport with the Maryland rules, which required that *nine* copies be filed. They needed another six copies of the brief, and the cost of photocopying would be $183. Because King was indigent, he had to write another six copies out by hand using a three-inch-long bendy plastic ballpoint pen. Every time he made a mistake, he started the page again from scratch. By the time he'd finished, he'd written more than three hundred pages in small, neat handwriting. The ordeal was particularly tedious because the medication he was taking gave him tremors in his hands. But he kept on writing. And because, like Brian, he'd been diagnosed with schizophrenia, his constant writing was regarded by Nurse Holt as a manifestation of his mental illness, a pathological compulsion.

In May, in an attempt to keep the nurse off his back, King took a break from his Herculean writ of habeas corpus to file a request for a protective order against Gloria Holt. The following week, when the nurse received her copy of the court papers, all hell broke loose. She didn't wait for the judge to decide whether the restraining order was justified; she didn't care. As King recalls it, she stormed into his room flanked by two security officers and told him he had ten minutes to set aside four sets of clothes.

Everything else, she told him, was going to be destroyed.

King didn't believe she'd do it. Still, he was worried enough to find a bag and fill it with clothes.

"Now stand aside," Nurse Holt said.

She ordered the two security officers to empty out the contents of King's locker, then told them get rid of everything in the room. King stood there and watched, mortified, as all his worldly possessions—the rest of his clothes, his paperwork, years of books, photographs, the nine copies of his handwritten brief to the Court of Special Appeals, and, the last straw, his Bible, in which he kept the "In Memoriam" card from the funeral of a beloved aunt who'd recently passed away—all were unceremoniously dumped into black trash bags.

King stared at Nurse Holt in horror.

"Now take everything outside and dump it in the green garbage can labeled 'Disposables,'" Nurse Holt said, throwing a smile in Mr. King's direction.

That night, he planned her murder.

A few days later, in the early hours of the morning, when the ward was quiet, Robert King slipped discreetly into the bathroom. Although the showers had been designed to reduce ligature danger, the faucet still had a small handle, and by wrapping a towel around it and applying all the pressure he could muster, he managed to unscrew the metal showerhead. He slipped it into his pants and then returned quietly to his room. There, on the back of an envelope that had managed to survive Nurse Holt's purgation, he wrote the words, "Out of Order."

He then put the metal showerhead inside one of his socks and tied the sock in a knot to make a flail.

King didn't go to breakfast that morning; he said he wasn't feeling well. He waited until everyone else had gone downstairs, then went back into the bathroom, taped the "Out of Order" sign to the broken shower, and hid himself in the cubicle next to it. Nurse Holt arrived on the ward every day after breakfast. King knew that as soon as she heard about the "Out of Order" sign, she'd want to see the broken shower for herself. He stood in the cubicle for almost thirty minutes, imagining how it would feel to strike the flail against the side of the nurse's head.

Nurse Holt arrived on the ward just before 8 a.m. as usual, when the patients had gotten back from breakfast. She checked in with the night nurse, who told her everything had been quiet and there were no pressing issues. She then wiped her hands with sanitizer and signed on to the computer to review the doctor's notes and look over his orders. She was about to start checking on the patients when one of them came up to the nurses' station and told her one of the showers was out of order.

Knowing that there was something wrong—the night nurse hadn't mentioned anything about a broken shower—Nurse Holt went into the bathroom and saw the notice: it was handwritten and obviously unofficial. She stepped into the cubicle to see if the faucet was working. Something hit the right side of her head; she stumbled, then found her footing. Something hit her again, even harder, and she fell.

"I wanted to kill her," Robert King told me. "I hit her over and over again. I'd never done anything like that before in my life, but that was the point she brought me to. I didn't care about the consequences." He was surprised the nurse wasn't more seriously hurt—in fact, she survived the attack with no permanent injuries and then retired from Perkins after filing a lawsuit against the hospital that was eventually settled out of court. King was found guilty of second-degree assault, sentenced to three years in prison, and transferred to Eastern Correctional Institution, a medium-security facility on Maryland's Eastern Shore. Compared to Perkins, he found life in prison surprisingly liberating. He was still inside a fence, but other than that, he could spend his time as he liked, and he wasn't constantly being judged, or analyzed for symptoms of mental illness. "In prison, I felt free," he told me. "I didn't have to do what people told me to. I could go to lunch or not go to lunch. I could stay in my cell all day. I could go to the gym. I could go to the library. I could go and lift weights." At Perkins, he'd been infantilized because of his purported incompetence, which, as an educated man, he found demeaning, but in prison, he was treated with respect because of his age. He kept to himself, and nobody interfered with him.

After three years, when his custodial sentence had been served, King was so reluctant to return to Perkins that he even petitioned the court to be allowed to stay in prison, but his request was denied. Against his will, he was sent back to Perkins to continue being "restored to competence."

"Perkins is supposed to be a hospital," he said, "but it's worse than a prison. In prison, you have some control over your life, some independence. It's not a lot, but it's enough to make you feel human."

A month after the attack on Nurse Holt, Brian went for another medical checkup and got some bad news. He had cancer—not in his lung, but in his left testicle. Could the shadow on his lung a year ago have been related? Possibly, the doctors said, but they didn't know for sure. They took him back to the University of Maryland Medical Center for tests, and it turned out his testicular cancer was already at stage three, which meant they'd have to remove his testicle. The guardianship order was still in place, so if he refused treatment, they'd treat him against his will. The matter was out of his hands.

In July 2006, Brian underwent a radical inguinal orchiectomy, followed by four cycles of chemotherapy. He was tired and miserable all the time. For months, he was in bed with a fever. When he wasn't feeling nauseated, he was frail, dehydrated, and depressed.

Going through chemotherapy seemed absurd. What was the point of recovering from cancer, he wondered, to return to a life that wasn't worth living?

16

Purgatory

When Brian was finally let out of restraints, it was on the condition that he take a high dose of meds—which were given by injection rather than by mouth, so there could be no more "checking." The drugs hypnotized him. He was always tired. When he wasn't sleeping, he tried not to draw attention to himself; at the same time, he struggled to stay alert, to keep his eyes and ears open. He hated to let his guard down. That ward was a godforsaken place, and its patients the scum of the earth.

Duquan Peoples, for example, was not only violent but also unpredictable. Brian didn't know why Peoples had been sent to Perkins, just that everybody avoided him—well, almost everybody. One day, an elderly patient, Mr. Adler, was on his way to the medical clinic when he heard grunting noises coming from the stairwell. Looking down, he saw Duquan Peoples and a female patient, Taneka Pierce, going at it hot and heavy. Concerned, Mr. Adler reported the incident to security staff, and Peoples was put in restraints, where he lay brooding on revenge. The first day he was back on the ward, he stabbed Mr. Adler in the face with a broken pool cue, causing so much damage that the victim's jaw had to be held together with metal plates. Meanwhile, news of the hookup had reached the female ward, and Breanna Hobelman, who considered herself Duquan's girl, was far from happy. Breanna, who'd been sent to Perkins for killing her daughter, attacked Taneka with the Perkins weapon of choice, a flail made from a sock. (Breanna stuffed hers with dominoes.)

Another dangerous character was Anthony Kelly, thirty-nine, who'd been found incompetent to stand trial after committing a series of high-profile crimes in Silver Spring, Maryland. Five years earlier, in March 2002, he'd beaten and raped a sixty-one-year-old woman in a quiet neighborhood. Three months after that, he'd forced a twenty-year-old woman into a stolen car at knifepoint, driven her to a wooded area, and raped her repeatedly. A few days later, wearing a wig and false beard, he'd broken into a house in Silver Spring, fatally shot a nine-year-old girl, then shot and killed her father, escaping from the scene with a Bible and a few dollar bills. Three nights later, he killed a tourist in a Metro station in Washington, DC.

Kelly had been sent to Perkins in June 2004 to be "restored to mental health," and he wasn't happy about it. (Perhaps he, too, wanted to be sent to prison.) Acting as his own attorney, he filed a civil action objecting to his competency evaluation and arguing that the doctor who had found him "incompetent to stand trial" was guilty of libel. He demanded compensation in the amount of $25,000 and accused the psychiatrist who'd performed the evaluation of "gross negligence" and "invasion of privacy." Unsurprisingly, his motion was dismissed. (The court ruled that the complaint was based on "indisputably meritless legal theory.") But it gave his doctors a heads-up: Kelly was a jailhouse lawyer.

At first, psychiatrists thought it would take less than a year to restore him to competency—despite his reputation for violence, he was a model patient who never required seclusion or restraint. When Brian was awake, he watched Kelly closely and noticed how clean he was and how nicely he dressed. He never caused trouble or drew attention to himself, but spent his time studying for correspondence courses. Still, the psychiatrists were convinced he was harboring a number of delusions, including the belief that he was sane, that he'd done nothing wrong, and that his arrest had been a terrible mistake.

Kelly's exceptional behavior caused a vexing problem for his doctors. On the one hand, as long as he remained delusional, he wouldn't be allowed to stand trial. On the other hand, it was unconstitutional to hold a defendant indefinitely without trial, and given that Kelly was behaving so peacefully on the ward, he'd have to be released from Perkins once the statutory time limit of ten years ran out—even if he was still mentally ill (and if he was, the doctors were confident he'd kill again).

His psychiatrists insisted that in order to be "restored to competence," Kelly needed medication, but he refused to take it. They tried to force him the same way they'd forced Brian: by "paneling" him. Once again, Kelly took his battle to the courts. First, he appealed to the Office of Administrative Hearings. When that office found in favor of Perkins, he appealed to the Circuit Court of Baltimore City, acting in his own defense.

In court, Kelly argued that because he hadn't been dangerous or disruptive on the ward, no one could argue he'd be a danger if he were released back into the community. To everyone's surprise, the judge found in his favor. If Kelly's psychiatrists wanted to medicate him by force or keep him at Perkins on the grounds that he was dangerous, the judge ruled, they couldn't simply claim that it wasn't safe to release him—they had to prove he was actually dangerous while on the ward.

This led to a troubling paradox. Kelly couldn't stand trial for his crimes because he wasn't mentally competent when he committed them. He could be made competent only with the help of medication, but he couldn't be medicated because he wasn't currently dangerous.

Anthony Kelly was a smart guy. If he held out for another seven years, they'd have to release him. Seven years was a long time, but if Kelly had a release date to look forward to, Brian thought he could probably make it.

People were drawn to Kelly; Brian couldn't understand why. He thought maybe it was because Kelly was so bright, or maybe it was just because his case was high profile. Brian had noticed that Joan Barnet, a social worker on minimum security, would come to maximum almost every day just to sit and talk to Kelly. The two would chat in the dayroom while Brian was slumped beside them on the sofa, apparently oblivious. He heard Joan trying to convince Kelly to plead not criminally responsible. If he did, Joan said, she'd try to get him out as soon as she could. But Kelly, wary of being railroaded, made no promises. He continued to file lawsuits: against the public defender who represented him in court, against his doctors, against Perkins staff, against the CEO, Sheilah Davenport. His motions were always dismissed, but Kelly didn't let this deter him.

Finally, in 2008, the psychiatrists signed off on Kelly's competency to stand trial—no doubt to ensure he wouldn't be released, as he was still unmedicated and apparently delusional. In court, against all advice, Kelly acted as his own attorney—because he'd been judged competent to stand trial, he could hardly be disqualified from defending himself on the grounds of his mental illness. Brian suspected Kelly was grandiose about his belief that he could represent himself at trial. He did know a little about the law, Brian thought, but not enough to know he was out of his depth.

Brian was right. Kelly won little sympathy from the jury, especially when he badgered his rape victims during cross-examination. The jury found him guilty of first-degree murder, and he was sentenced to four life sentences plus a hundred years in a maximum-security prison. However, Anthony Kelly left behind an important legacy at Perkins. In 2007, the State of Maryland passed the "Kelly law." According to *Maryland Department of Health and Mental Hygiene v. Anthony Kelly,* a patient couldn't be medicated against his will unless he displayed signs of dangerousness within the hospital.

Kelly wasn't the only unusual case on maximum security at the time, though he was perhaps the most high profile. Another was Norman Bell, whose bizarre diet made Brian rethink everything he'd been taught about germs and hygiene. Norman liked to eat strange things. This might seem like an odd habit, but it wasn't unheard of at Perkins, where patients had been known to swallow buttons, razor blades, batteries, and broken glass in order to get taken to a "real" hospital. In some cases, the act of swallowing inedible objects was symbolic, suggesting an unwillingness to let go of things, an illogical but instinctive response to the anonymity of institutional life. In a way, it made sense. When everything a person owned belonged to the institution, from their shirt and shoes to their comb and toothbrush, personal possessions were sacred. In these circumstances, collecting, hoarding, and even swallowing forbidden objects was a way to own things, to keep them private, to be different from others. But Norman Bell took the habit to a new level. He ate feces on a regular basis—not only fresh feces, but feces from toilets that had been clogged for a week. He also ate bugs, baby snakes, and, on one occasion, a large dead bird. To everyone's surprise, he never got sick; he never once had nausea or a stomachache. He never caught a cold in winter or got even so much as a runny nose.

Characters like Anthony Kelly and Norman Bell provided a short-lived distraction from the dull misery of life on the ward. The other thing that made this three-year stretch bearable for Brian was the allegiance of those who were suffering along with him, engaged in the same Sisyphean struggles. Two men in particular kept his spirits up, giving him legal advice and sharing their own battles against forced medication and their clashes with the court.

Brian's card partner, John Wesley Ray Jr., had come to Perkins in 2002 after allegedly trying to murder his ex-girlfriend. Ray, like Brian, had refused medication for his first two years at the hospital, taking it only after the court appointed his brother as his legal guardian. During the hearing, Assistant State's Attorney Lisa Marts testified that she'd received hundreds of letters from Ray, some threatening in tone, others offering clues to unsolved crimes. According to his doctors, Ray was a paranoid schizophrenic who refused medication because "he believed it impeded his psychic powers." He had, they said, "delusional beliefs that he was a psychic and wrote to government agencies claiming that he was helping to solve crimes."

This was the kind of conclusion Brian recognized from his own guardianship hearing, when Dr. Kim-Lee claimed that he had tried to escape from Perkins because he thought the world was going to end and "it was his responsibility to lead his people out of the hospital into the Amazon." In saying this, she'd conflated three things Brian had mentioned at different times and to different people: his plan to get sent to prison, his decoding of the Gospels, and his belief in the End Time. In Brian's view, the way Dr. Kim-Lee had added them together, putting her own twist on it, made him seem truly deluded. The same was true in the case of John Ray Jr. Brian knew Ray's psychiatrist's claims were exaggerated versions of a fact, which was that Ray had actually worked from time to time as a police informant.

There's no clear line between hyperbole and delusions. All "fixed beliefs," even psychotic ones, have their roots in lived experience; in fact, in the *DSM-5*, the definition of *delusion* no longer refers to "false beliefs." Delusions are now defined by the quality of a person's belief rather than its content. It's tempting to separate the "material" of a person's "madness" from the rest of that person—to see the mental illness, like physical illness, as something that "takes over" a person who was previously just like anyone else. In this way, we try to separate a person's malady from their character, motives, and life experiences. But that's not how it works. Delusions and "real life" are tangled together and comprised of the same material. They're part of who we are. They draw from our reservoir of lived experience, and in consequence, they're always meaningful. If taken seriously, they can shed light on what's most important to us, and why. But few psychiatrists have the time or inclination to analyze the meaning of a patient's delusions. Instead, they're generally seen as symptomatic, the product of misfiring neurons in a broken brain.

Leonard Dunmore was another friend who helped buoy Brian's spirits at this arduous time. Brian and Leonard had a lot in common. They were both mechanically minded and liked to design and invent things. Both had been at Perkins for longer than they believed necessary, and both wanted desperately to get out. Both were very smart, and both found it difficult to contain their contempt for the staff and administrators who kept them confined. When something made them angry, neither was able to contain himself. Their anger was triggered by the same thing: getting news that someone who'd committed a crime more serious than theirs had just been released. Their frustration was especially acute when these patients had been at Perkins for less than five years, like the petite Latina who was sent home just six months after killing her baby; or Leroy Jones, who left Perkins less than three years after murdering his mother with a sledgehammer. But if either Brian or Leonard expressed his frustration in therapy, it would go down in their file, causing them to sink more deeply into the quicksand.

Brian, Leonard, and John Ray Jr. would help one another with their legal research, drafting documents and editing motions as well as giving advice and moral support, reminding one another of the absurdity of things. More than any of the "treatments" he was offered at Perkins, Brian's friendships sustained his sense of self. They helped him look at things from an outside point of view. The three men would often talk about mental illness: what it was, whether it existed, and how it was connected to dangerousness. They wondered what the state had achieved by keeping them in Perkins for so long and restricting their lives so profoundly. They talked about how the law had defined them into oblivion, how their incapacity was never questioned, how they'd been dumped at Perkins and left to rot. Ultimately, the cases of John Ray Jr. and Leonard Dunmore renewed Brian's hopes, because both men managed to win their release through the courts and eventually lived lives on the outside that, while not always ideal, at least were of their own choosing.

In 2009, Brian received another risk assessment to see, yet again, if he was ready to move back to medium security. The psychiatrist administering the tests was Paulo Negro. Brian was fully cooperative with the interview and did his best to be honest. When he saw Dr. Negro's evaluation, he was surprised to learn that his diagnosis had been changed for a third time. Apparently, he no longer suffered from paranoid schizophrenia. (In fact, the diagnosis of "paranoid schizophrenia" would disappear completely four years later, when the *DSM-5* came out.) Now his Axis I diagnosis was "schizoaffective disorder, bipolar type." His Axis II diagnosis ("mixed personality disorder with narcissistic and antisocial features") remained unchanged. "Affect was reactive," Dr. Negro noted in his report. "Mood was neutral. There was no evidence of delusional content. Thought was coherent, logical, goal-directed.... He was pleasant and collaborative throughout the interview."

Knocked into a stupor by antipsychotics, Brian had done very little for the last three years other than sit in a chair in front of the television, so it was hardly surprising that Dr. Negro had noted that "he has been compliant with hospital rules, not engaged in power struggles, or evidenced unusual resentment towards the hospital and staff." In fact, Brian had maintained the highest privilege level all year. But instead of praising him for his "compliance," Dr. Negro assumed Brian was carefully hiding his dangerous psychosis. "Mr. Bechtold remains with significant structural risk for violent recidivism and escape," the doctor wrote.

He has a severe mental illness and history of recurrent violence and escape attempts associated with symptoms of his illness. The dangerousness is due to the combined effect of the mental illness and personality disorder. . . . [T]he behavioral pattern is characterized by unexpected, albeit planned, violence due to well concealed, but active, psychotic symptoms.

Dr. Negro did, at least, agree that Brian seemed to be more passive and obedient than he used to be, and he agreed that Brian should be permitted to return to medium security—with the caveat that a nine-hundred-milligram dose of lithium be added to his daily cocktail of medications. For once, Brian didn't complain. His daily regimen of Zyprexa and Abilify had left him apathetic, without drive, motivation, or purpose. The medications had cast their spell, and he'd lost the will to fight. Dulled, muted, and passive, he was finally considered "insightful" enough to move to a less secure environment.

17

Lady-Killer

In his medicated slump, Brian had temporarily lost his fighting spirit, but there were plenty of others doing battle, both patients and staff. According to state records, there were around 100 patient-on-patient attacks at Perkins in 2008, during which 26 patients were injured. By the end of 2009, these figures had increased to 129 attacks with 46 injuries (which didn't include assaults by staff on patients). One year later, 242 patient grievances were filed at the hospital, including complaints about staff members slapping patients on the buttocks in the showers; cursing at them; aggressively pulling out a patient's nasal draining tube; punching a patient in the stomach; slapping a patient in the face; hitting a patient in the head; refusing to change a patient's soiled diapers after he became incontinent; ripping off a patient's clothes; and shoving a patient against a wall and sexually abusing her. The vast majority of these complaints were dismissed, but five staff members were fired that year for using excessive force.

This rise in violence created a feverish atmosphere on the wards, and the tension was made worse by inconsistent leadership, a shortage of therapists, and shared rooms even among patients with violent histories. Boredom also played a role: there was nothing for patients to do in the evenings except watch television, and there was no opportunity for education, not even for them to complete their GEDs.

Understaffing at the hospital had always been a problem. In light of the risks they ran, security guards were woefully underpaid, and as a result, some of them didn't take their duties seriously. Although he'd never been on the internet or used a cell phone himself, Brian had seen aides, guards, and nurses texting and scrolling, checking their phones when they should have been checking on patients. Others would nap during their shifts, exhausted by the extra work they took on. The shortage of staff meant there were lucrative overtime opportunities for those who wanted them—and many did.

Hospital authorities relied heavily on the more experienced guards who'd been at Perkins for a long time and knew the patients' backgrounds. Due to their seniority, however, these were also the guards drawing the highest salaries, and they knew how to play the system. Brian had heard them talking in the dayroom or behind the desk at the nurses' station. They'd gossip and complain about the hospital and didn't care if they were overheard, as if patients didn't count as real people. Some guards incited violence deliberately, provoking patients into tantrums or panic attacks and then demanding the presence of extra staff to oversee the situation—which meant extra pay for their pals. If a guard sprained an ankle or wrist playing sports during the weekend, he might come in to work on Monday and blame the injury on the patients. Brian had seen it happen more than once. A sprain, if it was serious enough, could lead to a cash settlement and six months off work on full pay.

The CEO, Sheilah Davenport, solved the problem by replacing many of the older guards with younger ones, but this created its own set of difficulties. The older guards had been familiar with the patients' histories; the younger ones were too trusting and hadn't seen enough violence to understand how important it was to stay vigilant. Plus, the younger guards often wanted to show off and would exercise their power by victimizing certain patients—and Brian was one of them. He found it very difficult not to fight back— with his martial arts training, he could have caused serious injury with a well-placed kick—but he knew better. Acts of aggression led directly to the isolation cell.

By 2010, Brian had been at Perkins for eighteen years—longer than most of the doctors, nurses, and staff. He knew most of the other long-timers, some of whom had left Perkins only to return again, often multiple times. One of these patients was Saladin Taylor, who returned to Brian's medium-security ward in August of that year. Now, however, he went by the name El-Soudani El-Wahhabi. He told Brian he'd changed his name when his father converted the family to Wahhabism, a fundamentalist Islamic doctrine founded by eighteenth-century preacher Muhammad ibn Abd al-Wahhab. The new name was a mouthful, he agreed, adding that most people just called him "El."

El had originally come to Perkins in 1984, after being found what was then termed "not guilty by reason of insanity" for various crimes, including sexually assaulting his sister-in-law while wearing women's lingerie. After stabbing a female patient in the eye with a pencil, he'd been sent from Perkins to prison, and in early 1995, he'd been released on parole.

On the night of September 5 of that same year, Mona Johnson, twenty-six, was sexually assaulted and stabbed to death in a row house where she'd been renting a room. Another tenant of the house, located in the North Baltimore neighborhood of Madison Park, was Saladin Taylor, then thirty-four. At the crime scene, next to the victim's dead body, detectives found a piece of human tongue "the size of a quarter" that they believe the victim had bitten off during a long struggle with her killer.

The following day, Taylor's parole officer noticed that his client was mumbling uncharacteristically. The parole officer, who'd heard about the murder, reported the incident to the police, and Taylor was arrested. When interviewed by detectives, according to David Simon, writing in the *Baltimore Sun*, "Mr. Taylor contended that he injured himself outside his home and left the severed portion of his tongue on the street. He said he had no idea how it came to be found at the crime scene." Adjudged not criminally responsible, Saladin Taylor was sent back to Perkins in 1997. He'd been there ever since, although he and Brian had usually been on different wards.

El, a former security patrol officer, was handsome and strong, with rippling muscles. Brian thought he looked like a model from a men's fashion magazine. He usually kept to himself, so Brian was flattered when El sought him out to talk. Some people thought he was withdrawn and aloof, but Brian had always gotten along with him. They were both intelligent and ambitious, they both had a strong work ethic, and both had spent most of their adult lives at Perkins. In former times, before Brian had been so heavily medicated, he and El would play one-on-one basketball together. (El would always win.) Brian would sometimes watch him exercise and knew he was surprisingly vigorous—he'd do push-ups alone in his room and then follow them up with some exotic lifts at the gym.

When he wasn't working out, El could often be found quietly reading religious literature in a corner of the dayroom, a habit that led some of his fellow patients to regard him as a gentle, spiritual type. But Brian had known him for longer than anyone else on the ward, and he knew El was deeply confused, especially when it came to gender. The man was a paradox. Although he was physically tough, El had a feminine nature. He once told Brian that he was a woman trapped in a man's body. Those who'd shared a room with him whispered that he wore female underwear. At the same time, El had a distinctly unladylike fascination with violence; his favorite television shows were *Criminal Minds, Law and Order,* and *Conspiracy Theory with Jesse Ventura.*

But if El was a woman trapped in a man's body, he was the kind of woman who had no sexual interest in men. Brian had been at Perkins long enough to know there was plenty of action available for gay men—in fact, the hospital had a reputation in Maryland for being the state's most gay-friendly facility, as many of the guards and staff were gay. El certainly had plenty of admirers in that regard, but he was never interested. On the contrary, whenever a woman was transferred to the ward, El was the first to check her out. He was also obsessed with germs and bacteria and was convinced that HIV could be spread through flatulence. He'd launch into diatribes on the subject of inoculations. He believed bodily fluids had a magic power, and he was horrified if anyone close to him sneezed, blew their nose, wept, or drooled.

El wasn't the only patient transferred to Brian's ward in August: Susan Sachs arrived at around the same time. In 2004, Sachs, thirty-nine, had been found not criminally responsible for her role in the murder of therapist Dr. Joyce Hadl, seventy-one, whose body had been buried under a shed on an isolated farm in Montgomery County. Dr. Hadl was known in the community as a Good Samaritan who sometimes took in people like Susan, troubled patients who couldn't afford to pay rent. But Susan caused so many problems for Dr. Hadl that Hadl called the police to have her evicted. A few days later, Dr. Hadl disappeared. Eventually, Susan Sachs and two others were arrested for their involvement in her murder.

Brian found Susan sullen and unpleasant, although other patients were fond of her. He'd noticed El and Susan were very close, although their attachment didn't seem to be sexual or even romantic. What sealed their bond was their shared sense of gloom. They were a melancholy pair, sitting together in a corner of the dayroom, each feeding off the other's angst, treating every little setback as if it were the end of the world. A cloud of misery hung over them. They were like a pair of woeful ghouls, always talking about suicide. They often said they'd be better off dead, but no one took them seriously.

Until El strangled Susan to death with a shoelace.

Saturday, September 25, 2010, was a strange night for Brian. He stayed up late. That in itself was hardly unusual—he had more energy in the evening, and he'd pace around the ward for exercise when it was quiet. But on this occasion, he wasn't alone. Even more unusually, he stayed up talking about the Bible, which was something he'd learned not to do, for fear of being considered delusional. This evening, though, he got into a deep conversation with Susan's roommate, Felicia, who'd been asking him about his beliefs. Brian was glad for the chance to talk; most people weren't interested. The two of them stayed up until around 11:30 p.m. discussing biblical doctrine.

The following morning, Brian noticed that neither Felicia, Susan, nor El had come down to breakfast. Even more unusually, when the meal was over, instead of going back upstairs, the patients were all led to a ward that was furnished but currently vacant. Later, Brian learned from Felicia that Susan hadn't responded to the morning wake-up call. Seeing that her roommate was still in bed, Felicia told her it was time to get up. No reply. When Felicia turned the blanket down, she saw Susan lying facedown, motionless. Felicia shook her shoulders, but her roommate's body was stiff and cold.

On medium security, the patients' bedrooms had push-button controls on the inside that allowed them to let people in. These could be overridden by automatic locks controlled from the nurses' station, and all rooms were supposed to be locked automatically at night—but this didn't always happen. Patients often needed to get up in the night to use the bathroom or to get medication, and it was easier for guards to leave the doors unlocked than to keep getting up to open them.

Coincidentally, it was the day of the yearly minimum- and

medium-security picnic. A feast of ribs and shrimp had been ordered, and family and friends were due. That afternoon, staff fired up grills outside, and the cookout went ahead as though nothing had happened. But because the police investigation was still in progress, patients on Brian's ward weren't allowed to attend the picnic. They were kept in the vacant ward and had their ribs and shrimp brought up to them.

It was one of the strangest days of Brian's life. The get-together could hardly have been described as a party. There was a lot of hushed talk and whispered speculation. After the meal, the hospital CEO, Sheilah Davenport, came to the vacant ward to speak to the patients. Dr. Davenport asked everyone to be quiet. She said she had an announcement to make.

"A very serious crime was committed last night against a female patient on Four South," she said. "Some of you may be called to give interviews to the police."

"Is Susan okay?" someone asked.

"Sadly, no," Dr. Davenport said.

Patients, she added, would no longer be permitted to have shoelaces.

Everyone had heard Susan saying she wanted to die; still, it didn't seem right that her body was being taken to the morgue while everyone else was feasting on ribs and shrimp. News of the crime spread quickly, both inside and outside the hospital. As with Dr. Gopalani's "nervous breakdown," Perkins authorities tried to keep patients from seeing media coverage of the crime, but the embargo was pointless; before long, all the details were public knowledge.

The ward's security cameras had caught El entering Susan's room at around 10:50 p.m. (while Felicia was talking to Brian about the Bible), and leaving nine minutes later. The footage also showed major lapses in security. There were three guards assigned to the ward that night. They were supposed to check on patients every half hour, but at the time of the murder, one guard was sitting on a couch watching television, the second was at the nurses' station but had no view of the patients' rooms, and the third was nowhere in sight.

Footage of the days leading up to the murder contained shocking evidence. On numerous occasions between July and September, El could be seen collecting and consuming Susan's urine and feces in full view of the security cameras—and no one had noticed. No one had seen it happen at the time, and clearly, no one had watched the video footage. When questioned, El reiterated his belief that bodily fluids contained magic powers. Consuming Susan's urine and excrement, he believed, would make him into a woman, as nature had intended.

According to El, in March, six months before the murder, at an individual case conference that he hadn't been permitted to attend, Dr. Davenport and Dr. Mohammed Ajanah, the clinical director, had made the decision to discontinue his prescription for Risperdal. In June, El said he'd complained of "psychological problems" to a clinical social worker, who said his body was probably adjusting to the absence of antipsychotics.

On September 27, 2010, the *Baltimore Sun* published an interview with Robert Cure, a retired Perkins security sergeant, who testified that El would order bras and panties in the mail. Cure said he'd sometimes deliver the packages to El's room. "He was well-read and intelligent, but quiet and kept to himself," said Cure, adding that, in his opinion, El should never have been housed on the same hallway as female patients. "There are so many places Saladin Taylor should have been, as opposed to around women," Cure said, referring to El by his former name. "We knew that Saladin was a killer and that at no time can you relax on Saladin. He was absolutely a noted, documented killer of women."

Brian had to agree. He wasn't shocked by the murder; he'd always believed that El was a serial killer. Placing him on a coed ward, in Brian's opinion, was like housing a wolf with a pack of puppies.

Susan and El had been close friends, and people wondered about his motive. Some alleged the killing was a sex crime. El did admit to kissing Susan before he strangled her, and she was found naked from the waist down—the pink yoga pants she normally wore to bed were found balled up in her closet—but he denied there was a sexual motive to the murder. He claimed that he and Susan had a murder-suicide pact, and he'd even ordered a pair of extra-long shoelaces to use: one to strangle Susan and the other to hang himself. But strangling another person, he'd discovered, was a lot easier than strangling oneself.

A year and six months after the murder of Susan Sachs, El-Soudani El-Wahhabi, né Saladin Taylor, was found competent to stand trial. The prosecutor argued that if indeed there had been a murder-suicide pact, El had no intention of carrying out his half of the bargain. In order to strangle Susan so efficiently, the prosecutor explained, El had stood on top of her body and pulled the cord, leaving his footprint on her skin. As for hanging himself with the other shoelace, he hadn't even gotten around to taking it out of his shoe. The jury was deadlocked, a mistrial was declared, and the case went to court again a year later. This time, El-Soudani El-Wahhabi, by now fifty-two, was found guilty of first-degree murder and sent to North Branch Correctional Institution, a maximum-security prison in western Maryland.

The last anyone heard of El, he—or, rather, she—had taken the name Shawnté Anne Levy and was petitioning the court for gender reassignment surgery (so far, without success).

18

"Everybody Is Afraid"

Unsurprisingly, the murder of Susan Sachs put the hospital under enormous scrutiny. The three security guards who were working on Brian's ward that night all chose to retire (thereby keeping their benefits and state pensions). Four months later, to Brian's disappointment, the hospital CEO, Sheilah Davenport, also "stepped down." Brian thought Dr. Davenport had been doing a fine job and guessed that higher authorities had chosen to make made her a scapegoat for the murder. In response to the crime, extra guards were hired, night employees were watched more closely, additional security cameras were installed, a new female ward was created, and the state's attorney for the Department of Health and Mental Hygiene, Susan Steinberg, briefly took over as interim CEO until a new one was appointed.

Patients had died at Perkins before—from natural causes, illnesses, suicides, and accidents. But murder was different. Journalists, politicians, mental health advocates, and members of the public wanted to know how this crime had been allowed to happen. Why had a known sex offender with a history of violence against women been placed on a coed ward? Why had he been taken off his medication? How was he able to enter a woman's bedroom at night, unseen?

To those outside the hospital, the negligence was inexcusable. But those at Perkins knew that, especially compared to many of his fellow patients, who also had histories of violent crimes, El had been quiet, calm, and well behaved. He'd caused no trouble for years and had been found well-adjusted enough to be moved to medium security. His preoccupations were certainly unusual, but no more so than those of other patients—some of whom, before the incident leading to their committal, had been successful, high-functioning individuals.

One of these was Vitali Davydov, a young man who, like Brian, had dropped out of college in the middle of his second semester— although, unlike the Bechtolds in Brian's case, Vitali Davydov's parents were aware of, and deeply concerned about, their son's increasing paranoia. A student at the University of Tennessee at Knoxville, where he roomed with his twin brother, Vitali began calling home confused and agitated. Each time, his anxious parents drove down to Knoxville from Maryland in the middle of the night, but although he seemed restless at first, after a couple of days, Vitali was his old self again. Still, the Davydovs could tell something was wrong. Unlike the Bechtolds, they were a close-knit family, and Vitali's parents could recognize uncharacteristic behavior.

At the beginning of August 2006, Vitali appeared to be back to his old self, relaxed and easygoing. But as the month drew to a close, his symptoms returned, and so his father, Albert, made an appointment with Dr. Wayne Fenton, a prominent expert in schizophrenia with a private practice in Bethesda, Maryland. Fenton was an associate director of the National Institute of Mental Health and a psychiatrist well known for his courage in dealing with severely psychotic and often dangerous patients. Fenton generously agreed to see Vitali at 4 p.m. on the Sunday of Labor Day weekend, September 3, 2006, and Albert dropped him off at the doctor's office and then went to run some errands. When he returned to pick Vitali up, Albert saw with horror that his son's hands, shirt, and pants were dark with blood.

Albert ran over to the psychiatrist's office and looked through the window.

Dr. Fenton was lying facedown on a bloodied Oriental rug.

Vitali Davydov was sent to Perkins in April 2007, at the age of nineteen, after he was found not criminally responsible for the murder of Dr. Fenton. Smart and personable, Vitali had a huge advantage in the support of a close and loving family, who visited him whenever they could, bringing him food, clothes, and treats. When patients had such strong connections outside the hospital, they usually found it easier to obtain a release, especially if their friends or family could pay for the services of a private attorney. In some cases, of course, an early release was simply not possible. Vitali Davydov, for example, had committed a very high-profile crime. (Ironically, Dr. Fenton was one of the world's foremost experts on schizophrenia.) Vitali's attorney set up a release hearing after his client had been at Perkins for only three years, but even though a psychiatrist hired by the defense conducted an evaluation and concluded that Vitali was ready to be released, the jury disagreed.

Still, Vitali had done well at Perkins—well enough, in fact, to be moved to a medium-security ward, then to minimum security. There, he was given open-ward privileges, which meant he could come and go as he pleased and was trusted to follow the hospital rules of his own accord. He was doing so well, in fact, that he'd been on supervised trips outside the hospital and was permitted to lower his dose of antipsychotic medication. Before long, however—as with El—Vitali became unstable again and found it hard to regain his equilibrium. His psychiatrist tried out various combinations of drugs, but nothing seemed to restore his self-possession. Vitali became obsessive, paranoid, and delusional. He said Dr. Fenton had wanted to die, had asked to be killed. Sometimes, Vitali said his *father* had killed Dr. Fenton. At other times, he said his father wasn't actually his father, but an identical impostor (a delusion known as Capgras syndrome). Eventually, he was sent back to maximum security.

The most pervasive theme of Vitali's obsessions was anal rape. Sometimes he said he'd been anally raped by his father, and sometimes he'd say by his brother. Sometimes he claimed his father had anally raped his brother. He even said that Dr. Fenton had been anally raped. In light of Vitali's odd preoccupation, Brian found it disconcerting to learn that, in the fall of 2011, Vitali's roommate was David Rico-Noyola, a convicted sex offender. This twenty-two-year-old patient, known as Rico, had been sent to Perkins after being found not criminally responsible for murdering his mother three years earlier. Brian had always found Rico sneaky and devious. He didn't speak much English, got into a lot of fistfights, and was rumored to be a member of MS-13, a criminal gang of Salvadoran immigrants. Rico was openly gay, and on two separate occasions, when they were on the same ward, Brian had witnessed him trying to rape a patient named Delmus Kimble in the dayroom. Both times, Kimble had punched him in the stomach, but instead of fighting back, Rico would either try to kiss Kimble or grab hold of his underwear. By October of that year, Rico and Vitali Davydov had apparently been at odds for months, and staff knew it.

On the afternoon of October 21, 2011, about half an hour after the 2 p.m. bed check, Vitali Davydov came out of his room and approached a nurse.

"My roommate tried to rape me, so I beat him up," he told her.

When she entered the room, the nurse found Rico lying on the floor with his face covered in blood. He was taken to Howard County General Hospital, where he was pronounced dead on arrival.

The police were called, and Vitali was taken to headquarters. According to the coroner's report, David Rico-Noyola's cause of death was "blunt force trauma to the face and head," and Vitali's hands showed "blood and minor lacerations on and around the knuckle area." Vitali claimed he was defending himself against sexual assault. Later that night, he was charged with first-degree murder.

Louis, a patient in my group, was on the ward where the murder took place. "The white boy from Russia, he was already in here for killing somebody with his bare hands," Louis told me. "He was a strong guy, with a big upper body. And when you're sick and very aggressive, you get stronger. Although he didn't act out before that. He stopped taking his medication, and he started deteriorating. You have a right to stop taking medication, as long as you're not violent." On the evening of the murder, Louis was in the gym when he saw Rico's body being carried out on a stretcher. "There was a whole bunch of blood on his shirt," he said. "He was just lying there, dead."

It was just over a year since El's murder of Susan Sachs. The press and the public were outraged. Perkins authorities were defensive. The acting CEO, Susan Steinberg, announced that new security measures would be implemented. There'd be a new administration, she said. She insisted that nothing of the kind would ever be allowed to happen again.

But it did.

Eight days later.

Rogelio Mondragon, forty, had been sent to Perkins in 2010 after being found incompetent to stand trial on charges that he, along with two accomplices, raped an eleven-year-old girl in a Silver Spring apartment. On the morning of Thursday, October 28, 2011, at around ten o'clock, Mondragon, a slight Hispanic man who spoke very little English, was taken to Montgomery County Circuit Court for a competency hearing. The judge sent him back to Perkins for further treatment. At around seven o'clock that evening, on the same ward on which Vitali Davydov had killed David Rico-Noyola, a staff nurse performing a routine check on the patients' rooms found Rogelio Mondragon dead on the floor.

The police were alerted. Medics arrived. Once again, patients were rounded up and taken to another ward while the crime scene was taped off and the incident investigated. In the middle of all the confusion, Andre Mayo, forty-six, a patient with a long criminal history, quietly informed a nurse that he was the perpetrator. He'd punched Mondragon in the face, he said, and once he was on the ground, he'd beaten him to death with his fists. Mayo was kept on the ward in handcuffs and interviewed by the police, who stayed at Perkins all night, talking to patients and reviewing the evidence. Mayo, it turned out, was telling the truth: video surveillance tapes showed him entering and leaving Mondragon's room twice in half an hour. According to the autopsy report, death was caused by multiple blunt-force injuries to the face and neck.

In the press, the murder of Rogelio Mondragon was described as a "mystery." "He just killed the dude for no reason," Louis told me. But the crime was no mystery to Brian. He'd heard Andre Mayo say more than once that he'd be better off in prison than at Perkins. This was a strong indictment of the hospital, especially given that Mayo had been in prison before and had no illusions about life behind bars. Brian assumed that the Rico murder had given Mayo the idea. He chose the weakest man on the ward. Small and thin, Mondragon was a known child molester, and unpopular for that reason. On top of that, he had a private room. All in all, he was a perfect victim.

By issuing a statement the following day, the Maryland Department of Mental Health and Hygiene was clearly trying to preempt public criticism. "The events at the Clifton T. Perkins Hospital over the last week are tragic and unacceptable," said DMHH secretary Dr. Joshua Sharfstein. "Hospitals are places for healing, not violence. Perkins Hospital has taken many steps to strengthen the safety of its environment, but more needs to be done." Jonathan Fellner, Mondragon's attorney, was unconvinced. "Any time you have a client with mental health issues who's declared incompetent to stand trial, you expect the facility he's in to be a safe environment," he told Ian Duncan of the *Baltimore Sun*. "I was shocked and surprised when I found out that he was killed. He wasn't safe there."

Critics of the hospital blamed inconsistent leadership and inadequate staffing. Mental health advocates claimed the patients at Perkins were improperly medicated, and there weren't enough activities to keep them from getting bored in the evenings. Security guards complained about the absence of training and support, the lack of opportunities for advancement, the hostile work environment, and low pay. Overtime was a vexed issue, too. The hospital was subjected to a long and thorough review. New staff were appointed, and a new director brought in.

David S. Helsel, a seasoned and well-respected hospital leader, was transferred to Perkins from Spring Grove Hospital Center in Catonsville, Maryland. At a hastily arranged press conference, Dr. Helsel was asked about his plans to deal with violence and fear in the hospital.

Helsel was realistic. "I'm not sure it's possible to erase fear completely, but that would be the goal," he said. "With the nature of the patient population, everyone has to exercise caution, and there will be some degree of people looking over their shoulder." While he admitted the murders were disturbing, Dr. Helsel reminded everyone that people suffering from mental illness, including those in forensic hospitals, are rarely violent, and those who do commit a violent act rarely do so again.

Despite Dr. Helsel's reminder, the atmosphere at Perkins remained tense. Outside the hospital, representatives of advocate groups began to speak out for the rights of patients and staff. The union representing the hospital's security guards sent a letter to state officials claiming that violence was the inevitable result of constant paranoia. "Staff have seen doctors showing serious fear of clients," the letter claimed. "Some patients are under medicated and others are over-medicated."

As treatment teams did not get input from the direct-care staff, the union argued that they "are often out-of-touch and therefore make dangerous clinical decisions regarding these very dangerous clients."

"I'm in a room with two people," Louis told me. "I fear for my life all the time." Laura Cain of the Maryland Disability Law Center, a group that advocates for the rights of psychiatric patients, called on the state to address what she described as treatment problems and conditions that generated fear. Cain said that Perkins wasn't doing enough to protect patients. Instead of being treated with compassion after the murders, for example, the patients had been put in a state of near lockdown. She pointed out that none of them had been offered any kind of grief counseling; in the hospital itself, the murders had been swept under the rug or were discussed only in the vaguest terms—hardly a good example for a psychiatric institute. "The culture really needs to change, and the hospital leadership needs to find out ways to reduce that level of fear," Cain said. "Everybody is afraid."

Dr. Helsel's theory, which made sense to Brian, was that miserable people are dangerous, and happy people are safe. Consequently, Helsel ended the "no food trading" rule. He implemented a once-a-month takeout dinner (up to ten dollars in value), purchased an X-ray machine to scan food brought in by visitors, and every ward got satellite television. The improvements made a difference. Most people agreed that Perkins had become a better place.

On January 2, 2012, Brian was finally—yet again—moved from maximum to medium security. Escorted by five guards and wheeling a cart containing his few worldly goods, he walked the short distance down the hospital corridors to his new ward. His stigma, he felt, had been lifted. The path to freedom was no longer blocked. Now he'd have access to caffeine, money, food, and individual therapy.

Things quickly improved. He began therapy with a new psychologist he liked, Chelsea Howe. In June, he was evaluated by a psychiatrist named David Chandran, who concluded that "there was no evidence of any paranoia or any bizarre behavior or thinking. His thought process is very well organized at present. His mood has been stable. He has been compliant with treatment. The patient has not exhibited any mania, depression, suicidal ideation, or thoughts of hurting other people." Later that year, Brian got a new psychologist, Angela Onwuanibe (pronounced "on-WANNA-be"), who had a good reputation. Other patients had told him that if he ever got on to Dr. Onwuanibe's ward, it would be smooth sailing from there. She was known for getting patients out of the hospital quickly and efficiently.

The psychiatrist was an interesting character, a refreshing change from Brian's previous doctors. Every morning, bright and early, she'd come bouncing through the doors of the ward, bopping around like a teenager even though she was in her midfifties. She had an upbeat disposition and a winning, dimpled smile. Born and raised in Nigeria, she'd trained in London and was a die-hard fan of Arsenal, the English soccer team. Right away, Brian liked her attitude. She had a way of bringing everyone together to resolve conflicts and hostilities on the ward. At the same time, it sometimes crossed his mind that if she'd been a patient, she'd surely have been diagnosed as bipolar. Her manic energy sometimes seemed over the top for a woman her age. She told Brian she held three different jobs and said she sometimes interrupted people because she could read their minds and knew what they were about to say.

Still, her eccentricities didn't interfere with her can-do efficiency. On Dr. Onwuanibe's ward, Brian felt supported. It finally seemed that he was making progress toward an eventual release. One afternoon in 2013, after Brian had been on her ward for three months, Dr. Onwuanibe sat down next to him and told him that at the next meeting of the Clinical Forensic Review Board, she was going to recommend him for transfer to minimum security, with the understanding that shortly after that, he would be moved to a regional hospital.

Brian was elated. He'd been on minimum security before, ten years before, but a regional hospital was something new. He'd be getting out of Perkins at last. But before he'd even had time to absorb the news, Dr. Onwuanibe changed her mind. When she came back from the Clinical Forensic Review Board meeting, she said nothing about his release, and even started talking about increasing his medication. Brian realized that one of the other doctors must have warned her against treating him with too much leniency.

He tried to resist the increased dose—he felt just fine on his current regimen—but Dr. Onwuanibe made it clear that he wouldn't make any further progress toward release unless he changed his mind. The theme of her notes was always the same: that Brian had no "insight" into his illness because he distrusted the hospital, resisted medication, and didn't agree that he was mentally ill. In other words, the meanings ascribed to what Brian said weren't taken at face value, as they would have been with a healthy person, but were instead attributed to his mental illness. "SOMEWHAT HYPERVERBAL," Dr. Onwuanibe wrote in Brian's file.* "PATIENT IS PARANOID. Believes things are 'headed in a negative direction.' Insight is very limited to poor has made several bad decisions including refusing medication a few months back when frustrated. In addition has requested lower doses. REMAINS AMBIVALENT ABOUT MEDICATION CHANGES, CONTINUES TO REPORT THAT MEDICATION WILL NOT HELP HIM. FRUSTRATED AT THE LACK OF PROGRESS IN THE HOSPITAL BUT UNABLE to see his role in that especially with his drefusal to increased doses of medication and returning to lower doses." A month later, she complained that "HE REMAINS VERY UPSET TO SUGGESTIONS THAT MEDIATION MAY IMPROVE HIS CONSDITION><RE-PEATEDLY ASKING FOR TRIALS OFF MEDICATION SO HE 'CAN PROVE' that he plans to 'STAY IN A GOOD WAY' continues to misinterpret conversation and remains paranoid." She

---

* Quotations are verbatim, including misspellings, idiosyncratic spacing, and capital letters.

also refers to his "continued perseveration in long length of time here in the hospital" and "delusional beliefs that he is doing well."

There was nothing Brian could do. He accepted the higher dose. In August, Dr. Onwuanibe noted, "Mr Bechtold has been more open recently to medication CHANGES THOUGH HE STILL REPORTS IS AS 'I WILL DO WHAT THE HOSPITAL WANTS ESSENTIALLY SUCK IT UP.'" He stayed on the increased dose for months. The situation was intensely frustrating. For every step forward, there were at least two steps back. "Does not feel the hospital understands his position," Dr. Onwuanibe noted. "Feels that he has been stable for several m years and deserves the chance to transition to a less restrictive side . . . FEELS THAT THE HOSPITAL HAS NOT HELD UP 'THEIR SIDE OF THE BARGAIN.'"

The year 2013 was miserable for Brian in more ways than one. In the fall, he learned from Cathy that their older sister, Marcia, had passed away at the age of sixty-two. Brian hadn't known his oldest sister well, but he'd always loved her. He remembered her caring for him when he was a young child, and he'd been deeply touched by the way she stood by him after the crime. Marcia had been a master landscape gardener, and this had inspired Brian to request a job in horticulture at Perkins, although he was usually assigned to the kitchen or the laundry, as jobs involving outdoor work were offered only to particular low-security patients. Sadly, in recent years, Marcia had also suffered from mental illness, and although she'd never been diagnosed or hospitalized, she'd grown paranoid and irrational, and had turned into a hoarder. Cathy had taken Marcia into her home in Ohio for a while, but she'd proven to be unmanageable. At the time of her death, she'd been living in isolation. In a moment of clarity, she'd once admitted to Cathy that, like their father, she'd lost the ability to feel any emotion at all.

On the ward, Brian continued to follow all the rules. He assured his treatment team that he wouldn't be violent. He was open in therapy and compliant with his medications. A note in his file observed,

"It is the opinion of the treatment team at this time that he could be transferred to a less restrictive environment and given another opportunity at the regional hospital, which will assist him with his gradual transition back to the community."

And yet nothing changed. All year, Brian watched from the background while other patients were moved to minimum security, graduating through the hierarchy of privilege levels until they were released to supervised housing or even sent home. There were plenty of addicts, rapists, drug dealers, child molesters, and schizophrenics whom Dr. Onwuanibe seemed to have no problem moving through the system, or so it seemed to Brian. Some of them were young children when Brian first arrived at Perkins in 1992; some hadn't even been born.

The situation was intolerable. At the very least, he deserved a chance to prove himself. He decided it was time to force the issue. This time, instead of trying to escape, he tried the legitimate route and took the hospital to court.

19

Pro Se

As I've come to know the culture at Perkins, I've learned that psychiatric hospitals, like prisons, are fertile ground for the cultivation of jailhouse lawyers. Long-term patients, especially those who feel mistreated, indignant, and vengeful, often turn to the courts in search of justice and, ideally, retribution. Some become very knowledgeable about the law, and courts are encouraged to give special leniency to pro se litigants.

Some patients' pro se cases are well argued and articulate; others may be repetitious and even meaningless. In psychiatric literature, those who turn obsessively to the courts are known as "querulous patients"; in legal discourse, as "vexatious litigants." These personalities, according to those familiar with them, are usually well-educated males between forty and sixty years of age, of above-average intelligence, often coldly rational, and "abnormally difficult and disputatious" in character. They generally have an impressive (albeit superficial) working knowledge of the law and of legal terminology; they may be slightly unkempt; they sometimes carry around a bag or briefcase bulging with documents; they may be blindly obsessed by personal vindication. To their doctors, this constant litigation is proof of their paranoia. Robert Wisner-Carlson, one of the Perkins psychiatrists treating Anthony Kelly, described his patient in court as "argumentative, litigious, peevish; he will often file numerous complaints, lawsuits, grievances, this sort of thing, and will do so when there doesn't seem to be merit."

Judges, as well as psychiatrists, may find themselves growing impatient with litigants like Anthony Kelly and Robert King. Patients at hospitals like Perkins file pro se petitions all the time; their documents are usually handwritten and may be incomplete or difficult to understand. The response from the Court of Special Appeals in July 1980 to a pleading from a pro se defendant at Perkins named John Alan Langworthy, for example, begins, "Virtually every judge in southern Maryland has, upon some hearing, trial or motion, lavished attention upon John Alan Langworthy." The court goes on to complain:

> This record is choked with scores of variegated pleadings, hundreds upon hundreds of tightly scripted pages of *pro se* letters. . . . It would be an exercise in futility to inventory them all. In essence, the appellant was a loose cannon upon the trial deck, and his chaotic lurchings made the orderly passage of his case impossible. Every constituent element of the criminal justice system extended itself commendably to move this case forward but was continuously frustrated by the appellant's strewing of procedural obstacles in the path, compounded by his obstreperous and truculent disruptiveness at every turn.

As this response indicates, members of the judiciary may grow frustrated by their obligation to respond to such unruly petitions, which may be unhinged or abusive in tone, even personally derogatory to the judge and designed to stir his or her anger. In May 2016, for example, Donald Gary Rembold, a patient at Spring Grove Hospital Center, filed a civil rights action in the U.S. Court for the District of Maryland challenging his confinement on the grounds that he had been "unlawfully admitted," and he demanded monetary damages for "202 days of ignominy." The case was assigned to Maryland District Court judge Paul Grimm, who, in his response, described Rembold's petition as "rife with language that a Billingsgate fishmonger would think twice before using." This response angered Rembold, who filed an addendum asking that the case be given to a different judge. The addendum, addressed to Grimm, began, "Hey, Asshole," and concluded, "Get off my case asshole!"

While courts are encouraged to grant special leeway to pro se litigants, they're clearly under no obligation to ignore this kind of contempt. Petitions like Rembold's are part of the reason judges, in general, don't get involved with the mental health system. They're especially reluctant to act against the decisions of those working in the day-to-day environment of the clinic, who are (presumably) the people most familiar with the patients and their case histories. Rarely will a judge release a patient from a psychiatric hospital when their treatment team doesn't believe they're ready, especially if they've committed violent crimes in the past. The prevailing judicial attitude is that, as with the Department of Corrections, state authorities should have autonomy over their own fiefdoms.

Still, when judges refuse to get involved in the question of whether someone should be committed, restrained, or medicated against their will, they give psychiatrists the power to decide not only medical questions, but legal and ethical ones, too. And psychiatrists, however good their intentions, tend to find what they've been trained to look for.

"Litigious mania" is widely considered a symptom of paranoid or delusional disorders—and no doubt this is often the case. At the same time, however, anyone who's been incarcerated for more than twenty years, whether they have a mental illness or not, might naturally experience "a keen desire for moral vindication." If "querulous litigants" are paranoid and unstable personalities, it's possible they've become that way because their rights have been violated many times in egregious ways. Their complaints may be neither unfounded nor unreasonable.

It may be difficult for members of the judiciary to overcome their prejudices against persistent pro se petitioners, especially those who are incarcerated or clearly unhinged. In this light, it would hardly be unusual if Montgomery County Circuit Court judge Richard Jordan, who presided over *Brian Bechtold v. Maryland Department of Health and Mental Hygiene*, already had misgivings about the plaintiff's state of mind. If so, he can hardly have been reassured to learn, shortly after the opening of proceedings on the morning of February 10, 2014, that, as in his guardianship hearing, Brian had just fired his public defender and wanted to represent himself.

This public defender was Brad Hersey, a neat young man in glasses. As the attorney assigned to the Maryland attorney general's Department of Health and Mental Hygiene, Hersey represented every patient in Perkins other than the small handful able to afford a private lawyer. Most of his clients had active legal cases in the sense that they were either fighting their involuntary commitment, battling their security level, or protesting their medication regime.

After learning that the plaintiff intended to represent himself, Judge Jordan asked Brian to step forward. Brian's legs were shackled with a fifteen-inch chain, so it was more a shuffle than a step.

"Mr. Bechtold," the judge said, "why do you want to fire your attorney?"

"Mr. Hersey's very busy," Brian said. "At Clifton T. Perkins, there's about two hundred patients, and each patient is entitled to one court date a year. And I'm just one of those patients out of the two hundred, so it's very difficult for him to have enough time to manage a case like this."

"So, you think you can handle a trial in front of a jury better than Mr. Hersey?" the judge asked skeptically. "He's been to law school. He's passed the bar, and he has a lot of experience in this area."

There was a long pause. Brian gave the question serious thought.

"I think I'll be comparable, if not better," he said finally. "I'm very familiar with my charting and the documents that are held in my name at Perkins hospital, and it would be almost impossible for Mr. Hersey to go through all the volumes of material and know where to look and how to look for information pertaining to this case."

Jordan was still reluctant. "Do you understand that having an attorney is almost always far and away better than not having an attorney assist you?" he asked Brian. "Do you understand that?"

"Yes, Your Honor," Brian said. "But being that this trial is based upon who I am, and what I'm able to do, and think, and understand, I think the jury will be better served to see me actually participate more in my petition for release, because if I just sit back and let the attorney handle everything, there's some question mark as to my competency and my mental state that might be relevant to the trial itself."

At the time, Brian's decision to represent himself struck everyone as a spontaneous, spur-of-the-moment one—otherwise, why leave it to the last minute to fire his lawyer? In fact, as on the occasion of his guardianship hearing, it was a deliberate and strategic move. He knew that Rhonda Edwards, the Maryland assistant state's attorney assigned to the agency's Department of Health and Mental Hygiene, was used to arguing against Brad Hersey and would have been familiar with his methods and techniques. No doubt she'd already prepared a defense against them. But she wouldn't have a clue what direction Brian himself was going to take.

The judge continued to advise Brian very seriously against defending himself, but Brian stood his ground. Finally, Jordan conceded that if Hersey believed his client was competent to do so, he couldn't prevent Brian from acting as his own attorney. Brad Hersey agreed that

Brian knew what he was doing, and the judge allowed Brian's shackles to be removed—they were replaced with "tight coverage" by two deputies—and called the jury pool into the room.

The judge introduced the parties involved, gave the potential jurors an overview of Brian's petition and his crime, and made sure none of them had any connections to anyone involved with the case. From the pool, the jury members were selected—two attorneys, two doctors, an information technology consultant, and a nurse. A couple of them had known someone who suffered from mental illness, but all felt they were able to be impartial. Judge Jordan then outlined the issues they'd be asked to consider: Does Mr. Bechtold currently have a mental disorder? If so, would he, by reason of his mental disorder, be a danger to himself, others, or the property of others if he were released from the hospital? And if not, should the court impose conditions upon his release?

After a short break, Brian presented his opening statement. Dressed in a royal blue Jordan jogging suit, he read from a piece of paper covered with handwritten notes. His case, he explained, hinged on the question of free will. He asked the jury to imagine a normally peaceful person who, in their old age, developed Alzheimer's disease. If this person failed to recognize a family member and became violent because they believed a stranger was invading their home, nobody would hold them accountable for their actions. However, unlike mental illness, he explained, Alzheimer's is a very specific disease that all doctors recognize and understand. But in his own case, while everyone agreed that at the time he committed his crime he was in the grips of a condition that overwhelmed his free will, no one seemed to be able to say what that condition was or how it affected his personality, and so no one could say for sure when it had gone.

"In the case of mental illness, the waters are so muddy that even the courts and the hospital disagree in fundamental ways," he went on. "Let's go back to the Alzheimer's patient who becomes violent with the family member. If their condition radically improved, should they still be locked away? I honestly believe most people would say, 'Of course not.' However, if you put a mentally ill person in the same scenario, would you have the same compassion and understanding? Would you have the same ability to forgive?"

It was a compelling argument, and Brian, although nervous, spoke fluently and from the heart. He came across as open, affable, and intelligent and gave no obvious signs of mental illness. But Assistant State's Attorney Rhonda Edwards was poised and confident. The crime that Brian committed, while terrible, had occurred a long time ago, she conceded. She allowed that Brian appeared to be "a pleasant guy." But she wanted the jury to know they shouldn't be fooled by appearances: mental illness isn't always obvious, and according to his doctors, Brian was mentally ill and prone to dangerous outbursts of violence.

"You'll hear from the doctors that, since Mr. Bechtold has been at Perkins Hospital Center, he's tried to escape," Edwards told the jury. "In doing so, he took a hostage with a metal object. That was in 1999. . . . And then, in 2006, Mr. Bechtold again tried to escape from the hospital. . . . He'd been looking for a pathway out through the ceiling of his room. He was unable to find one, and so he made a shank, a metal shank, from the ceiling tiles. . . . Mr. Bechtold tried to assault a social worker." Brian's doctors thought he was too dangerous to be released into the community, Ms. Edwards concluded—and surely, they were the experts.

Because he was acting as his own attorney, and had no witnesses testifying on his behalf, Brian faced an uphill battle. He had to defend himself against four psychiatrists called by the state. If he tried to argue that he wasn't paranoid and dangerous, all the doctors had to do was refer to the "evidence" in his files. It didn't make any difference that, as Brian saw it, these documents were riddled with errors and misinterpretations. The opinions of psychiatrists, he'd learned, were tantamount to "scientific facts," and the only acceptable attitude in the face of their opinions seemed to be an almost religious humility.

The state kicked off with Rosha Hebsur, a thirty-one-year-old psychologist who specialized in the treatment of eating disorders. Dr. Hebsur, who didn't know Brian, had conducted a risk evaluation for the purposes of the court hearing. Her assessment, she explained, took place over two days. (Brian recalled her speaking with him for a couple of hours each day.) She said she'd conducted a close reading of Brian's history, followed by a series of tests and an interview.

In his direct examination, Brian asked Dr. Hebsur about his current diagnosis, and she replied that he'd been diagnosed with schizoaffective disorder and mixed personality disorder with narcissistic and antisocial features. Brian asked her to explain what personality disorders were, and she defined them as disorders that "are typically demonstrated in early adulthood or young adolescence" and are "pervasive and enduring."

Brian pointed out that he'd only recently been diagnosed with a personality disorder, which meant that it couldn't have begun in "early adulthood," and it couldn't have been "pervasive" or "enduring."

"Your disorder has been modified in the twenty-two years based on observation and demonstration of symptoms," she replied.

"It's been modified," Brian said. "Does that mean it's changed?"

"Based on new information and symptoms, diagnoses can change, yes."

"Is that typical? Does somebody typically change their personality?"

"That's not typical," Dr. Hebsur replied.

"Okay."

"However, sometimes it's difficult to identify features based on who's doing the observation."

"So, this has more to do with different doctors having different opinions, correct?"

"I wouldn't say that's correct."

Brian wanted to make the jury aware of the stark inconsistencies in his diagnoses over the years, including the fact that, according to his psychiatrists, he "became a psychopath at age 34." He also let the jury know that his escape attempt was a response to his despair at being medicated into a stupor, his sense that he'd never get out of the hospital, and his belief he'd be better off in prison.

During the state's cross-examination, Rhonda Edwards asked Dr. Hebsur to explain why she predicted that Brian was at "high risk" for future violence. In reply, Hebsur referred to

> his previous history of violence, history of childhood behavioral problems, history of substance abuse, a number of non-violent criminal offenses, his relatively young age at his most violent offense, employment instability, a diagnosis of major mental illness, a personality disorder, prior supervision failures, escape attempt without hospital approval, and he also falls within a moderate degree of psychopathy.

After a short break, the state's next witness took the stand. Sybil Smith-Gray, fifty-six, was a clinical social worker who specialized in the educational psychology of deaf children. It was difficult to understand why the state had asked her to testify. She had a weakness for Latin and medical terms. When Brian asked her if she'd read through his older records, she replied that she hadn't considered "previous iterations." When he asked her if she'd read his current documents, she said she hadn't read them "in toto."

As he'd done with Dr. Hebsur, Brian began by asking Dr. Smith-Gray about his diagnosis. Specifically, he asked her to explain his "antisocial features."

Dr. Smith-Gray spoke solemnly and with dignity, but her answer was confused and redundant.

> Antisocial personality disorder involves the violation of major rights and the violation of the rights of individuals. It involves major rule

breaking. It involves minor rule breaking. Individuals with antisocial personality disorder think the rules don't apply to them, that they're different, that they're special, that they can break the rules and get away with it. That's what antisocial personality disorder involves, as well as narcissistic personality disorder. . . . In my opinion, the anti-social personality disorder presentation in any individual, it dates back in history. In fact, the onset of it can typically take the form of something that is called "conduct disorder" in early childhood. That is the reason why your risk factor for early childhood maladjustment is a significant risk factor in your evaluation. So, there is a trajectory of early childhood maladjustment that looks like conduct disorder. And involves rule breaking. And that can go on to take the form of antisocial personality disorder in adulthood.

When Brian pointed out that he had, over the last five years, maintained a high level of privilege at Perkins, which wasn't consistent with "a pervasive pattern of rule breaking," Dr. Smith-Gray said this was clear evidence that he was planning future violence.

The privilege system is a qualitative examination of how a person is behaving on the unit at any given point in time. It would not be unusual, and it would not be unusual at all, for an individual with antisocial personality disorder, and a person with at least average cognitive abilities, to be able to manipulate the privilege level systems so that they can present in a way that looks very positive with underlying plans for alternative behaviors.

Furthermore, while the jury knew that Brian had murdered his parents, they'd been told that the crime wasn't part of the current trial and shouldn't be taken into account as evidence. Judge Jordan had told them that they should decide the case "based solely on the evidence that is presented in court." In this light, Dr. Smith-Gray's response to Brian's next question was a dirty blow:

Brian: You testified that Brian Bechtold has a problem with
breaking the rules?

Dr. Smith-Gray: Yes. Murder is an example of breaking the rules.

After a short break, the state's third witness took the stand. Forensic psychiatrist Dr. Inna Taller was, at the time, the clinical director
of Perkins; she had an eastern European accent and spoke in a short,
clipped tone that made her seem formal and competent but not especially warm. She, too, admitted that even though she was the hospital's
chief psychiatrist, she'd had very little contact with Brian. She'd never
treated him, she said. She'd spent about an hour interviewing him in
preparation for the trial—Brian recalls it as more of a casual chat—
and she'd looked over his records. After a lot of back-and-forth over
the nature of Brian's diagnosis and how far he'd progressed in his
twenty years at Perkins, Dr. Taller finally stated that, although on the
surface Brian might appear to be perfectly functional, in fact, he had
a very subtle mental illness that could be understood only by experienced psychiatrists who'd known him and studied him for a long time.
"The symptoms that Mr. Bechtold exhibits right now . . . are difficult
to see," she told the jury. "But with experience and with time, they
become apparent to the clinical and mental health professionals."

Here, many of the jurors shifted in their seats, turned from Dr.
Taller, and began looking curiously at Brian instead, as if hoping for
a glimpse of his barely perceptible psychopathy.

On the following morning, February 11, 2014, Dr. Angela
Onwuanibe took the stand—the only witness who knew Brian well.
She introduced herself as a board-certified psychiatrist with twenty-
six years of experience in general medicine and twelve years of experience in psychiatry and psychopharmacology. She spoke very quickly
in a soft, deep voice with a strong Nigerian accent that sometimes
made her a little difficult to understand. When she addressed Brian,
her tone was gentle and concerned, even maternal, and her voice occa-
sionally descended to a soft whisper.

Dr. Onwuanibe was on the stand longer than any other witness. She never seemed to waver in her confidence, although her answers to Brian's questions on direct were vague, rambling, and insubstantial. When he asked her to give examples of behavior that characterized his Axis II diagnosis of mixed personality disorder with narcissistic and antisocial features, for example, she replied as if addressing a young child:

> [O]f the narcissistic and the antisocial and the mixed? Well, I think part of the narcissistic part—it's just that it's really hard to tease out what is currently active and the reason why it's hard to tease out what is currently active is that you still have an active Axis I. And as you know with the same case in IV. With all of us. If anybody who—any of us have ever been ill in the hospital, we don't—we're just nastier when we're sick. Some people are just nasty when they're sick. So, I really wouldn't put as much weight in terms of which one do you currently exhibit. I think you do have a narcissistic part sometimes when you feel that your rights are not being recognized or you feel easily injured if somebody says something or if somebody disagrees with you. So, I think that's part of the thing. But like I said, Mr. Bechtold, you're a very pleasant guy. We enjoy working with you. We're just so saddened that the illness is alive and well. That's the only thing that saddens us.

After his direct examination of Dr. Onwuanibe, Brian felt as if the evidence spoke for itself. He believed he'd shown the jury his own presence of mind and the vagueness of the case against him. If they weren't persuaded, he thought, there was nothing more he could do. And while he was satisfied with his performance in the courtroom, he was hurt and disturbed by Dr. Onwuanibe's response to his final question:

Q: What is the plan with Mr. Bechtold? To keep him for life?
A: It's not sure.

To Brian, this was a betrayal. He'd thought Dr. Onwuanibe was on his side, working hard to get him out of the hospital. He thought she had a release date in mind. It was painful to hear her admit she was uncertain about his future.

When all the testimony was over, but before the jury was sent away to deliberate, Rhonda Edwards, for the state, requested a motion for summary judgment, which meant she was asking the judge to rule that Brian's case was so insubstantial that no reasonable jury could decide in his favor. The judge granted her request in regard to the question of whether Brian currently had a mental disorder. Because he'd already been diagnosed with one, the judge argued, that part of the question wasn't up for debate. On the second and third parts of the question, however—whether Brian would, if released, be a danger to himself, others, or the property of others, and whether he should be released unconditionally—the judge deferred his decision until after the verdict. This meant that even if the jury decided Brian should be released, the judge still had a right to grant the state's motion for summary judgment and overturn the verdict.

"This being a civil case, I'm allowed under the rules to reserve ruling on the motion—to see what happens with the verdict—then that also makes for a record," he told Brian. "If you win with the jury, and you lose with me on the motion, then you've got a complete record. You could appeal. If it goes down that the jury says 'release,' and I say, 'I'm now going to rule on that motion I deferred earlier,' and I grant it, then you've got a conflicting result. My own decision, if I decided to go there, would control. But you would have the right to appeal, and you would have the benefit of the verdict to go up on appeal, and if I'm proved wrong, on appeal, you could reserve the right to have a verdict entered, rather than go through all this again."

In short, the judge was hedging his bets. He didn't want Brian to be released, it seemed, because he didn't want to be held liable for any act of violence he might commit, but he wanted the jury to make the decision—to make it himself, unilaterally, would seem to undermine the whole point of the trial.

The jury retired to confer. They continued to debate until the end of the day. The following day, February 12, 2014, they deliberated from 9:15 a.m. until 4 p.m., with a short lunch break. At 4 p.m., they sent a note to the judge saying they were unable to reach a verdict. The judge issued a modified Allen charge (an instruction encouraging jurors in the minority to reconsider), and they continued to debate for three more hours before returning to the courtroom.

The first thing Brian noticed was that several members of the jury were smiling. For a moment, he thought they were mocking him and that he'd made a fool of himself, but then he realized it was more likely they were on his side. He felt his heart rising. They were a smart group of people, he remembered, but were they smart enough to see through the psychiatric jargon and lies? Had they come down in his favor? Were they going to set him free at last?

Brian tried to slow his breathing. He looked again at the faces of the jurors, most of them pleasant and encouraging. He looked at the judge; he looked at the plate behind the judge, which bore the State of Maryland coat of arms. Brian couldn't stop his heart from racing. He could feel it in his blood. He'd proven his sanity.

The jury foreman stepped up and handed the judge a note. The judge opened it and read the following words:

"We have consulted with each other and deliberated with a view to reaching an agreement. We have discussed, examined, and re-examined our views. In order not to surrender each of our honest beliefs as to the weight or effect of the evidence, we are not able to come to a unanimous verdict."

The courtroom fell silent.

The judge pursed his lips and folded up the note. "I'm inclined not to require that they deliberate any further and determine them unable to reach a verdict," he said.

Brian braced himself. Another mistrial.

"Mr. Bechtold," said Judge Jordan. "You have been perhaps the most consummate gentleman in this courtroom that I've seen, and you've been superb in how you've handled yourself. . . . At this point, I'm going to rule on the motion for judgment. I took it under advisement. I'm going to grant the motion for judgment for the defense. For the department. Which means it goes against you."

For a moment, Brian couldn't believe what he was hearing. Then it sank in. He'd lost the case. He was going back to Perkins—indefinitely.

"I want to say to you, I'm not only impressed with how you've handled yourself, I have an enormous amount of empathy and sympathy for the position you're in," the judge continued. "On a personal level, you seem like just a great guy. A very likeable, affable person."

His dignity, Brian realized, was the only thing he had left.

"I'm fine with it, Your Honor," Brian said. "I think you've been an excellent judge. It's been a fair trial. It's been my first fair trial in many years, and I think it's due to you presiding over the case. And I really thank you for it."

"I appreciate that, Mr. Bechtold," the judge said.

20

Until Sanity Is Restored

On November 7, 1974, a *New York Times* editorial column described the case of Kenneth Donaldson, who, after being told by a judge that he was being sent away for "a few weeks" to "take some of this new medication," spent fifteen years in Florida State Hospital, with no medication and no treatment. "There are dark corners in America where people are trampled, broken and forgotten," the column reminded its readers. "The saddest of these—and the most demeaning to our society—are those institutions, paid for and run by the public, where people are stashed away for the safety and convenience of the rest of us and then left to rot untouched by the collective conscience of the community."

In a similar and more recent case, a man named John Maxwell Montin was confined to a psychiatric hospital in Nebraska in 1992 because he was suffering from delusions. The doctors based their diagnosis on a police report of Montin's unusual behavior, ignoring

Montin's own account of the events. In fact, Montin was regarded as being delusional for insisting that the police report was mistaken, and his efforts to be released from the hospital were treated as psychotic symptoms. Against the objections of his attorney and Montin's own insistence that he was not suffering from a delusional disorder, he remained confined for the next twenty years, despite the fact that his case was annually reviewed. In 2012, Montin's attorney was finally able to convince his psychiatrist to take his client's case seriously and read the five-hundred-page transcript of his 1992 trial. The psychiatrist immediately revised his diagnosis of Montin, who was finally released.

People are sometimes incarcerated for crimes they didn't commit; in the same way, people find themselves locked up in psychiatric hospitals when they're not mentally ill. Of course, this is not what happened to Brian—as he himself admits, he suffered from a serious mental illness for many years, which caused him to commit a terrible crime. This fact, however, has made it even more difficult for his treatment team to accept that he "recovered his sanity" long ago and is being kept at Perkins only because, it appears, he still retains dignity, faith, and hope for a better life to come.

Although many things remain the same (and some get worse), there have been gradual improvements at Perkins. Some are due to an increased public awareness of the stigma borne by the mentally ill. In 2016, for example, the hospital was successfully sued by a former patient known only as Jane Doe, who claimed she'd been raped in a bathroom by an HIV-positive male patient while staff was supposed to be monitoring them. She complained to Perkins staff, but they didn't believe the sex was nonconsensual, even though a psychiatrist later testified to state police that Jane Doe didn't have the cognitive ability to consent to sex. Doe was granted $400,000 in damages, and Perkins introduced various reforms to prevent similar sexual assaults in the future.

The food for patients has improved (although it still has to be eaten with a plastic spoon). Those on minimum security can choose to eat in the staff cafeteria. (Patients have to pay for food here, but the prices are very reasonable.) "Every day, I eat a salad, French fries, fruit. Last night we had fish, which was pretty good. Fried fish in a bun, with lettuce, tomato, and cheese on top," Louis told me. There were even options for vegetarians. "They've got vegetarian patties, vegetarian chicken nuggets, sauerkraut, pork substitute, vegetarian egg rolls. . . . The vegetarian egg rolls are very good," he added. "They have kind of a vinegar taste to them. For dessert you can get a piece of fruit or a Nutri-Grain bar."

Access to staff at Perkins has also improved (a little). "We have an individual treatment plan, and meet with our treatment team every other month," Jeremy told me. "There's also a sign-in sheet that the doctors post up somewhere on each ward. So, if a need arises, you can either go to the nursing station and tell them you're having an episode, or you can just sign on the sheet."

But Brian was still seen as an escape risk for many years and wasn't even permitted into the yard unescorted. Whenever he asked for a chaperone, they told him no one was available. By April 2016, he hadn't been allowed outside for almost a year and was suffering from vitamin D deficiency due to lack of sunlight. He filed a complaint with the Patients' Grievance Committee, but nothing came of it. "Fresh air is not a human right," he was told.

Around a third of forensic patients, after their first psychotic break, once diagnosed and given treatment, will never commit another act of violence. The second third will never hurt anyone else, though they might hurt themselves and may even commit suicide. The last third will need constant evaluation through middle age and sometimes beyond, as their psychosis remains active. All indications suggest that Brian is part of the first group, those who, after the initial catastrophe, will never be violent again.

Brian readily admits that at the time of the offense, he was severely mentally ill. Twenty-seven years later, however, he believes his illness has been in remission for decades, and he no longer suffers from paranoid schizophrenia. He recognizes that he has "odd thoughts" and can be suspicious, distrustful, and hypervigilant; he even accepts that he may have a mild form of mental illness as a result of his prolonged incarceration, but he knows he isn't psychotic, and he certainly isn't dangerous. Whatever may be wrong with him now, it doesn't seem to be any of the five different personality disorders he's been diagnosed with over the last three decades.

For a long time, Brian was convinced he'd die in Perkins. He believed this not only because of the way he'd been treated, but because of what he saw around him every day. In theory, Perkins is a place where patients stay while undergoing treatment that will restore them to mental health. In truth, however, many patients never leave the hospital. They're being warehoused. Relatives often find themselves unable to deal with chronic mentally ill family members. Friends get burned out. Even when someone seems to be making progress, they'll often decline, rally again, decompensate, go off their medication, and regress. If released, many of them would end up on the streets because there's nowhere else for them to go.

With this in mind, it's particularly difficult for me to understand why the hospital is so reluctant to release Brian, even to a regional hospital or residential treatment program. I was told many times that no one was kept at Perkins for longer than was absolutely necessary. In fact, there's a very high threshold for being considered disturbed enough to get a bed, and patients are discharged as soon as possible, often without meaningful recovery. There's fierce competition for space—so much so that on July 12, 2017, Perkins was held in civil contempt over delays in providing psychiatric hospital beds to defendants referred by the courts. (The suit was overturned on appeal.)

Of course, things could always be worse. There are patients who've been at Perkins for longer than Brian (including a man who's been there since 1968). And Brian still has visitors. His best friend,

Kyu, visits him whenever he can; former patients stay in touch. His sister Cathy does her best to fight for him from her home in Ohio and has offered to take care of Brian once he's released. For the last three years, he's been a minimum-security patient, and he's currently on a coed ward. (Recent years have seen an increase in the number of females pleading not criminally responsible.) In July 2019, he was allowed to leave the hospital for the first time since his escape. In the company of a clinical supervisor, Brian and another patient were taken to spend two hours in the Walmart in Laurel, Maryland, about seven miles away from Perkins. Brian was impressed by the size of the shopping center, but other than that, the world of 2019 didn't seem much different from the one he remembered. He bought a jar of coffee and a mug.

Brian's sister Cathy can't understand why her brother is still in the hospital. She doesn't believe he's dangerous or even mentally ill, although she does suspect he has some kind of nonverbal learning disability. His friend Kyu feels the same way. "There's no reason to keep him there," Kyu told me. "Brian's not going to hurt anybody. I think he should be released." And he's not alone. Dr. Hertzberg, the forensic psychiatrist hired by Brian's public defender, has agreed to testify on Brian's behalf if he should go to court for another release hearing in the next few years. But his fee, he told Brian, would be $7,500, and Brian's income is limited to a small Social Security payment and his negligible Perkins wages—$7,500 is more than he makes in a year.

Sometimes, at night, Brian's mind takes him back to a period when he was ten or eleven, after Cathy had left home. It seems to sum up his childhood. His father tried to reach out to him, to forge a bond. He took Brian to a place in Maryland called Solomons Island, where he'd been working on a project to transform a former naval base into a recreation area for U.S. Navy veterans. Brian was thrilled to get a chance to go on vacation with his dad, just the two of them. He imagined them exploring the island together, defusing unexploded mines. But when they arrived, he was disappointed to find it wasn't an island at all, but an empty military base at the tip of a peninsula with a few houses and an abandoned movie theater. His father ignored his son and spent the whole time working while Brian wandered alone, up and down the desolate, windswept streets.

Illustrations

Notes

5: Day of Reckoning

criminologist Kathleen M. Heide: "Parents Who Get Killed and the Children Who Kill Them," *Journal of Interpersonal Violence*, vol. 8 no. 4, December 1993, 531–44.

6: Focus on Fiction

Chesterton: "Orthodoxy," *The Collected Works of G. K. Chesterton, Vol. 1: Heretics, Orthodoxy, the Blatchford Controversies* (San Francisco: Ignatius Press, 1986), 81.

7: Ward 8

an eight-state study: L. A. Callahan, H. J. Steadman, M. A. McGreevy, and P. C. Robbins, "The Volume and Characteristics of Insanity Defense Pleas," *Bulletin of the American Academy of Psychiatry and the Law*, 1991, 19 (4), 331–8.

8: Rehab and Risperdal

Rosenhan: David Rosenhan, "On Being Sane in Insane Places," *Science*, vol. 179, no. 4070 (January 19, 1973), 250–58. Note that the validity of the Rosenhan experiment has recently been questioned.

HIPAA regulations: The Health Insurance Portability and Accountability Act of 1996 (HIPAA), Public Law 104-191, was enacted on August 21, 1996. Sections 261–64 of HIPAA require the secretary of the Department of Health and Human Services to publicize standards for the electronic exchange, privacy, and security of health information.

twilight state: Joanna Moncrieff, "Magic Bullets for Mental Disorders: The Emergence of the Concept of an 'Antipsychotic' Drug," *Journal of the History of Neuroscience*, January 2013; 22(1): 30–46.

9: "Untying the Straitjacket"

Untying the Straitjacket: A&E home video, November 1, 2004; produced by David Heilbroner, hosted by Bill Kurtis. Available to view online at Western Connecticut State University Media Library, https://media.wcsu.edu/media/Investigative+Reports+-+Untying+the+Strait+Jacket/1_30jm467h.

The Insanity Defense Reform Act: Signed into law on October 12, 1984, this was the first comprehensive federal legislation governing the insanity defense and the disposition of individuals suffering from a mental disease or defect who are involved in the criminal justice system.

Birnbaum: Dr. Morton Birnbaum, MD, "The Right to Treatment," *American Bar Association Journal* 46.5 (May 1960), 499–505.

10: "Hyper-religious"

Elyn Saks: See *The Center Cannot Hold: My Journey Through Madness* (New York: Hachette Books, 2008), 12–13.

another first-person account: Anonymous, "Language Games, Paranoia and Psychosis," *Schizophrenia Bulletin* vol. 37, issue 6, November 2011, 1099.

12: Medicine Man

Thomas Insel: "Antipsychotics: Taking the Long View," NIMH blog post at https://www.nimh.nih.gov/about/directors/thomas-insel/blog/2013/antipsychotics-taking-the-long-view.shtml, August 28, 2013.

Nancy Andreasen: Nancy C. Andreasen, Peg Nopoulos, Vincent Magnotta, Ronald Pierson, Steven Ziebell, and Beng-Choon Ho, "Progressive Brain Change in Schizophrenia: A Prospective Longitudinal Study of First-Episode Schizophrenia," *Biological Psychiatry* 2011, October 1 70 (7), 672–79, published online July 23, 2011.

Germán E. Berríos, Rogelio Luque, and José M. Villargrán: "Schizophrenia: A Conceptual History," *International Journal of Psychology and Psychological Therapy*, vol. 3, no. 2, December 2003, 111–40.

14: Thought Crimes

Kenneth Donaldson: see *Insanity Inside Out* (New York: Crown, 1976).

19: Pro Se

Robert Wisner-Carlson: see Kelly v. State of Maryland, No. 07–7576 (4th Cir. 2008).

John Allan Langworthy: See 46 Md. App. 116 (1980), John Allen Langworthy v. State of Maryland, 416 A.2d 1287 No. 848, September Term, 1977, Court of Special Appeals of Maryland. Decided July 9, 1980.

Donald Gary Rembold: See United States Court for the District of Maryland, July 14, 2016, Donald Gary Rembold v. David Helsel, et al., Civil Action no. PWG-16-1569.

litigious mania: See C. Adam Coffey, MS, Stanley L. Brodsky, PhD, and David J. Sams, JD, LLM, "I'll See You in Court . . . Again: Psychopathology and Hyperlitigious Litigants," *Journal of the American Academy of Psychiatry and the Law* 45: 62–71, 2017.

20: Until Sanity Is Restored

Kenneth Donaldson: "Society's Warehouses," *New York Times*, November 12, 1974.

Montin: See Marc W. Pearce, JD, PhD, "No Remedy for Dubious Insanity Commitment," *American Psychological Association Monitor*, June 2016, vol. 47, no. 6, 24.

Jane Doe: See United State District Court for the District of Maryland, Jane Doe v. Maryland Department of Health and Mental Hygiene, Civil Action No. WMN-14-3906.

About the Author

Mikita Brottman is an Oxford-educated scholar and psycho-analyst and the author of several previous books, including *An Unexplained Death*, *The Great Grisby*, and *The Maximum Security Book Club*. She is a professor in the Department of Humanistic Studies at the Maryland Institute College of Art in Baltimore.